# MAURICE SCÈVE: POET OF LOVE

# MAURICE SCÈVE
# POET OF LOVE
## Tradition and Originality

DOROTHY GABE COLEMAN

*Lecturer in French in the University of Cambridge*
*and Fellow of New Hall*

CAMBRIDGE UNIVERSITY PRESS
CAMBRIDGE
LONDON · NEW YORK · MELBOURNE

Published by the Syndics of the Cambridge University Press
The Pitt Building, Trumpington Street, Cambridge CB2 1RP
Bentley House, 200 Euston Road, London NW1 2DB
32 East 57th Street, New York, NY 10022, USA
296 Beaconsfield Parade, Middle Park, Melbourne 3206, Australia

Library of Congress Catalogue Card Number: 74-31794

ISBN: 0 521 20745 2

First published 1975

Printed in Great Britain
at the University Printing House, Cambridge
(Euan Phillips, University Printer)

# CONTENTS

# TO ODETTE

Who first gave me love for Scève

# PREFACE

To avoid repeating what earlier critics and scholars have said
about Scève, I have omitted from this study all biograpy of
the poet and all references to contemporary events, unless they
are essential to the argument. Quotations are from the edition
of *Délie* by Professor I. D. McFarlane (C.U.P., 1966). Other
works written by Scève are not considered in this study.
Following Leonard Forster in his book *The Icy Fire* (C.U.P., 1969),
I have distinguished throughout between Petrarchan (appertaining to Petrarch himself) with a capital, and petrarchism,
petrarchist, etc., in lower case.

My thanks are due to the editorial boards of *French Studies*,
*Studi Francesi* and the *Kentucky Romance Quarterly* for allowing
me to make use of my material previously published in their
periodicals. I am very grateful to Michael Black and my
husband, for reading and criticising the work. My deepest debt,
however, is to the critic, Odette de Mourgues, who has stimulated, encouraged and enlightened me with intellectual acumen,
poetic humour and warm affection. *Merci.*

*May* 1975                                                    D.G.C.

# ABBREVIATIONS

| | |
|---|---|
| *BHR* | Bibliothèque d'Humanisme et Renaissance (Geneva, Droz) |
| *BN* | Bibliothèque Nationale, Paris |
| *FS* | French Studies |
| Huguet | E. Huguet, *Dictionnaire de la langue française du seizième siècle* |
| *MLR* | Modern Language Review |
| *SF* | Studi Francesi |

# I

# INTRODUCTION

'The poet makes poetry, the metaphysician makes metaphysics, the bee makes honey, the spider secretes a filament; you can hardly say that any of these agents believes: he merely does.' This statement of fact by Eliot (*Selected Essays*, London, 1953, p. 138) draws approving astonishment from every abecedarian teacher of the rudiments of poetry. For we as teachers never turn to Dante for a résumé of Aquinas' thought nor do we run straightway to Aquinas for an explanation of the concept of sin when we are reading the *Inferno*. The former is a poet, the latter a theologian, and Aquinas' dismissal of poetry as 'infirma inter omnes doctrinas' was shared by all the scholastics who moralised and didacticised about the non-philosophical arts. Still less do we leaf through Aristotle's rules for drama when we are reading a tragedy. He had a brilliant intellect, but he was not a poet.

The metaphysical assumptions of a poet are, of course, important if we are examining the climate of ideas that produced such and such a poem, in order to explain part of the historical context in which the poet was working. This is a perfectly legitimate procedure for the reconstruction of various elements that went to the making of a poem, and any aesthetic analysis must, if it hopes to illuminate a particular work, function through the particular literature, born in a particular context, not outside or against it. But there is no *need*, strictly speaking, to know first of all the poem by Petrarch which is a relevant source for a dizain by Scève. A knowledge of Petrarch's poem may well add to our understanding of it. But poetry is written and read at several levels. Dylan Thomas described his falling in love with nursery rhymes in this way,

I had come to love just the words of them, the words alone. What the words stood for, symbolized or meant, was of very secondary import-ance; what mattered was the sound of them as I heard them for the first time on the lips of the remote and incomprehensible grown-ups who seemed, for some reason, to be living in my world.

(*The colour of saying*, ed. R. Maud and Aneurin Talfan Davies, London, 1963, p. xix.)

1

At this level – which is perhaps the lowest – we can enjoy the sounds of the words pirouetting, as it were, in the air, playing symphonies together or merely vibrating as a pattern in our minds; and, like children, we gasp with delight as the sequence of words becomes a glittering catherine-wheel bursting against the backcloth of our sensitivity. The act of enjoying poetry is slightly different from the act of understanding it. At this stage, we may not understand the poem. How many of us savoured sensually the sound of the Psalms years before we knew what, for instance, this meant?

The Lord is my shepherd; I shall not want. He maketh me to lie down in green pastures: he leadeth me beside the still waters. He restoreth my soul: he leadeth me in the paths of righteousness for his name's sake. Yea, though I walk through the valley of the shadow of death, I will fear no evil: for thou art with me; thy rod and thy staff they comfort me...

It is with the imagination that we enter the universe of the poet, and that universe is totally different from the ordinary one we live our daily lives in. Furthermore we are different people when engaged in reading poetry. And we do not judge the poem on first acquaintance.

Many scholars insist that a reader must have an immense apparatus of scholarship before he can read a poem. But this is to bypass the first essential step in dealing with literature, which is intelligent, close, critical, active reading. Professor I. A. Richards said in 1929,

We speak *to say something*, and when we listen we expect something to be said. We use words to direct our hearers' attention upon some state of affairs, to present to them some items for consideration and to excite in them some thoughts for these items.

(*Practical Criticism*, London, 1929, p. 181.)

We read poetry not because we have the scholarship to reconstruct the poet's intention (we may never understand that more than partially, and what is perhaps more relevant in the present instance, this critical procedure itself was not applicable in the Renaissance, when most critics were looking at what poetry achieved in the mind of the reader rather than what any particular poet felt or intended) but because we feel certain human emotions in their intensity and have a certain appreciation of the artistic process by which they are presented in the poetry. Indeed, we are energised by a spark of fire in a particular poem, which generates heat in our intellect, emotions, senses, memory. Perhaps later we may be driven into scholarship to make the implicit appeal of particular effects more explicit and to redefine continually our personal conception of poetry; we may be urged by our own re-reading of the poem to tease out bits of syntax, to unravel the meanings of a word, to follow through the clues of a complex structure, or to suck out the marrow of a poet's imagery. This deepening of our awareness of a poem starts a two-way process in us: our experience helps us to unravel the meaning of a poem and conversely the poem helps us to appreciate our experience. Reading the poem becomes a network of criss-cross relations. Our impressions of human love are disorganised and, in one way, we do not realise that we have to be taught how to be free to appreciate it. And literature comes to our aid and shows us how many things co-ordinate between life and art. We associate the poems we read not so much with the men or women who wrote them: we associate them indirectly with ourselves and directly with other poems we have read.

One problem that faces us immediately in reading Scève's poems is their difficulty. On a simple level the purely phonetic impressions are felt with particular vividness when we are approaching a foreign language. We delight in French words like *opoponax, popincourt, brouhaha, croquer* and so on. Childish fantasy, perhaps, but serious when we are considering a language. On another level Scève would be regarded a difficult poet for syntactic, grammatical, semantic, symbolic reasons. But let us get at the problem by examining three poems from three different periods of literature: a sonnet by Mallarmé, an ode of Horace and a dizain of Scève. Let us approach these three poems first through the sensory quality of words, through imagery and metrical, rhythmic movement without thinking on evaluation, judgement or what they have in common. We shall take Mallarmé's poem first:

> A la Nue accablante tu
> Basse de basalte et de laves
> A même les échos esclaves
> Par une trompe sans vertu
>
> Quel sépulcral naufrage (tu
> Le sais, écume, mais y baves)

Suprême une entre les épaves
Abolit le mât dévêtu

Ou cela que furibond faute
De quelque perdition haute
Tout l'abîme vain éployé

Dans le si blanc cheveu qui traîne
Avarement aura noyé
Le flanc enfant d'une sirène.

(*Œuvres complètes*, Pléiade edition, Paris, 1945, p. 76)

When this famous sonnet is read aloud a strange feeling of incomprehension paralyses us. We do not understand it. The language seems straightforward but the syntax is difficult; the absence of punctuation (except for the two very emphatic commas in line 6) means that the reader does not know which word goes with which other word. The logical syntax of non-literary prose has been shattered. Language is playing tricks. The very harmless word *nue* could be an adjective; as it is feminine it could mean a naked woman or a naked girl; but on the other hand it could be a noun meaning, poetically and rather archaically, a high cloud or, collectively, clouds. *Furibond faute* (line 9) at first suggests an adjective followed by a noun, but on second glance the adjective does not agree with the noun. The rhyming position of *tu...tu* suggests that they are different words; the second person singular and the past participle of *taire*, but there is no way of telling which is which. Whole phrases might be in apposition to a single word, and the tone of a rhetorical question underlies the poem. It is a visual representation of words on the page with, seemingly, an emphasis not on the sequence of ideas but rather on arbitrary aesthetic concepts. Arbitrary, because so far the reader is unable to see reasons for them. However, he is excited by the sheer linguistic difficulty and the sonorous musicality of the words, and he feels that he must get something to bite on in this smooth-polished artefact. The internal rhymes in the first line, the alternation in the octave between *tu...vertu...tu...dévêtu* with the heavy *laves... esclaves...baves...épaves* thudding the rhyme, the alliteration in line 2 between *basse* and *basalte*, the sound of *Abolit le mât dévêtu* and the insistently recurring *a* sounds (e.g. lines 1, 2, 13) the diphthong *au* (lines 9 and 10 in the rhyme) – all stir the reader's musical sensibility. The first eight lines are a piling up of words with hardly any visual dramatization, simply an abstract pattern of notes around the *Quel sépulcral naufrage* of line 5. The speed of reading is painfully slow: consonants split up the lines into laboured fragments which, perhaps, imitate a visual impression of a shipwreck. One sinuous sentence, enunciated with difficulty, brings to mind, perhaps, the weight and blackness of storm clouds preceding or following the wreck. Complex, disorientating, astonishing. We are excited by the poem.

Now let us read aloud an ode by Horace to see whether we can make as little out of it as we have done for Mallarmé.

> O fons Bandusiae, splendidior vitro,
> dulci digne mero non sine floribus,
>     cras donaberis haedo,
>   cui frons turgida cornibus
> primis et Venerem et proelia destinat.
> frustra: nam gelidos inficiet tibi
>     rubro sanguine rivos
>     lascivi suboles gregis.
> te flagrantis atrox hora Caniculae
> nescit tangere, tu frigus amabile
>     fessis vomere tauris
>   praebes et pecori vago.
> fies nobilium tu quoque fontium,
> me dicente cavis impositam ilicem
>     saxis, unde loquaces
> lymphae desiliunt tuae.                    (*Odes*, III.13)[1]

Latin, being an inflected language, lacks articles, but its case endings define the relationship between subject, object and modifiers. The first words are in the vocative so that we hear an *I* talking to a *you: o fons Bandusiae* seems to be an address to the fountain in the vocative. The immediate impression is that it is a hymn, it is almost as if the fountain were subsumed under a

---

[1] O spring of Bandusia, more shining than glass, deserving of sweet wine and flowers, tomorrow you will be presented with a kid whose forehead, swelling with the tips of horns, gives promise of both love and battles; in vain: for he, the offspring of a playful flock, shall stain for you your chill waters with his red blood.

The black hour of the flaring Dog-Star knows no means to touch you: you provide pleasing coolness for tired oxen and the straggling herd.

You also shall become one of the famous fountains, since I describe the oak-tree planted over your hollowed rocks from which your chattering waters jump down.

(Translated by Gordon Williams in *The Third Book of Horace's Odes*, Oxford, 1969.)

god's name. As we note the number of times *tibi, te, tu, tuae* enter the poem we come to feel that it is a dramatic monologue, in which the poet has used the 'I' who speaks and a second person singular to whom he talks. In line 14 *me dicente* suggests that the 'I' is singing of the glories of this fountain in Bandusia, echoing perhaps the Greek poets who were always singing of fountains; perhaps this fountain will be greater than any other because this 'I' is singing of it. Our first reading of this Horatian Ode will have demonstrated that there are some clues, like the musicality – the slow start to each line and the falling cadence of $-\smile\smile-\smile-$ in the first, second and fourth lines of each stanza – which imprint themselves on our memory. But again we do not yet understand the poem.

Finally let us listen to a poem by Scève.

> A si hault bien de tant saincte amytié
> Facilement te deburoit inciter,
> Sinon debuoir, ou honneste pitié,
> A tout le moins mon loyal persister,
> Pour vnyment, & ensemble assister
> Lassus en paix en nostre eternel throsne.
>    N'apperçoy tu de l'Occident le Rhosne
> Se destourner, & vers Midy courir,
> Pour seulement se conioindre a sa Saone
> Iusqu'a leur Mer, ou tous deux vont mourir?    (dizain 346)

Again, there is a feeling of not understanding. The first six lines are syntactically difficult, but certain lines have embedded themselves in our mind, like the splendid 'A si hault bien de tant saincte amytié'. The last four lines are simple; they convey their meaning more clearly than Mallarmé's sonnet or the Horatian ode. Yet, reading these three poems is much more difficult than enjoying a poem by Ovid, or by Verlaine or one of Marot's chansons. We are in a state of baffled astonishment; there is a sense in which something is working to get hold of our minds.

All three examples are difficult and they are difficult in many different ways. But they share certain qualities and values. Mallarmé is difficult syntactically and in the way the metaphors work – and that is like Scève. Horace represents the domestication of a foreign literary tradition, and that, as we shall see later, is like Scève. But they have something else in common. We realise that each poet is going to make us work. The three poets share the same attitude towards the reader; he is not a member of the *vulgus;* he can be expected to tease out the syntax, the vocabulary, the images and sound patterns of the poem, precisely because his emotional sense has been aroused. He knows that the points are going to be made more by implication than explicitly. The emotional reaction to the three poems is tied to sound. The reader may have a tremendous emotional uplift in being carried hither and thither as dictated by a phrase, a musical line or by whole sentences.

On our first reading our sensibility as well as our intellect is fired. We can say that foreign languages do not prevent us from 'feeling' certain things in word-patterns and sounds and that we are in the same position as the child who savours sensually a psalm without understanding it fully.

Therefore it is not so much that difficult languages face us when we read the three poems; it is more a feeling of the complexity of the artistic process. The difficulty of Scève lies more in the working out of a rich and allusive arrangement of words than in the words themselves. Commentators on Scève from Brunetière to McFarlane stress the difficulties. Brunetière put forward a theory purporting to explain the architecture of *Délie* by means of the number symbolism of the Cabbala; Saulnier saw Scève as a forerunner of Valéry; Odette de Mourgues saw the intellectual content behind the emotion; McFarlane took scrupulous pains to ease the linguistic difficulty for us.[1] But it is the reader's enjoyment, his elucidation and ultimately his participation in the fullest sense which must work with all three poets. By reading the poems again we can try and work out something of value (even though it will not be a full understanding) without relying at this point on the knowledge, the background and the tradition in which each poet was working.

We shall start with the Horace poem – because for many reasons it is the easiest and clearest. The word *fons* generates a number of related words. The water is so clear, so perfected by nature that it seems far 'outsplendouring glass'. Its transparency is so bright that it seems to take on the brilliance of the

---

[1] McFarlane, in the notes to the dizains in his edition and in 'Notes on Maurice Scève's *Délie*', FS, XIII, 1959, pp. 99–111; F. Brunetière in 'Un précurseur de la Pléiade', *Études critiques sur l'histoire de la littérature française*, 6e série, Paris, 1899; V. L. Saulnier, *Maurice Scève*, Paris, 1948–9, 2 vols; O. de Mourgues, *Metaphysical, Baroque and Précieux Poetry*, Oxford, 1953, pp. 12–22.

midday sun. With the comparative adjective *splendidior* Horace expresses the sparkling nature of the water in its quintessence. In the second verse, he has *gelidos...rivos*: we have passed from the fountain's outward semblance to something which evokes for the reader the sense of touch; for it is icy, very, very cold – a mountain stream on a hot day. This icy transparency is then contrasted with the poet's sacrifice of the warm blood of a kid (*gelidos* implies *tepido*, *rubro* implies *liquidos* – an economic device of complementarity that Horace is fond of in descriptive contrasts). With the word *haedo* Horace suggests a pathetically young animal (contrast the other two words for goats – *hircus* and *caper* – which he might have used); and this has one association, which is the right one here – the wantonness and lasciviousness of a young goat, and especially the poignancy of these qualities unfulfilled (note *destinat*). The next verse guides the effect of icy by using *frigus*, which is slightly less cold than *gelidus*, in combination with *amabile* to evoke a pleasant sense of taste and touch – the cool, refreshing loveliness of a stream on a hot summer's day. The last verse has the sound of the fountain: *loquaces/lymphae desiliunt tuae*. *Loquaces* means 'babbling'; *lymphae* is a poetic synonym for *aquae*, and carries the underlying association that Roman poets would make between *Lymphae* and *Nymphae*; *desiliunt* means leap down, tumble and fall. (See Ronsard's rendering of this in *A la Fontaine Bellerie*, Odes, ii, 9, where everything that has been implicitly suggested by Horace, is brought out in the open and made explicit e.g. the *Nymphes*.) The sensations in the images impinge on the reader's mind, and through their artistic patterning remain there underlying the poem after one has finished reading it.

Let us look at the content. There is a balance of two verses and two verses; the first half conveys the offer of a sacrifice, the second half extolls the spring's benefactions. The contrast between today and tomorrow is identified with that between icy-coldness and blood-heat; the young kid will be sacrificed. The explicit contrast in the second half is between the labour of the oxen as they pull their ploughs and the pastoral herds which provide milk, wool and meat. And there is an implied contrast finally between *me dicente* and the non-articulate *vulgus*.[1] Horace

---

[1] I cannot agree with N. E. Collinge, who says (*The Structure of Horace's Odes*, Oxford, 1961, p. 106) that this last stanza is 'self-advertisement for the poet'. That seems a rather crude interpretation of a suggestive and only implied intimacy with the audience.

was ready to acknowledge that, technically, he was the offspring of the lyric poets of Greece, and this is implicit in the choice of an Asclepiad metre. But for Horace it was important that he should bring all his technical excellence, his own personality, to this complex work of art. When we look for the unity of the poem, it is true that we can see the separate elements, the parallels, the contrasts and the comparisons; but ultimately everything is brought together by the poetic character into a little scene, where the poet seems to be talking rather casually about springs, sacrifices and wanton young goats. When we read it we are struck by the way he interweaves sensations, ideas, common everyday things from nature, almost as if there was no art in it at all. The poet is giving us an experience or several experiences in a seemingly simple form – *ars sine arte*.

The core of our response to a Mallarmé sonnet lies in the state of suspension of the intellect while all the possible suggestions of the imagination are stirred, allowed to run their full course, interacting with one another, and then blotted out. The glories of this imaginative activity, though illusory, are intensely exciting, and in the best poems they are pushed to their extreme in a spectacle of intense light. This is not the same process as in Scève or Horace; for one thing, in the nineteenth century the imagination is the centre of the poetic universe.[1]

The long phrase of the tercets, hinged on the subject, *Tout l'abîme* suggesting an alternative to the shipwreck image, culminates in nothingness, all the weight in the sky, all the violent forces of sky and sea converge to conjure up the illusory child of the siren. Mallarmé's negative technique, precisely because it makes greater demands on the reader's intellect, his powers of imagination and association, takes us actively rather than passively through the poetic experience. At its logical extreme, this negative technique would lead to an impasse of non-communication between the poet and his reader. In the best poems the reader *has* to co-operate, because his emotions and sensibility are moved and demand a resolution. The effect of Mallarmé's syntax is initially disorientating, but instead of leaving it unresolved, the reader has to work out the kind of

---

[1] This will be clearer later on, especially the beginning of Chapter 3. But see the fine article by J. M. Cocking, 'Imagination as Order and as Adventure', in *Order and Adventure in Post-Romantic French Poetry. Essays presented to C. A. Hackett.* Edited by E. M. Beaumont, J. M. Cocking and J. Cruickshank, Oxford, 1973, pp. 257–69.

multiple reaction the poet describes in *Crise de Vers*. The resolution depends on intellect: the reader has to piece together the words, in order to see whether the first *tu* is indeed the second person singular or the past participle of *taire*; he has to repeat the process when he comes across the second *tu*. Mallarmé's effort at compressing multifarious threads through syntax reveals an approach which demands that the reader do a great deal of the work: the juxtaposition, the appositions may be whole phrases, they may be little words; the imagination is involved through association. For example, *basse* in the second line has its musical associations confirmed by *trompe* in line 4; so that *basse* might mean that weighting of sound in an orchestral score which the bass-parts provide; *sans vertu* would have as one sense distant or faint, scarcely reaching the hearer; yet *trompe* makes the musical element explicit. Mallarmé's trumpets characteristically *announce* things. The series of *a* vowels describes the low, heavy black cloud – but also the sounds that are scarcely identified; a heavy, crushing silence is implied by the first *tu* which is isolated and has the whole weight of the line pressing on it. The metaphors are so tenuous that they almost do not function: e.g. *les échos esclaves*; or personifications like *écume...baves*. At the end of the poem even the metaphorical siren has only a chimerical child, and from this intense abstraction comes our feeling that we must start again and see more.

Let us now look at the Scève dizain. It is the finest poem of persuasion that he wrote. He sets out to convince Délie of the sacred necessity and worth of their union. He proceeds at first by abstract argument: in the first four lines he argues from *debuoir*: it is her duty to obey a decree of nature or love, first from *honneste pitié* which should spring from her heart and affections, her sympathy for his suffering, and finally because of *mon loyal persister*, his perseverance, which should be capable of breaking down her resistance. The syntactical anomaly, the inversion of subject and verb and predicate, places the emphasis on the sacred worth of their friendship. So *A si hault bien de tant saincte amytié* properly comes first in the poem. Lines 5–6 suggest the goal to which they would aspire, or the reward that this friendship would bring:

> Pour vnyment, & ensemble assister
> Lassus en paix en nostre eternel throsne.

*Vnyment* and *ensemble*, far from being superfluous synonyms
suggest the two aspects of union: two persons in one, and both
persons together. *Assister* from the Latin *adsistere* means 'to be
present side by side', *Lassus* suggests *là-haut*. These six lines have
been described by Boutang[1] as an 'ascension dure' where the
summit is reached in the confident-sounding line 6, which
radiates peace and the timelessness of eternity. From this peak
(which is at once the summit of the abstract argument and
suggestive of the geographical summit of Mont Fourvière in
Lyon with the river at its feet) the poet seems to turn to Délie,
almost as if the abstractions of an argument on love were
pointless in the face of his desperate need for her to feel his
presence, and we visualise her by his side as he shows her from
that high point how the Rhône changes its course in order to
join the Saône. Scève gives this rhetorical question, which
expects the answer 'yes', as the final, unquestionable proof that
the two lovers are meant for each other.

> N'apperçoy tu de l'Occident le Rhosne
> Se destourner, & vers Midy courir.

How can Délie discount this proof from the world of verifiable
fact? The two rivers are bound together as if by fate. The two
possessive adjectives *sa Saone* and *leur Mer* reinforce the notion
of their belonging to each other, and their final union. So the
whole logical argument is brought into this poem to corroborate
an emotional phenomenon – the poet trying every means to
persuade Délie of the sacredness of their friendship.

This dizain often lacks articles – for instance in line 3, where
the relationship between modifiers is changed by inversion, and
this alerts the reader to the fact that this is the kind of
poem-structure where he and the poet must work simultaneously. For the reader is not so much concerned with the
sense sequence as with following the arrangement of the words.
Scève has put more emphasis on aesthetic or emotional words,
and one has to work it all out in the same way as a Mallarmé
sonnet. The striking thing is that there is a tacit assumption in
all three poets that the very physiognomy of words is important.
Thus with Horace the underlying association between *Lymphae*
and *Nymphae* has to be 'heard' by the reader. With Scève the

---

[1] P. Boutang, *Commentaire sur quarante-neuf dizains de la 'Délie'*, Paris, 1953, p.
114. Boutang further calls it 'la montée du Fourvière intérieur' (p. 115).

reader has to 'hear' the difference between *vnyment* and *en-semble*. And with Mallarmé nuances of sound and meaning are conjured up with vibratory magic. As he said in *Les Mots Anglais*,

le Mot présente, dans ses voyelles et ses diphtongues, comme une chair; et, dans ses consonnes, comme une ossature délicate à disséquer.

(ed. op. cit., p. 901)

The linguistic difficulty in the three poets arises precisely because poetry is not non-literary prose. And this puts the onus on the poet: he *has* to create a language which, while it respects the conventions of language, is in a different dimension to the language he speaks or reads. Therefore, as Valéry said,

Les rimes, l'inversion, les figures développées, les symétries et les images, tout ceci, trouvailles ou conventions, sont autant de moyens de s'opposer au penchant prosaïque du lecteur (comme les 'règles' fameuses de l'art poétique ont pour effet de rappeler sans cesse au poète l'*univers complexe* de cet art.)

(*Œuvres*, Pléiade edition, t. i, p. 1294)

The question of the affinity between Horace, Mallarmé and Scève is one that contains and embodies certain basic elements in European thinking about poetry. Certainly, all three poets are working with different raw materials, different conventions and different backgrounds. But all three are part of a larger tradition. The problem is too complicated and vast to deal with in this book. Yet one of its facets deserves some discussion, however brief. It is a commonplace notion that obscurity in the very best poets is not intended to puzzle the reader. As Valéry said in a letter to Aimé Lafont on this question,

Je ne veux jamais être obscur, et quand je le suis,– je veux dire: quand je le suis pour un lecteur lettré, et non superficiel,– je le suis par l'impuissance de ne pas l'être. (op. cit., vol. i, p. 1625)

This emphasis on *pour un lecteur lettré* removes one element of difficulty: the naive reader who expects that he will understand a poem on the first reading. The second point – Valéry's insistence on his *impuissance de ne pas l'être* – is valid for Horace, Scève and Mallarmé. For Horace told the Pisones that what he found very difficult in practice was

Brevis esse laboro
Obscurus fio... (*Ars poetica*, lines 25–6)

Horace points to one of his faults – if it can be called a fault – namely the desire to be short and dense, without being unintelligible, in an ironic, colloquial, highly stylised and highly conscious art-produced artefact. Readers of his poetry regard his 'obscurity' and 'difficulty' in the same way as they regard these qualities in Scève or Mallarmé: a difficulty inherent in writers to 'translate' intellectual and emotional inner thoughts on to a public platform.

In the elucidation of these three poems, the intellect has played a capital role. And this process is difficult; but there is not the difficulty of certain Surrealist poems, nor the original, but to a large extent, private symbolism of Blake. Poetry is, in one sense, myth and symbol and as it is almost impossible to make up one's own language and still be understood; it follows that intelligibility depends largely on heritage. One thing remains in our minds after this analysis of three poems: in terms of linguistic patterning, Scève is easier to understand if we look backwards to Augustan Rome and forwards to the nineteenth century in France. There is something we will have to look at more closely – and that something is called rhetorical tradition.

Poetry tends to be allusive and the central things in the poetry of modern Western civilisation are the Greek and Roman classics, the Bible and the native tradition in which the poem was written.

Every poem is irremediably rooted in its past; it has a relationship with a tradition, and its meanings are clarified and enriched by a knowledge of previous contexts. The poem has the power of evoking a deep response in the reader if that reader is aware both sensitively and intellectually of the literary tradition that the poet, consciously or unconsciously, was taking for granted. The literary analysis should lead one back into a deepened state of excitement. Any poet who thrills us '*d'un frisson fraternel*' on first reading him, who activates in us a sense of 'awe' and a feeling of half-recognition of permanent themes and problems transmuted into poetry establishes immediately a relationship between himself as poet and his readers. Every great poet starts out with his own raw and crude emotions, but the tradition within which he is working plays a dominant role in moulding and crystallising his feelings.

The broad framework in which Scève was working provides

difficulty for twentieth-century readers. The outline of the tradition of Western European love poetry up to the French Renaissance is too well known to need repeating. Scève's greatness as a love poet does not automatically lie in the novelty of his themes. Indeed, it is rare for a person to be great in the sense of being a new emotional being, capable of registering the novelty of feelings and, as it were, proving himself to be interesting precisely because of newness. If one recalls Proust in describing Swann in love thus,

Se sentir transformé en une créature étrangère à l'humanité, aveugle, dépourvue de facultés logiques, presque une fantastique licorne, une créature chimérique ne percevant le monde que par l'ouïe.

(Pléiade edition, Paris, 1954, vol. 1, p. 237)

is this not common to all people in love? This 'volupté d'être amoureux, de ne vivre que d'amour' (p. 267) is deeply felt by lovers anywhere. But it requires, say, Proust or Scève to give it verbal expression. There is no décalage between what we as ordinary beings experience and what writers experience: the material is the same. The crudeness of the emotion does not imply anything about its intensity. If we return for a brief moment to the Proust quotation, is it surprising that the analogy should be exactly the same as in dizain 6 of Scève – the unicorn? Is it surprising that the senses of the lover are disorganised and that many of the dizains in Scève focus the loss of sight? We can find the same sort of correlation between any two artists and it is partly our task as serious readers of literature to interpret every work in the light of those works we know. We use our knowledge to clarify the poems and enrich the reader's appreciation of them. It is certainly possible to appreciate a number of Scève's dizains by training on them no more than our sensibility and some intellectual nimbleness. It has been done brilliantly for instance by Boutang. He starts from a personal evaluation of a dizain: for example, the way in which *A si hault bien de tant saincte amytié* (no. 346) makes its effect on him; he then moves on to examine the first six lines and the last four and finally comments – 'La gloire commune ou l'immortalité est mieux comprise au moyen de cette interprétation mystique de la vallée du Rhône. L'élévation égale et monotone se justifie par le spectacle qu'elle permet de contempler.'[1] This is possible

---

[1] Boutang, op. cit., p. 115.

because a great deal of *Délie* is concerned with such fundamental aspects of love as to be in some ways timeless. Yet every age reacts to a dizain in very different ways. For instance, the dizains of Scève chosen by Sainte-Beuve are not ones that a twentieth-century critic would automatically choose as the best. But, paradoxically, this timeless relevance becomes even more obvious when we try to read Scève with a knowledge of literary tradition and literary scholarship.

Undoubtedly the sixteenth-century reader found Scève a difficult poet, much as Valéry did not reveal himself to the great academic critics fifty years ago. But how much more difficult it is for the modern reader who, on opening his copy of *Délie*, is immediately puzzled by what might be the relevance of the woodcuts and mottoes; who, when reading the dizains experiences an uneasy feeling of frustration as he gropes for associations so distant in the past as to appear out of reach. The more frustrated if he is fully conscious of the fact (he may have already read James Joyce or Ezra Pound) that the difficult writer, writing for an élite, relies on the knowledge and culture of his reader.

The present study does not boast of having removed all the difficulties in the text of *Délie* nor would one condone the use of erudition for erudition's sake. What is intended is simply to show how our appreciation of Scève, as the poet of love, is at the same time made truly critical and very much intensified when we realise the conventions which moulded his work and the wealth of literary culture he was entitled to draw from.

In the sixteenth century petrarchism was the accepted style for elevated expression in amatory verse. But the petrarchist tradition did not give poets a vision of the love-experience. The tradition needed to be given a particular direction or emotional orientation by each poet in order to make an impact on the reader.

The literary tradition of the Renaissance comprised not only petrarchist themes, conceits and terminology and Neo-Platonic metaphysical ideas. It was a beneficiary too of the love poetry of Rome. Catullus, Propertius, Tibullus and Ovid had turned the Hellenistic epigram (as exemplified in *The Greek Anthology*) into personal lyrical poems. The love poets had steeped themselves in the literary forms used by the Greeks, in the myths which the Greeks had exploited; they had mastered the verbal technicalities demanded of a poet by the Latin language; they had explored the allusive resources of their inherited poetic tradition and enriched it by their own originality in matters of form and content. Scève had a complete mastery of linguistic technique by the time he published *Délie* in 1544. He had translated a Spanish story into French; he had written Neo-Latin verse; he had contributed to the *Blasons* match that Marot had started; and he had tried his hand at Vergilian imitation in an eclogue called *Arion*.

He had experimented with the two languages of the bilingual Renaissance in France – French and Latin – and had decided in favour of writing a *canzoniere* in French. He knew that writing love poetry was fashionable, that Petrarch, 'ce Thuscan Apollo' (dizain 417) was avant-garde in France (Scève himself had been involved in the affair of 'discovering' Laura's tomb at Avignon in 1533); he was aware that Italy was the centre of European culture at the time (in 1547 an edition of Dante's *La Divina Commedia* by Jean de Tournes was dedicated to Scève). In Lyon he was the master of Italian culture and he realised that love poetry was the climax of Italy's maturation in Ancient literary civilisation.

The decision to write love poetry entailed certain standard themes or topics such as the *innamoramento* or the 'falling in love', the praise or dispraise of the lady, the description of certain experiences – for example the sudden and inexplicable changes from joy to sadness in the lover, or the physical transformations from heat to cold when the lover was in the presence of his mistress, the protestations of fidelity or railings against fickleness, the singing of happiness and the recording of misery. The lover only existed in what he loved and thought on; his soul became transferred to his lady so that it no longer belonged to him; if his love were returned, then he possessed her soul, while his soul lived in her; if his love were not returned, then he lost his soul and had nothing in return and thus was left only half-living. These are all aspects of a relationship experienced or imagined between two people, and it is the poet's task to make the relationship intensely felt by his readers. He has to express the passion he feels (or imagines or puts forward that he is feeling). Now it is not for us as serious readers to construct a theory of the passions, doctrines about Scève's love

or even prove that he was a good lover. To quote Rush Rhees'
statements,

Evidently none can write about love. Gifted writers don't try. (Stendhal
– but has anyone else?) When anyone does, the result is commonplace
and boring. Not because love is boring. It is the theme of poems and
plays and stories more frequently, perhaps, than any other. And a new
portrayal of it by any real writer will always hold us. But if he starts to
tell us *about* love, we stop reading.

('The Tree of Nebuchadnezzar', *The Human World*,
no. 4 (1971), p. 24)

But we must know various things that were embedded in the
European tradition first. Beneath the various traditional modes
of expressing features of a love-affair lie the basic psychological,
moral, metaphysical and social attitudes. Thus, for example, the
whole machinery of Cupid, Eros, Anteros, Venus or the God of
Love is merely a means of expressing initially the inexplicability
of falling in love. This is an emotion that is not easily expressed,
catalogued nor understood. Moreover the mystery of why one
should fall in love with a particular person has to be rationalised
and explored *after* the event. The traditional mode of expression, cast in mythological form, entailed more often than not
leaving the initiative to Cupid. The initial battle was between
Cupid (or Eros or Venus), set forth as a god with manifold tricks
and powers, and the lover who was *surprised*: in other words an
active agent against a passive victim. Poets had expressed this in
different ways: for instance, 'falling in love' was represented as
the God of Love taking vengeance on indifferent youth or Cupid
maliciously trapping innocent and carefree hearts. Even when
we recognise the mythological machinery of love as outmoded
we must recognise at the same time that it is trying to explain
the inexplicable.

In Scève's *Délie* a dizain may be a dense fabric, interweaving
abstract and concrete with a constant incorporation of detailed
verbal echoes from the petrarchist stock-in-trade. Like all his
French contemporaries Scève remembers or borrows evocative
images, key ideas on love, familiar phrases and lines from
Petrarch and from poets who are within the petrarchist tradition. But he has changed a number of features in the petrarchist
convention and this puts a totally new emotional orientation on
his own experience of love. McFarlane in the introduction to

17

his fine edition of *Délie* (p. 27) is hesitant about the amount of Graeco-Roman tradition there was in Scève:

What is rather unexpected is that Scève, whose links with the humanists and the Neo-Latin poets of the Lyon *sodalitium* are well known, and who himself had written quite a lot of Latin verse, should have introduced such a minute number of classical echoes of a textual nature.

Instead of looking further at the assumptions and attitudes that Scève was formulating Professor McFarlane concludes his survey of merely textual correspondences with the words 'At all events the total is negligible.' In fact a greater affinity between Scève and the Roman love poets than between Scève and Petrarch may often be seen, once one has gone beyond the textual dependence and examined the vision of the love experience. In fact, the three main streams of tradition in the sixteenth century – the Biblical, the Roman or classical and the petrarchist – will play their own roles in *Délie*. Sometimes they will be conjured up together in a particular dizain; sometimes the orientation will be created through a clash or a warring of the three traditions; and sometimes the poet will be creating a fusion, entirely individual to the dizain he is composing, between the three traditions. This study will, to a large extent, be examining the traditions in order to make articulate the 'voices of silence' that Scève needs to establish his individual talent. And it will also be analysis via scholarship and scholarship via analysis. We shall look at the first stage in the next chapter – the *innamoramento* – where we shall start to hear those voices from past tradition.

# 2

# 'INNAMORAMENTO'

The tradition that Scève was working in was broadly the Graeco-Roman one, more narrowly the fashionable petrarchist one. As with any work of art the adequate response is not automatic; the process of getting to know the work is a long one; it is not only living in, so to speak, a well-stocked reference library. Every poet is a painter of *papiers collés*: to design his own *collage* is to take existing forms, existing themes – be they intellectual ideas, emotional or literary feelings – and make a new form of poetry out of them. In every form of art our personal experience is crucial but it is only the starting point in deepening our experience; we need also to steep ourselves in the knowledge of the background that is necessary to understand emotionally and intellectually the works of art of any century.

Since Scève, the author of *Délie*, is a love poet, and every great love poet has to start with the experience of falling in love let us look first at three descriptions of this *innamoramento* to see what the comparison reveals: the first elegy of Propertius' *monobiblos*, Petrarch's first sonnet and Scève's first dizain.[1]

[1] There can be no doubt that Scève had read Propertius. The *editio princeps* of Propertius was published in Venice, 1472 and the best edition throughout the sixteenth century was Beroaldus' which first came out in Bologna, in 1487. In a Latin epigram (in Guégan, *Œuvres poétiques complètes de Maurice Scève*, Paris, 1927, p. 312) Scève is reminiscent of Propertius, e.g.

> Si nimis ardenti, nimis o tibi Gellia friget:
> Non mirum: tua nam Gellia tota gelu est.
> Delia si laetis blandum mihi ridet ocellis:
> Non mirum: mea nam Delia delitiae est.
> (first four lines of the epigram to Ducher)

And in dizain 408 of *Délie* there is an allusion to the Mausoleum or Pyramid erected for Mausolus, satrap of Caria, by his widow Artemisia which is a direct reminiscence of the four lines in Propertius, III.2.19–24,

> nam neque pyramidum sumptus ad sidera ducti
> nec Iouis Elei caelum imitata domus
> nec Mausolei dives fortuna sepulcri
> mortis ab extrema condicione vacant.

[*Note 1 continued*]

> *Cynthia prima suis miserum me cepit ocellis*
>     *contactum nullis ante cupidinibus.*
> *tum mihi constantis deiecit lumina fastus,*
>     *et caput inpositis pressit Amor pedibus,*
> *donec me docuit castas odisse puellas*
>     *inprobus et nullo vivere consilio.*
> *et mihi iam toto furor hic non deficit anno,*
>     *cum tamen adversos cogor habere deos.*
> *Milanion nullos fugiendo, Tulle, labores*
>     *saevitiam durae contudit Iasidos.*
> *nam modo Partheniis amens errabat in antris,*
>     *ibat et hirsutas ille videre feras;*
> *ille etiam Hylaei percussus vulnere rami*
>     *saucius Arcadiis rupibus ingemuit.*
> *ergo velocem potuit domuisse puellam:*
>     *tantum in amore preces et benefacta valent.*
> *in me tardus Amor non ullas cogitat artes,*
>     *nec meminit notas, ut prius, ire vias.*
> *at vos, deductae quibus est fallacia lunae*
>     *et labor in magicis sacra piare focis,*
> *en agedum dominae mentem convertite nostrae*
>     *et facite illa meo palleat ore magis!*
> *tunc ego crediderim vobis et sidera et amnes*
>     *posse Cytaeines ducere carminibus.*
> *aut vos, qui sero lapsum revocatis, amici,*
>     *quaerite non sani pectoris auxilia.*
> *fortiter et ferrum saevos patiemur et ignes,*
>     *sit modo libertas, quae velit ira, loqui.*
> *ferte per extremas gentes et ferte per undas,*
>     *qua non ulla meum femina norit iter:*
> *vos remanete, quibus facili deus annuit aure,*
>     *sitis et in tuto semper amore pares!*
> *in me nostra Venus noctes exercet amaras,*
>     *et nullo vacuus tempore defit Amor.*
> *hoc, moneo, vitate malum: sua quemque moretur*
>     *cura, neque assueto mutet amore locum.*
> *quodsi quis monitis tardas adverterit aures,*
>     *heu referet quanto verba dolore mea!*     (*Propertius*, I.I.I)

[Cynthia it was who first captured me with her eyes, poor wretch that I was and untouched till then by any desires. Then Love caused eyes that had been steadfast in disdain to be lowered and placing his feet on my head pressed down on me till unrelenting he taught me to hate girls that are chaste and to live a life of recklessness. A year has passed and my madness does not pass away, even though my suit has the gods against it. It was by shirking no toils, Tullus, that Milanion crushed the spirit of the cruel daughter of Iasion. For once *he* was wandering out of his mind amidst the hollows of Mount Parthenium and came face to face with the shaggy wild beasts, he too struck by a blow from Hylaeus' club, groaned in pain among the crags of Arcadia. And so he was able to tame the fleet-footed girl. That's how much prayer and good deeds are worth in love. But as for me, slow witted Love has lost his art and does not remember to tread the paths that once he trod. But you who beguile men's hearts by charming down the moon from heaven and who

## 'INNAMORAMENTO'

The opening couplet of Propertius' poem is arresting:

> Cynthia prima suis miserum me cepit ocellis,
> contactum nullis ante cupidinibus.

The first word the poet utters is *Cynthia*. Its choice directs the reader's mind along a track of associations – Cynthia the radiant Moon Goddess, Diana the goddess of chastity, the maiden huntress, and as the *Dea Triformis* (Selene in heaven, Artemis on earth, Hecate in hell) and the goddess of magicians – which is supplied by mythology and had claims to be a poetic language centuries before Propertius called his mistress Cynthia. Proper-

---

labour to consecrate your rites on magic altars, go change my mistress's mind and make her face more pale than mine. Then will I trust your claim to have power over stars and rivers to lead them where you will by Colchian charms. Or else, my friends, you who would recall me too late from the downward path seek all the remedies for a diseased heart. I will bravely bear the savage fires and the knife if only I may win liberty to speak the words my anger prompts. Bear me far through nations and seas at the world's end where never a woman may trace my path. Stay at home you to whose prayer the god gives easy audience and answers 'Yes' and each to each give equal response of safe love. Against me our Venus plies nights of bitterness, and Love that has no respite faileth never. Lovers, I warn you all. Flee the woe that is now mine: cling each one to his own beloved, and never change when love has found its home. But if any all too late give ear to these my warnings, with what agony will he recall my words!]

(I have used the Carducci edition of Petrarch's *Rime*, Florence, 1957.)

> Voi ch'ascoltate in rime sparse il suono
>   Di quei sospiri ond'io nudriva'l core
>   In su'l mio primo giovenile errore,
>   Quand'era in parte altr'uom da quel ch'i' sono;
> Del vario stile, in ch'io piango e ragiono
>   Fra le vane speranze e'l van dolore,
>   Ove sia chi per prova intenda amore,
>   Spero trovar pietà non che perdono.
> Ma ben veggio or sí come al popol tutto
>   Favola fui gran tempo, onde sovente
>   Di me medesmo meco mi vergogno;
> E del mio vaneggiar vergogna è'l frutto,
>   E'l pentersi, e'l conoscer chiaramente
>   Che quanto piace al mondo è breve sogno.

> L'Œil trop ardent en mes ieunes erreurs
> Girouettoit, mal cault, a l'impourueue:
> Voicy (ô paour d'agreables terreurs)
> Mon Basilique auec sa poingnant' veue
> Perçant Corps, Coeur, & Raison despourueue,
> Vint penetrer en l'Ame de mon Ame.
>   Grand fut le coup, qui sans tranchante lame
> Fait, que viuant le Corps, l'Esprit desuie,
> Piteuse hostie au conspect de toy, Dame,
> Constituée Idole de ma vie.

tius' use of mythology introduces an element of mystery which adds a further poetical dimension to what he is going to say. *Cynthia prima* tells the reader that this relationship comes first and is unique. (Whether or not this is historically true is irrelevant, for this is a phrase in a poem and not the first words of an autobiographical or real statement.) *Suis...me* posits a relationship between the first person and the third person i.e. Cynthia is not *addressed*; the *me* is going to see it from a personal point of view (incidentally Propertius uses the first person far more often than other Roman poets), and this *persona* of the poet is a private personal one quite unlike the public *persona* he will use in other poems (e.g. IV.9; IV.18; V.6). *Miserum...cepit ocellis*: the *coup de foudre* of the *innamoramento*; she captured me not with her *oculis* but with her *ocellis* – the diminutive is endearing. Allusions to the beauty of Cynthia's eyes occur again and again after this first one (e.g. III.3.23) and we feel a thrill of admiration, since sight is our most powerful sense. *Miserum* calls to mind all the suffering and hardship of love: for instance, the very famous poem of Catullus (no. 8) starts,

> Miser Catulle, desinas ineptire...

The ironic, self-mocking use of *miser* in Catullus invites the reader inside the poet's situation, recalling all the associations of melancholy, wretchedness, sickness of heart, complete weariness, violence and excess in love (cf. Vergil, *Aen.*, 5.655) but at the same time puts the reader at a distance, to share with Catullus the poet the spectacle of Catullus the lover. Similarly, Propertius introduces an ambivalent note with his *miserum*: we have to take his role or his *persona* seriously and yet it is at once both real and exaggerated; his anguish must be taken seriously and yet intellectually it is seen for what it is. He follows it immediately by *cepit ocellis*: there is no God of Love here; rather it is the poet's mistress who has done the capturing and made a piteous being out of someone who was not before pitiable. Propertius rounds off the starting point of his *innamoramento* in the second line: '*I* have never been affected emotionally before, never been touched (*contactum* perhaps suggesting disease, viz. the *insania* of love. Contrast this with II.12.19, *intactos isto satius temptare veneno*) by *cupidinibus*, carnal desires, lusts or sex impulses. This is the first love affair and there never will be another one quite like this one (cf. I.12.20, *Cynthia prima fuit*,

*Cynthia finis erit*). *I* am going to analyse what this one feels like within me.'

What is distinctive about these lines is their exciting and disturbing nature: the poet is not singing of the joy or misery of the 'falling in love' but is putting into words what many humans experience when they fall in love. Moreover, the linguistic formulation is entrenched in the allusive tradition. For example, every word laconically conveys more than it says: Cynthia brings in mythology, *miser* recalls all the lovers that the Graeco-Roman world has sung about, *cupidinibus* refers to the machinery of love, the relationship (or rather what *she* has done to *me*) is between 'me and her', and these two pronouns compose the world which Propertius analyses. The poet invites us to share the experience that the poem is about to offer, and the difficulty of the language (later in the poem) is over-shadowed by the difficulty inherent in the poet's thinking process.

If we turn to the opening lines of Petrarch's first sonnet,

> Voi ch'ascoltate in rime sparse il suono
> Di quei sospiri ond'io nudriva'l core
> In su'l mio primo giovenile errore...

we are surprised to find that Petrarch has not begun with the *innamoramento*; that has to wait until the second sonnet. The angle of vision of the reader is entirely focussed on the poet's justifications for 'falling in love'. Already there is a slackening off of human intensity about a love relationship. The poet must come to grips with self-examination or conscience; the relationship is seen from a psychological point of view, but it is really not a double relationship but a single one – the poet in a human predicament explaining the causes to the readers. In other words the poem is not concerned with the internal motivation to love; rather it is dealing with the external cause of Petrarch's love. The main concern in the poem is self-knowledge and the power of the will against the passion roused in the poet by this mortal love. *In su'l mio primo giovenile errore* reminds us of *error* in Roman love poetry, an error in the sense of delusion, distraction, insanity and every kind of derangement of love (e.g. Vergil, *Ecl.*, 8.41). But, whereas the word in classical Latin very rarely carries with it moral implications, for Petrarch it has ethical and theological considerations built into it. Some of Petrarch's comments on his love poetry show that this love affair is seen primarily from a Christian point of view: for instance,

Hinc illa vulgaria iuvenilium laborum meorum cantica, quorum hodie pudet ac poenitet, sed eodem morbo affectis, ut videmus, acceptissima...[1]

The self-recrimination and the guilty conscience are present in Petrarch's *canzoniere* right from these first few lines and provide a different orientation from Propertius.

Let us now look at the first lines of Scève,

> L'Œil trop ardent en mes ieunes erreurs
> Girouettoit, mal cault, a l'impourueue:
> Voicy (ô paour d'agreables terreurs)
> Mon Basilisque auec sa poingnant' veue
> Perçant Corps, Coeur, & Raison despourueue,
> Vint penetrer en l'Ame de mon Ame.

This time the first word is *L'Œil*: but it is the poet's eye, not the mistress's as it was in Propertius. Scève incorporates Petrarch's *errore* in *erreurs*: he can arouse the expectation of a familiar phrase in a reader who is as steeped as he is in Petrarch's poetry (and of course the petrarchists; for the phrase *giovenile errore* is used by Serafino and Bembo for instance and in fact in the *Hecatomphila* of L. B. Alberti, the plural *quelli miei giovanili errori* is used in the first poem) and then obliterate it. By recasting it in a different language and pluralising the abstract noun (so making it concrete; a characteristic device of Roman poetry) he creates something very different out of the phrase. Whereas the *errore* would be the abstract fault or error, its plural is part of a larger more specific thing – the wanderings of carefree youth. There is very little of Petrarch's attitude or his conception of *errore* in his sonnet; Scève's use of the phrase places his dizain in a Petrarchan cast, but any distinctively Petrarchan meaning is immediately cancelled by the different words that form the context. Readers would be reminded of Petrarch's phrase but on looking closely at the Scève dizain would be aware of a significant dissimilarity. For Scève's *erreurs* are tied to the action of the roving eye: it conjures up the youthful lover, falling in love many times, becoming infatuated by passing and random love affairs and perhaps standing around to admire pretty girls

---

[1] *Epistolae de rebus familiaribus et Variae*, ed. Gius. Fracassetti, Florence, 1863, VIII, 3.

as they pass. The word here has no moral or theological connotation. The next line with the very emphatic *girouettoit* (which, according to McFarlane, is a neologism) captures the reckless character of the eye, darting hither and thither like a weathercock blown by the winds of fancy. If we read the next line slowly and notice its abstract words we can feel the anticipation which is resolved by the fourth line. *L'Œil* has intersected with the sharp-pointed stab of the lady's eye; the impact of her transfixing gaze on his own eye tears piercingly through every faculty and penetrates his innermost being. This is the *innamoramento*, and one sees it through the coupling of two pairs of eyes: *ardent, girouettoit, poingnant' veue, perçant* and *penetrer*.

Scève has altered a number of features of the petrarchist convention in these first six lines in *Délie*: the gods are forgotten – Cupid or Eros, Venus or Love do not manipulate the poet and his mistress – and the poem is not Christian at all. Even the comparison of the lady's eyes with those of a basilisk brings into the poem associations with fire, death and sexuality.[1] The description of the basilisk is a literary tradition derived mainly from the full account given by Pliny the Elder (*Nat. Hist.* 8.33) where he says

duodenum non amplius digitorum magnitudine, candida in capite macula, ut quodam diademate insignem...nec flexu multiplici, ut reliquae (serpentes) corpus impellit, sed celsus et erectus in medio incedens.

It is a kind of lizard or snake, the deadly power of whose eyes and breath is capable of killing any man or beast that approaches. In the context of the Neo-Platonic theory of love *Mon Basilisque* would be readily understood by Scève's contemporaries. Ficino in his *Commentaire sur le Banquet de Platon* (ed. Raymond Marcel, Paris, 1956, 2e discours, Ch. 8) insists upon the idea that the lover dies in himself when he 'falls in love' but is resurrected in his beloved if his love is returned, since he is then able to find himself in the object of his love,

Cet amant...est une âme morte dans son propre corps et vivante dans le corps d'un autre...l'amant qui n'est pas aimé est complètement mort...         (pp. 155–6)

---

[1] See also D. Fenoaltea, 'Three animal images in the *Délie*: new perspectives on Scève's use of Petrarch's *Rime*', *BHR*, t. xxxiv, pp. 413–26, 1972 for a discussion on Scève's and Petrarch's use of the basilisk image.

In this linguistic exploration of the relationship between the poet and his mistress there is an intellectual quality that owes nothing to Petrarch or to the petrarchist convention. We have a personal reaction to the *innamoramento* without any of the religious feelings that are the conceptual base of Petrarch's whole examination of love. It is clear that Propertius and Scève are dealing with human love in an intensely emotional yet intensely intellectualised way. Petrarch, by contrast, is singing about his love in an uncomplicated manner.

The next few lines of Propertius,

> tum mihi constantis deiecit lumina fastus,
>    et caput inpositis pressit Amor pedibus,
> donec me docuit castas odisse puellas
>    inprobus et nullo vivere consilio...         (lines 3–6)

start with a *tum* which fixes the moment abruptly, and this leads us into the analysis of the complete dejection into which, from that precise point in time, the poet is cast. The *ocellis* are powerful not only because of their beauty but because they have completely subjected the poet's resolute disdain. Various problems are raised here by the complexity of mythological allusion, the boldness of the imagery and persistent obscurity. The difficulty of the poem lies in the apparent rationality of his statements underlaid by non-rational meanings: associative words, images, key-ideas upset the rationality of the poem. Take for example the use of *Amor* in the fourth line. It looks tired and hackneyed like the icy heart of an Italian lady in the fifteenth century. But in fact it is like Racine's

> Brûlé de plus de feux que je n'en allumai,
>                 (*Andromaque*, I. 4)

which far from being only a brilliant but empty conceit condenses into one line a number of leit-motifs of the play. For *Amor* is not only the God of Love, its obvious and immediate sense in the context, but also the power of love, inside or outside a person, driving him to 'fall in love' and the thing love – what one feels inside oneself, ranging from carnal desire to the sexual act itself. Another example is the Atalanta allusion that comes shortly afterwards:

> Milanion nullos fugiendo, Tulle, labores
>    saevitiam durae contudit Iasidos.

nam modo Partheniis amens errabat in antris,
   ibat et hirsutas ille videre feras;
ille etiam Hylaei percussus vulnere rami
   saucius Arcadiis rupibus ingemuit.
ergo velocem potuit domuisse puellam:
   tantum in amore preces et benefacta valent.

(lines 9–16)

She was a huntress-maiden won by Milanion after a violent fight
with the centaurs who attacked her. Key-words like *saevitiam,
furor, amens errabat, velocem, durae, saucius* could all be applied
to the poet's own feelings but by an artistic illusion they are put
within Milanion's story and only reverberate onto Propertius
himself. Line 15 with *domuisse* has echoes throughout *Délie*. *Domo*
has as an original meaning 'to tame or domesticate' or to bring
someone to a state which is opposed to brutish animals. This
meaning of *domo* is very Roman and was widely used in love
poetry (cf. Horace, *Odes*, I.27.14, 'quae te cumque domat Venus';
and also in Cicero, *de Or.* I.194, 'domitas habere libidines,
coercere omnes cupiditates'). Scève uses *domestiquer* more than
once. For instance, the 48th woodcut contains the fly, which
sixteenth-century mythographers took as a symbol of 'untamed-
ness'.[1] For the dizain (429) describes the nature and attitude of
Délie in terms of *rusticité* (a Latinism meaning the habits of the
country, *sauvagerie* almost):

      Ia soit ce encor, que l'importunité
      Par le priué de frequentation
      Puisse polir toute rusticité
      Tant ennemye a reputation:
      Et qu'en son cœur face habitation
      A la vertu gentilesse adonnée,
      Estant en mœurs mieulx conditionée,
      Que nul, qui soit quelque part, qu'elle voyse:
      Elle est (pourtant) en amours si mal née,
      Que plus y hante, & moins s'y appriuoyse.

[1] It is possible that Scève borrowed this idea from Serafino, who has the
following lines in his 22nd Sonnet (*Opere del facundissimo Seraphino Aquilano
collette per Francesco Flavio*, Venetia, 1502) B.N. copy, Rés. Yd. 1344.

      Tu nocte e giorno fra le gente stai
      Et pur domesticar mai non ti puoi.
      Io da che preso fui converso assai
      Con vaghe donne: et con legami suoi
      Mio cor domesticar non potten mai.

Serafino is comparing himself with a bird; the tone of the courtly poem
contrasts sharply with the dizain of Scève.

2-2

The general belief (lines 1–4) forms part of a concessive clause, and is followed (lines 5–8) by another concessive, narrowed from the general to the particular, to Délie, who has *gentilesse* and is better *conditionée en mœurs* than anyone else. But in spite of this she is like the fly. This dizain is a recognition of the poet's failure to 'domesticate' her, and may be contrasted with dizain 287 where he has succeeded for a brief moment in taming her,

> Fortune en fin te peut domestiquer,
> Ou les trauaulx de ma si longue queste,
> Te contraignant par pitié d'appliquer
> L'oreille sourde a ma iuste requeste.

Sensual satisfaction (excluded by both Petrarch and the petrarchists almost by definition) is not excluded in Scève. Both Propertius and Scève know that one of the powerful effects of love is precisely to change *rusticité* into *gentilesse* and that love alone can effect such a metamorphosis. The duality of Délie's nature – chaste and carnal at the same time – is the basis of the cycle's structure and the themes that Scève is exploiting branch out from this central position. We shall look at this duality of love in a later chapter.

In Propertius the Cynthia–Moon associations of the mythological tradition implicit in the choice of name are exploited:

> at vos, deductae quibus est fallacia lunae
> et labor in magicis sacra piare focis,
> en agedum dominae mentem convertite nostrae
> et facite illa meo palleat ore magis!        (lines 19–22)

where the charming of the Moon is taken as representative of the magicians' rites, and they are challenged to demonstrate their powers by charming Cynthia. But the poet is only allowing these irrational impulses sway because he hopes for a stable relationship – which intellectually he knows is impossible. Propertius sees all that he experiences quite clearly but he cannot prevent himself from experiencing it.

If we look at Petrarch's sonnet it is clear that the analysis is not intellectual but moral and spiritual. For example in line 4 he mentions that when he fell in love he was

> altr'uom da quel ch'i'sono.

Like Propertius he places the experience in the past, but in order to pass censure on himself and see what a fool he had been

Favola fui gran tempo, onde sovente
Di me medesmo meco mi vergogno:

He knows shame, repentance and self-consciousness as a result
of his love. Sixteenth-century comments on Petrarch's first sonnet
put it in the proper perspective: for instance, Giovanni Talen-
toni in his *Lettione sopra'l principio del Canzoniere del Petrarca* (1587)
says that this sonnet is acceptable since Petrarch's confession is
present and his apology for his varied style, 'si da a conoscere
per huomo costumato, e buono, e perciò si rende l'auditor docile,
cioè, disposto a comprender quel, che poi si tratta'.[1] The moral
lessons taught arise from the great superiority of Petrarch over
his predecessors and this superiority is that of the Christian
religion over paganism. Or Nicolò Franco who in his dialogue,
*Il Petrarchista* (Venice, 1539) points this difference between
Petrarch and the Augustan Latin love poets rather sharply. He
stresses the stability of Petrarch's love as contrasted with
Propertius and his Cynthia and says that Petrarch's qualities
were moral ones. He is to be admired for his substance as well
as for his style, and indeed for his character as a man,

chi puo dire quanti e quali sentimenti de la diuina, e de la humana
philosophia si stieno ascosi ne le sue rime? Quanto e egli (O Dio
immortale) modesto? Quanto terso, e netto d'ogni lasciua ruggine?
Quanto senza lasciuia leggiadro? Quanto e religioso ne i pensieri?
Quanto e casto ne la mente? Quanto e Platonico nel suo amore?[2]

There is an awareness that love is sinful: to record one's *errore*
is therefore to take a Christian attitude to love which is totally
different from that of either Propertius or Scève. Nor is our
conclusion about Petrarch modified when we turn to the second
sonnet on the *innamoramento. Per fare una leggiadra sua vendetta*
is situationalized as Love taking vengeance on the poet for
his *ben mille offese*. The poet is immediately on the defensive,
Love on the offensive, crafty and cunning, taking up his bow
*celatemente* and dealing his victim a mortal blow. Love is the
enemy of God, that is the Christian God; the poet's defence
would be repentance and weeping, but the God of Love aims
his arrow to strike home so irretrievably that the poet is left with
no defence 'né vigor né spazio'; he was not even able to retire
from the fray. The human encounter between the poet and his

[1] Cited on p. 224–5, vol. I, Bernard Weinberg, *A History of Literary Criticism in
the Italian Renaissance*, University of Chicago Press, 1961.
[2] Cited by Weinberg, vol. I, p. 263.

lady is really not there at all.[1] In both Propertius and Scève the incident is depicted entirely in human terms; it is not a battle between the poet and the God of Love, though the image of Amor with his foot on Propertius' head in an attitude of triumph draws on the conventional battle of Eros versus the lover. Scève's dizain does not give us a static account of all the faculties taking up siege positions while the handsome Cupid comes to take them by surprise. It is a direct contact between himself and his mistress. In the last four lines,

> Grand fut le coup, qui sans tranchante lame
> Fait, que viuant le Corps, l'Esprit desuie,
> Piteuse hostie au conspect de toy, Dame,
> Constituée Idole de ma vie.

he analyses the effect on his body and soul: it seems as if he has been killed, because he is really unconscious of anything else save his basilisk's gaze. *L'esprit desuie* – the mind is lifeless, only the body is still alive. Note the tenses here: from the imperfect *girouettoit* to a past historic *vint* to the present *fait*; in this eternal present all the other words are heaped up around the verb – *hostie, au conspect de* and *constituée Idole*. The permanent place of his mistress within him is established in this first dizain. Furthermore, by choosing the term *hostie* from the Eucharist in the last but one line Scève does suggest communion, though in an entirely different way from Proust whose Marcel is given it by his mother

> et me l'avait tendue comme une hostie pour une communion de paix où mes lèvres puiseraient sa présence réelle et le pouvoir de m'endormir.                                      (op. cit. t. I, p. 13)

For the poet is transfixed into a complete loss of identity which is like the ecstacy that mystical poets find often in receiving on their tongues the Lord's wafer.

Through this analysis we can see how completely Scève departed from Petrarch in his treatment of the fragile relationship between two people in love. Quite apart from the *way* Scève expresses the experience, the orientation and attitude are totally different from Petrarch. The first dizain gives one the shock of

---

[1] This is true also of the third sonnet, *Era il giorno ch'al sol si scoloraro* in which the encounter between the lady and the poet takes place on a specific day – Good Friday. Indeed it almost hints at the fact that religious images are going to be inherent in Petrarch's *canzoniere* whereas they are not in Scève or Propertius and the moral evaluation of Petrarch's experience in love is totally different from the other two poets.

human experience which conditions the whole cycle. Scève fails in a large number of poems because he tries to convince through intellectual argument alone, but in the best poems the combination of emotional power and intellect transmutes the verse into poetry. In all love poetry there is a certain repetitiousness, but in both Propertius and Scève the intellectual qualities in their linguistic exploitation of the love relationship make it exciting and disturbing.

This shock of human experience in falling in love makes Scève experiment artistically with the veerings of personal feeling around the coupling of two pairs of eyes. He returns again and again to it; McFarlane (p. 34) says 'he is trying with all sorts of "approximations" to give perfect expression to the sentiment from which the whole book derives' and Staub in *Le Curieux Désir* (Geneva, 1967, p. 37) states that 'Scève est d'abord poète du regard; il le sera d'un bout à l'autre de ce recueil qui commence par le mot "l'Œil".' This key feeling runs through the cycle as a leit-motif and we shall see it more closely later on. Propertius in his first elegy shows brilliantly how tense was his mood of powerless awareness, and the emphasis in him and in Scève is on the poem itself as a piece of imaginative argument. Both are intellectual and both are obscure – but their obscurity comes from their conception of the poem as a delicately complex, richly allusive development of ideas and feelings. Perhaps we are now in a better position to see how different Scève's obscurity is from, say, Blake's. His best dizains have an immediate emotive appeal for the reader: words and images imprint themselves on one's mind before the argument is fully understood. Even at a first or second reading many dizains are illuminated by shafts of light – startling analogies, suggestive comparisons, insistently repeated words and vowel and consonantal harmony. Isolated lines of *Délie* like 'A l'embrunir des heures tenebreuses' (dizain 126), or 'De toute Mer tout long, & large espace' (259), or single images like 'Comme le Lieure accroppy en son giste' (129) or 'Tu me seras la Myrrhe incorruptible/Contre les vers de ma mortalité' (378) or the epigrammatic last line like 'Mort de ma mort, & vie de ma vie' (167) or the last three lines of dizain 35

> Car le mourir en ceste longue absence
> (Non toutesfois sans viure en toy) me semble
> Seruice esgal au souffrir en presence.

impinge on the reader's mind whether or not he grasps the lines in the context of the overall argument of the poem. Ideally, these echoes stimulate the reader not to enjoy them in isolation but to look further and fit them gradually into the pattern of the poem, which only fully reveals itself with close reading. The reader can allow himself to be played upon by the poet who is trying to awaken the right body of associations needed to understand his allusive technique. This power of suggestion is one of the marked characteristics of Scève and we shall have now to look at his setting in the France of the sixteenth century to see whether it is a unique characteristic and whether we understand it correctly.

# 3
# TRADITION

Tes vers sont beaux, & bien luysants,
Graves, & pleins de majesté:
Mais pour leur haulteur moins plaisants,
Car certes la difficulté
Le grand plaisir en a osté.
Brief, ilz ne quierent un Lecteur,
Mais la commune autorité
Dit qu'ilz requierent un Docteur.
(Charles Fontaine, *La Fontaine d'amour, contenant Elegies,
Epistres & Epigrammes*, Paris, 1545, miiij v°)

In the twentieth century there is still a Romantic tendency to
assume that the poet is a more sensitive and sincere member of
the community. Even Dr Leavis in his *New Bearings in English
Poetry* (London, 1932, ed. used 1967, p. 19) states '[the poet] is
unusually sensitive, unusually aware, more sincere and more
himself than the ordinary man can be. He knows what he feels
and knows what he is interested in.' Only in modern times has
sincerity become a value in itself. The apparent exception to this
rule in Horace's suggestion,

si vis me flere, dolendum est primum ipsi tibi
(*Ars Poetica*, line 102)

is only apparent. The stress is not on sincerity as an end in itself
but on sincerity as a means of poetic efficacy. The opposition
between a poet and an ordinary man is irrelevant. But the
tradition of poetry inducing poetry, the source of inspiration
being art rather than nature – whether one is exceptionally
sensitive to nature or not – is something that we must stress.
David Jones in *Epoch and Artist* (London, 1959, p. 29) makes
these important points when he says,

The artist, no matter of what sort or what his medium, must be moved
by the nature of whatever art he practises...The artist is not, necessarily, a person vastly more aware than his friends and relations of the
beauty of nature (or of anything), but rather he is the person most
aware of the nature of an art. The inception or renewal or deepening

33

of some artistic vitality comes to the artist via some other artist or some pre-existing art-form, not via nature.

The fundamental issue is whether a poet or artist or architect can in any century start and finish with sensitivity to nature – human or otherwise. Imitating nature on the lowest level in the sixteenth century meant the realistic or almost facsimile depiction of visible nature: for example the canvases of Flemish painters (objected to strongly by Michelangelo) crowded with literal detail – kettle, frying-pans, dripping pans and chafing dishes. On this view the challenge of art is to produce lifelike semblance: for instance, one would applaud the painting of a fish so succulent that it made one's mouth water. But even such an insister on exact and scientific observation of the things of the visible world as Leonardo da Vinci moves into another realm for his theory of painting – and that is creativity. In fact the painter or poet *selects* from nature and creates a work of art. There is no conflict between 'natural' and 'artificial' in the Renaissance because art was formally rather than naturalistically conceived. The actual imposing of form was not thought to set the poet in opposition to nature.

In the twentieth century many scholar-critics tend to assert that a poem is not *there on the page at all*.[1] There are marks on a printed sheet of paper but their meaning is not there. To discover their meaning – and thus their form and nature – we have to ask what the author intended to express when he laid one word following the other. And this is somewhat of a fallacy. For how can you discover what the author really meant unless you are that author? No-one can tell what a poet himself had in mind when he composed the poem. 'What did the author set out to do? And how far did he succeed in carrying it out?' are two questions that are, in my opinion, irrelevant. Aesthetic effects are not determined by intention. And the modern preference for Intentionalism is due to the belief that the reconstruction of

[1] In the verbal match which Dr Leavis played against Mr Bateson in *Scrutiny*, 1953 the latter says, 'Dr Leavis does not explain, however, in what sense the poem is *there* (wherever *there* is). I imagine he must mean that the poem, as we meet it on the printed page, consists of certain specific words arranged in a certain determinate order. But strictly speaking, of course, there is nothing *there*, nothing objectively apprehensible, except a number of conventional black marks. The meanings of the words, and therefore *a fortiori* the meaning of the whole poem, are emphatically not *there*.' (*A Selection from Scrutiny*, compiled by F. R. Leavis, vol. 2, p. 307).

intention in a writer is virtually history and history offers the promise of greater 'certainty'. All we can ask is what does the poem mean in terms of its context, its connotations and its historical, cultural, stylistic, intellectual and social assumptions. The meanings of words are created by the poet in the poem and nowhere else and part of our critical task is to try and recognise them. It is a vastly delicate task but it is not trying to invent the meanings ourselves.[1] I have insisted on these points not to join in the theoretical discussion of modern critics but because one element of subjectivism will, inevitably, be there in studying Scève. Yet the knowledge of tradition is essential in our perspective of him.

Furthermore, we half-forget that the basic power of poetry is to stir the emotions, to affect profoundly and to hold the reader at the poet's complete mercy, 'me tournant ça et là à son plaisir' as Du Bellay said. If the poem is 'une sorte de machine à produire l'état poétique au moyen des mots' (Valéry), if the poet is to be

industrieux à esmouvoir les passions et affections de l'ame, car c'est la meilleure partie de ton mestier, par des carmes qui t'esmouveront le premier, soit à rire ou à pleurer, afin que les lecteurs en facent autant apres toy...
(Ronsard, *Œuvres complètes*, Pléiade edition, Paris, 1950, t. II, p. 1024)

then the power of poetry is dependent on the poet's complete understanding of the means and devices in his native tongue. Poetry is not a deviant form of prose but a special form of language with its own unique function to perform. Valéry said in his 'Situation de Baudelaire' (*Œuvres*, Pléiade ed., vol. I, p. 611)

Le devoir, le travail, la fonction du poète sont de mettre en évidence et en action ces puissances de mouvement et d'enchantement, ces excitants de la vie affective et de la sensibilité intellectuelle, qui sont confondus dans le langage usuel avec les signes et les moyens de communication de la vie ordinaire et superficielle.

There is the same preoccupation with the differences between poetry and prose in Ronsard and the whole of the sixteenth

---

[1] In fact it is what Dr Leavis calls 'contextual' reading. His rejoinder to Mr Bateson in *Scrutiny* 1953 stresses what knowledge any critic must have, 'the most essential kind of knowledge can come only from an intelligent frequentation of the poetry – the poetry of the age in question, and the poetry of other ages...Some of the essential meanings that one has to recognize are *created* by the poet...' (*A Selection*, op. cit. vol. 2, pp. 312–13.)

century: the language – the concept of a poet working through the operation of his creating language – must be 'quasi séparer du langage commun...eslongnées presque du tout, ou pour le moins séparées de la Prose triviale et vulgaire (car le style prosaïque est ennemy capital de l'eloquence poëtique)'. (Ronsard, op. cit., t. II, p. 1015). Poetry does not aim primarily at communicating information; it is not exhaustible. The poet must revitalise language and be a master of every technical device, able to capture every word and emotion. For example, a realisation of what a certain kind of comparison can effect in a particular context will increase our awareness of a tragic situation and will strike home the full significance of the event. So that when Dido, rejected by Aeneas, has fallen upon her sword (a present from Aeneas) Vergil uses a comparison with larger things, with the fall of mighty cities like Carthage or Tyre, in order to bring out the full tragedy and the magnitude of her fall:

> lamentis gemituque et femineo ululatu
> tecta fremunt, resonat magnis plangoribus aether,
> non aliter quam si immissis ruat hostibus omnis
> Karthago aut antiqua Tyros, flammaeque furentes
> culmina perque hominum volvantur perque deorum.
>
> (*Aeneid*, IV. lines 667–71)

> [All was weeping and wailing, the streets were filled with a
>     keening
> Of women, the air resounded with terrible lamentations,
> It was as if Carthage or ancient Tyre should be falling,
> With enemy troops breaking into the town and a
>     conflagration
> Furiously sweeping over the abodes of men and of gods.]
>
> (C. Day Lewis' translation)

What we have here is a moving of the reader – by emotive and intellectual means first – the pressure is artistic not personal. The moving quality of poetry, its aptness to direct the will and passions, is always the important thing.

In the poem by Charles Fontaine which we quoted as a preliminary to this chapter we notice two things: the impression that Scève gave of being 'docte' and the notion that his lines are 'graves'. These are important for an understanding of sixteenth-century poetics and we now move on to discuss them in turn.

Many artists say little or nothing about the theoretical framework which surrounds their art. It is no paradox that Scève did not leave to posterity a convenient compendium of his own thoughts about poetry. For instance, we do not know what he thought about the 'originality' of his poetry. We saw in the last chapter that in his first dizain on 'falling in love' he was weaving in threads of Graeco-Roman literature and drawing on the contemporary petrarchist and Neo-Platonic conventions. Could we in any sense call his first dizain original? One must distinguish between two meanings of originality: the Romantic criterion of spontaneity – a work of literature which is not an imitation of previous works and in which a writer demonstrates his individuality, authenticity and sincerity by the degree to which he can compose new and personal human emotion in literature. And secondly, something which is native to a specific writer, invention and creativeness. We are not concerned with the first sense at all in the sixteenth century, for 'original' began to take on connotations of the Romantic and modern sense only in the seventeenth century.[1] The second sense had been a commonplace in antiquity, for 'While they affirmed that his (i.e. man's) arts are the products of naturally given faculties, imitate natural processes, use natural material, and assist natural evolutionary tendencies, they recognized a point where the conditioning influence of nature ends (both within and outside human beings) with man's free and rational creative power coming into play.'[2] The term 'original' had not yet been coined. But ideas exist without the terminology that later ages give them. Terms like rationalist, fideist or materialist were only begotten by the nineteenth century, and yet one could fairly argue that Montaigne was a fideist. We are not being unhistorical if we simply superimpose a structure of language on previously blurred outlines. To Febvre's argument that incredulity, rationalism or libertinism could not exist in the sixteenth century because the terms to describe these attitudes were not born we can reply with Busson

Non seulement nous n'acceptons pas ce paradoxe que l'incrédulité est impossible au XVIe siècle; nous dirions plutôt qu'elle a toujours existé. Parce que le mot *rationalisme* n'a été employé qu'au XIXe siècle quel historien de la philosophie raccourcira à ce point la vie de ce système?

---

[1] For the shift between the ancient and modern meanings of originality see G. Castor, *Pléiade Poetics*, C.U.P., 1964, esp. Ch. 7.

[2] A. J. Close 'Art and Nature in Antiquity and the Renaissance' in *Journal of the History of Ideas*, xxx, no. 4, 1969, p. 483.

Parce que le mot *fidéisme* date de 1838 quel historien de la théologie refusera de voir du fidéisme jusque dans le moyen age?[1]

In the same way it is not unhistorical to talk of originality in the sixteenth century. We mean 'being natural to what the poet does, *naïf*, natural, pertaining to the individual we are talking about.'[2] The originality of a given poet may operate within, be dependent on, tradition, and this very dependence may be the most important factor in his originality. And in this sense we can see seeds of originality in Scève's first dizain: enmeshed in past conventions it is stating in an individual and personal way how he fell in love. The dizain evokes the transition from the carefreeness before meeting Délie to the fixity and immobility after his whole being had been enslaved and this is emphasised by the language and the syntax: for example, the isolation of *Dame* slows down line 9 and the last line demands a stress on both *Constituée* and *Idole* thus creating an effect of firmness and solidity as contrasted with the movement of verbs and adverbs in the first two lines. Thus, although we saw in the last chapter how imitative the dizain is of Augustan love elegy and petrarchism, we can still see its originality. Echoing poets of previous ages or of different countries was to pay a debt to the past and was the greatest compliment that a poet could bestow on those poets whom he loved. Writing in the poet's native language of Provençal, as Dante did when describing Arnaut Daniel in the *Purgatorio* 26. 139ff., was an even greater compliment.

If I say that imitation is part of his originality what is the precise relation between the two? Imitation like originality has two meanings: mimesis – or imitation of nature – and literary allusiveness. Or, in more specific terms, the Aristotelian mimesis which had successive religious and philosophical layers encrusted around it and imitation of the works of previous authors, mostly Greek and Latin ones.[3] French poets in the sixteenth century thought that they had invented theories which were, if

---

[1] L. Febvre, *Le problème de l'incroyance au XVIe siècle. La religion de Rabelais*, Paris, 1944 and H. Busson, 'Les noms des incrédules au XVIe siècle', *BHR*, t. XVI, 1954, p. 282.

[2] See O. de Mourgues on 'originality' in *Actes du IVe Congrès de l'Association Internationale de littérature comparée*, The Hague–Paris, 1966, pp. 1261ff.

[3] For a fuller account of Aristotelian mimesis see G. Castor, op. cit., pp. 51–62, where he gives the definition of it in terms of imitation: 'it designated the relationship between the poem and a "subject" derived in some way from things which exist, from Nature, however interpreted'.

I may put it this way, pure imitations from the Graeco-Roman world; there was little that was new in Du Bellay's or Ronsard's theorising about poetry – but they both wrote excellent poetry. If we do not separate the meaning of mimesis from literary allusiveness we are in something of a quandary with Scève. For since his *Délie* came out before the (real) beginning of vernacular criticism in the French Renaissance and since he did not write an *Art of Poetry*, he offers little on the mimesis-imitation theme. And yet, literary allusiveness is one of the most pointed features of his poetry. Marot had been until the recent edition of his works by Professor C. A. Mayer in the same position: like Scève he did not hold forth theoretically upon poetry, and like Scève too his experimentation, his attempts at innovation and his break with the *Rhétoriqueurs* were unsung by the Pléiade who took for themselves the mantle of poetry and insisted that they, and they alone, could speak in public about the art of being a poet. Supposing that that were actually a major transgression it could have been rectified by more accurate literary historians. It is more than that: for not appearing to have mimesis in their minds when creating poetry Marot and Scève are damned by some scholars and critics. And yet, it is precisely mimesis that has led critics astray.

The first-rate poets in France were not thinking primarily in terms of a metaphysical framework; they were pragmatists in the theory of criticism; they were concerned, when writing poetry, not so much with the Aristotelian mimesis theory of imitation as with the tradition of literary allusiveness.[1] This allusive process entrenched in the Graeco-Roman culture is the one living, vital and dynamic aspect in the poetics of sixteenth-century France. The poets knew perfectly well what they were trying to do: re-grafting the tradition of Graeco-Roman culture on to the tree of French poetry. The tradition they were grasping towards was neither Platonic nor Aristotelian. It was literary.

It is difficult to say whether the literary or pseudo-scientific Aristotelian criticism was even read by Horace for example,[2]

---

[1] For a different view see G. Castor, op. cit. esp., Chs 5 and 6.
[2] See C. O. Brink, *Horace on Poetry: The 'Ars Poetica'*, Cambridge, 1971, esp. the Preface; see also his *Horace on Poetry. Prolegomena to the Literary Epistles*, Cambridge 1963, where on p. 140 he says 'I know no evidence of any first-hand knowledge of Aristotle's *Poetics* in Horace's time.'

and furthermore Catullus, Vergil, Propertius, Tibullus and Ovid cannot be understood as being only fine practitioners of rhetorical communication. The rhetorical education implicit in Cicero and Quintilian is one that *all* Romans who were educated at all had experienced. And so naturally Du Bellay's case for the development of French language and literature was based on the Romans' case for developing Latin. His view of his native tongue is coloured by the Romans' view of their language vis à vis Greek. Quintilian was acutely aware of the limitations of Latin as compared with Greek and insisted on the need to use all the resources of the language to show it at its best advantage. Latin, according to him, could not afford to aim at simplicity or bareness of style:

Sensus sublimes variique eruantur: permovendi omnes adfectus erunt, oratio translationum nitore inluminanda. non possumus esse tam graciles, simus fortiores: subtilitate vincimur, valeamus pondere: proprietas penes illos est certior, copia vincamus.     (Quintilian, XII.10.36)

In order to rival Greek, Latin had to use ornament since it did not possess the innate charm of Greek: Du Bellay had a similar inferiority complex vis à vis Italian and thus it seems that the principle of imitation was peculiarly appropriate.

Now in the early decades of the sixteenth century there was a spate of books and editions of Cicero and Quintilian which accept their views on the writing of poetry. We know the battle that went on between Bembo and Pico della Mirandola about the hierarchy of Latin authors.[1] We know too that in 1526 Erasmus wrote the dialogue *Ciceronianus* to combat the excessive ciceronianising that was rampant in Italy and France at the time. But, in fact, among poets and prose writers even if not among rhetorical pedants, it was the unconscious assimilation of classical and, of course, Italian literature, at which they were aiming. It was the innutrition of authors that they had in mind. They were already what Montaigne would call towards the end of the century 'digestors',

ainsi les pieces empruntées d'autruy, il les transformera et confondra, pour en faire un ouvrage tout sien, à sçavoir son jugement.
                                                                    (*Essais*, 1.26)

[1] See *Le Epistole 'De Imitatione' di Gianfrancesco Pico della Mirandola e di Pietro Bembo*, ed. G. Santangelo, Florence, 1954.

Past literature will be devoured by the poet, will be held within his being, will be changed by him, re-transformed by him and bodied forth in a new way by him. This is the exciting discovery that first-rate poets made during the sixteenth century: they see 'des visages plus riches' (Montaigne, 1.25) in Plutarch or Pindar or Propertius. Perhaps the first stage of their assimilation of classical authors was similar to the mental process which will be that of twentieth-century readers of Proust, who says of them,

Car ils ne seraient pas, selon moi, mes lecteurs, mais les propres lecteurs d'eux-mêmes, mon livre n'étant qu'une sorte de ces verres grossissants comme ceux que tendait à un acheteur l'opticien de Combray; mon livre, grâce auquel je leur fournirais le moyen de lire en eux-mêmes.

(*À la recherche du temps perdu*, op. cit., t. III, p. 1033)

So that sixteenth-century poets read the ancients as the modern reader reads Proust but of course the modern reader of Proust stops there and does not use his subjective reading of *Le Temps Perdu* to create another work of art. The poets did not grovel around ancient books looking for the appropriate quotation or the appropriate passage to package in their own poems. They rather assumed that their reading public would recognize the quotation, then perhaps look it up in the original Latin, Greek or Italian and be doubly delighted to compare the two in their own minds.

The first attempts at reform or criticism are bound to be concerned with technical details rather than with general principles. Where Bembo got absorbed in Ciceronian ideas about poetry – ideas in fact that were already old-fashioned in Cicero's day – Du Bellay by steeping himself in the poetry of the Latin Augustan age was able to come up with the view that French writers were to 'convertir en sang et nourriture' all that they had learnt about the writing of poetry from Greece and Rome. A twentieth-century reader knows – and this is a large assumption to make – his Horace, his Ronsard, his Scève and his Du Bellay. Naturally, the sixteenth-century poet, like any other poet, might be making implicit references to classical literature again and again, and one cannot recognize all of them (even a contemporary reader could hardly follow Scève's mind in the process of composing, so there are parts which are absolutely secret), but we know the text of *Délie*, we know he was not appealing to the *vulgus* and we know that he was consciously re-grafting the Roman tradition on to his poetry.

Literary imitation was the principle on which all pre-eighteenth-century poetry was based and Renaissance imitation must be seen in the much wider perspective that the Graeco-Roman tradition gives it. We must dwell a minute on this apparently servile principle which was so popular.

The sixteenth century's mesmerised worship of the Ancients, as well as the Italians, was based on the assumption that the French language was weak and bare and this nakedness was a weakness and not a strength. In other words it was a sign of poverty not of elegant simplicity. From this assertion of a negative fact the French tradition in modern, post-Renaissance poetic theory was born. French writers took over from the Ancient writers a whole scale of cultural values which held the stage until the twentieth century. For instance, the whole of the classical period, 1660–85, was entrenched in the same literary world as was the Renaissance. The cultural values were still Ancient and it was still their aim as French writers to create within this tradition. One can go further than this and say that for poets like Baudelaire, Nerval, Mallarmé and Valéry the whole principle of *copia* in language comes to the foreground again. Indeed, there are aspects of their poetic theory which are nothing but a sophisticated working out of Ancient rhetorical theory.

The common cultural heritage and background of general ideas that make up in any age the philosophy of the average unsystematic mind was present in the Renaissance but there was also the relatively new, artificial (in the original non-pejorative sense of the word – derived from *artifex*, something you fashioned in an artefact, produced by art) sense of the past. Now although Scève's *Délie* came out in 1544 and Du Bellay's *Deffence et illustration de la langue françoise* in 1549, it becomes clear in the course of examining Scève that the ideas 'in the air' in the 1530s and 1540s in France are essentially the same as those expressed by the Pléiade. The Pléiade too rejects the whole of the poetry that came from the French tradition they knew (and of course this did not include the greatest poetry of the Middle Ages like for instance *La Chanson de Roland* – which they did not even know existed), all the myths and legends that would have been such rich source material for their poetry; instead they vitalised poetry through another stream – the Graeco-Roman one. The *imitateur* practised innutrition: like an organist playing variations on a theme, where the variations themselves conform to a pattern, as for instance in Bach's Choral Preludes or Canonic Variations, but where the listeners could hear the originality of the composer or organist who would be making his own improvisation. The very tradition served to spark off the creative resources of the musician.

The famous *univers livresque* of Scève and Ronsard is only a fault if looked at through parochial twentieth-century eyes. For the whole of the Graeco-Roman poetic universe was *livresque* and we misunderstand a literary culture if we denigrate it for having recourse to previous features in the tradition.

The basic problem for a sixteenth-century poet like Scève was a technical one, as indeed it had been for the poets of the Augustan era in Rome (from about 31 B.C. to A.D. 14). For it was during this epoch that a new Roman classical literature came to maturity, based on the classical literature of the Greek world. The principles of enrichment, imitation and allusiveness were important catalysts in the production of an entirely new, original, complex art. Horace was a poet and a critic in the same way as were Eliot or Valéry, and one who, in the process of writing creative poetry, was intensely self-critical. The reader is urged to participate in the poet's work by the exercise of his own sensitivity, imagination and intellect. There is the same mystery of complexity and of understatement in Horace's *Ars poetica* as there is in Eliot's famous essay, *Tradition and the Individual Talent*. With Horace (and Vergil, Propertius and Tibullus) there is a breaking loose from rhetoric for a short time – and it is this unleashing of poetry that is not taken into account by most scholars of the Renaissance.[1]

It is precisely to the Augustan Latin poets that the French poets turned – and, perhaps crucially, Horace hardly took account of the Aristotelian mimesis theory because imitation, for him, meant literary allusiveness. What distorts this for *us* is the importance *we* assign to Plato and Aristotle – the theoreticians and not the poets. When we see literary allusiveness from the angle of poets writing poetry there is something 'docte', and

[1] For a full discussion of this period of literature see K. Quinn, *Latin Explorations*, London, 1963, esp. Ch. 6; and G. Williams, *Tradition and Originality in Roman Poetry*, Oxford, 1968.

something exciting and new in it. It is this conscious process that Scève exploits in *Délie* and this was something frowned upon by Charles Fontaine in his poem –

> Brief, ilz ne quierent un Lecteur,
> Mais la commune autorité
> Dit qu'ilz requierent un Docteur.

Let us move on now to the second thing that Charles Fontaine said – that the lines were certainly beautiful but were also 'Graves, & pleins de majesté'. To demonstrate these qualities and give a concrete example of allusiveness I take the preliminary huitain to the 449 dizains of *Délie*. We shall here see more clearly what I have been trying to say about literary imitation.

> Non de Venus les ardentz estincelles,
> Et moins les traictz, desquelz Cupido tire:
> Mais bien les mortz, qu'en moy tu renouelles
> Ie t'ay voulu en cest Œuure descrire.
>   Ie sçay asses, que tu y pourras lire
> Mainte erreur, mesme en si durs Epygrammes:
> Amour (pourtant) les me voyant escrire
> En ta faueur, les passa par ses flammes.

Scève invites his readers, clearly but unobtrusively, to place his love cycle in a poetic tradition. He starts with a negative device – *Non...Et moins...* – followed by a positive assertion – *Mais bien ...*This statement of intention takes the shape of a Hellenistic *recusatio*, that is a refusal by the poet of certain themes, genres and styles. Scève is more or less saying, 'I am not going to write about the earthly love symbolized by Venus and Cupid but about the pangs of passion (*mortz* in petrarchistic terms equals both the utmost point of passion and death) you ceaselessly awake in me; my humble talent will not rise to other subjects but only the love that you make me experience.' Now in this statement the poet uses a *persona* which is public. (In *Délie* generally it seems to me Scève holds a mid-way position between speaking in the character of a poet, assuming the same reactions as other poets, and speaking as a distinct private individual.) In dizain 18 he alludes more explicitly to the Roman literary tradition: the more elevated mood, tones and styles of epic or heroic odes, the more lowly moods of satire, the more comic style of farces, these he is not attempting; to sing of love alone is his aim and lot. Sublimity and soaring aspirations are cancelled out; he is not even trying to sing of his love *manifeste*; all he can do is *crier mercy, mercy, mercy*. Neither poem (the huitain and dizain 18) must be taken at surface value: the literary confession they make has the effect of leading readers away from certain genres and on to Scève's own commitment. That the pursuit of fame was not Scève's intention has always been implied by scholars; as far back as 1927 the great critic Marcel Raymond stated that Scève was 'insoucieux du grand public'[1] and this view has been largely followed.

Of course, Scève's quiet unobtrusiveness is far removed from the showy, glittering preface to Ronsard's *Amours*, with the name of the poet engraved by the Muses for eternity,

> Ronsard, affin que le siecle a venir,
> De pere en filz se puisse souvenir,
> D'une beauté qui sagement affole,
> De la main dextre apprend a nostre autel,
> L'humble discours de son livre immortel,
> Son cuœur de l'autre, aux pieds de ceste idole.
>
> (The *Voeu* at the beginning of *Les Amours*, 1552-3)

Nevertheless, Scève asserts himself positively, through the highly wrought humility, the ambiguity that the whole work shows vis à vis Venus and Cupid, his self-confidence and the purely secular dedication to a still living Délie. These are clues to the love tradition of Western Europe. But there is more than this in the poem: what does the phrase *durs Epygrammes* mean exactly and what associations underlie the word *durs?* Is this one adjective part of a literary tradition which takes us back to Augustan Rome? We may remember Horace's two adjectives *molle atque facetum* as the distinctive characteristic of Vergil's bucolic poetry and maybe half-recall his judgement on Lucilius (*Ars poetica*, 86–131) that he composed *durus...versus* – he was rough in his language and versification. We are forced then to ask the question: did *durus* have special connotations for Roman writers?[2]

---

[1] In *L'Influence de Ronsard sur la poésie française (1550–1585)*, Geneva, 1927, reprinted 1965, p. 16.

[2] V. L. Saulnier, *Maurice Scève*, op. cit., t. II, p. 120, footnote (57) takes *durs* in the sense of Latin *rudis*, or *mal équarris*. In the first volume, p. 279, he says 'Il fait le modeste. Peu de textes, dans notre littérature apparaissent comme le fruit d'une pareille densité de travail artistique.' Saulnier has very suggestively stopped there; we hope to go a little further into the key-word *durs*. W. Niedermann, *Versuch über Maurice Scèves Dichtung*, Zurich, 1950, Ch. 1, sees in the phrase the clarity and difficulty of form. W. Fowlie, in *Sixty poems of*

The term *durus* had three connotations: first, it was a term of rhetoric, secondly it denoted a genre or style and thirdly it was bound up with the attitude towards composition. We shall look at the three in turn.

If we turn to a lexicon of Latin rhetoric we find *durus* compared to *asper* and contrasted with *enervis* and *effeminatus*.[1] For example, Quintilian, IX.4.142, says, 'In universum autem, si sit necesse, duram potius atque asperam compositionem malim esse, quam effeminatam et enervem, qualis apud multos.'[2] Now the slight metaphors in this statement reveal fully the rhetorical assumptions in Quintilian: the analogy between a fine healthy body and good rhetoric puts the emphasis on health and proper functioning rather than on decoration and superficial beauty. We can press the analogy further to make the blood, muscle and strength of a human body correspond to particular elements in an organised piece of writing. Terms of approbation

*Scève. Introduction, translation and comment by Wallace Fowlie*, New York, 1949, translated the phrase as *closed epigrams*. It is rather difficult to interpret this unless it be the contrast between the *open* form of say an epic and the *closed* form of a sonnet or dizain. This does not take us very far. Jean Attal in *Etat présent des études scéviennes*, in *Critique*, janvier 1960, pp. 3–24, interprets *durs* as *rudis, mal équarris* the same as Saulnier and sees Scève as rejecting facility and harmony in the writing of poetry. But then he brings this in line with English Metaphysical poetry with their strong lines, description of familiar and humble objects, their wit and their colloquial language. One is perhaps not prepared to go that far with Attal's evidence. Hans Staub in his book, *Le Curieux Désir*, op. cit., p. 61, says 'Scève a fait de la forme du dizain un instrument merveilleusement apte à sa quête. Il porte à l'extrême le caractère fermé de la strophe carrée de dix fois dix syllabes dans ses 'durs epigrammes' (sic), comme il appelle ses dizains dans la dédicace *A sa Délie.*' This is not an explanation of *durs* at all. Robert in his dictionary gives *un style dur* as *heurté, rocailleux, sec* and quotes Boileau on an *auteur dur* thus

> Maudit soit l'auteur dur dont l'apre et rude verve...

When we turn to Boileau's epigram we find that this line is followed by three others,

> Son cerveau tenaillant, rima malgré Minerve;
> Et, de son lourd marteau martelant le bon sens,
> A fait de méchans vers douze fois douze cents.

The pejorative use of *dur* here is applied firstly to a poet rushing in to poetry and secondly, to the actual prosodic composition. These remarks are suggestive and will be borne in mind during our discussion.

[1] I. Chr. Ernesti, *Lexicon technologiae latinorum rhetoricae*, Leipzig, 1797 (reprinted, Hildesheim, 1962).

[2] Cf. Jacques Peletier du Mans, *L'Art Poétique*, ed. Boulanger, Paris, 1930, p. 143, 'Qui veut etre facile, il devient mol, efemine et sans ners' (see also Horace, *Ars poetica*, 25–30). This contrast between the effeminate style and the hard style is a constant assertion among Roman writers.

in Roman rhetorical criticism reveal the authors' constant mental habit of regarding the details of a particular man's style in terms of this analogy. Thus, for example, Quintilian praises Demosthenes – 'Tanta vis in eo, tam densa omnia, ita quibusdam nervis intenta sunt.' Conversely terms of disapproval echo the same analogy: Cicero castigates philosophers' style in this way – 'tamen horum oratio neque nervos neque aculeos oratorios ac forenses habet'. (*Orator*, 62.)[1] Terms such as *nitor, nitidus* and *nitere* were often applied by Quintilian to style and they carry with them the full associations of the sheen and glow of health. A further extension of the metaphor is the element of virility, of masculinity even, approved of in style: for instance Quintilian speaks with pleasure of 'hic ornatus...virilis et fortis et sanctus sit nec effeminatam levitatem et fuco ementitum colorem amet: sanguine et viribus niteat'. (VIII.3.6.)[2] The use of words like *sanguis, nervi, caro* and *sucus* for praising someone's style is clearly an appreciation of the richness, appropriateness and success of that style – much like the peak of fitness achieved by an athlete's body. Thus *durus* is the opposite to an effeminate style; it is one that has the nerves of a good style.[3]

In discussing *durus* Ernesti has a paraphrase from the passage in Cicero which is rather puzzling. In his *Orator*, 16, Cicero seems to state

ubi lenitati et aequabilitati, et puro candidoque generi dicendi, quod maxime in suavi verborum forma, iunctura et compositione cernitur, duritas et severitas verborum, et orationis quasi maestitia opponitur.

*Durus* has here rather pejorative connotations: it is opposed to flexibility and modulation. Ernesti gives as a conclusion a definition of *durus*,

Si quid tamen definiendum sit, ego ita distinxerim, ut dura sit, quae sonos literarum cum ictu et pulsu duriori exprimit...rigida vero, cui illa flexibilis opponatur, hoc est, semper unisona, paucas aut nullas flexiones habens.

Hard-hitting compactness, virile body – these seem to be appropriate to Scève's style – but there is a pejorative association which

---

[1] Cf. Quintilian qualifying Archilochus as having 'plurimum sanguinis atque nervorum'. X.1.60.

[2] Both Quintilian and Cicero speak with obvious distaste of an anaemic, flabby, soft, sinewless style (e.g. Quintilian, X.10.13 or XII.10.25).

[3] See Carl Newell Jackson, '*Molle atque facetum*', in *Harvard Studies in Classical Philology*, vol. XXV, 1914, pp. 117–37 on the usage of rhetorical terms like *durus* used in opposition to *mollis*.

is a refusal of flexibility of sound. This aspect is taken up by Quintilian, for instance, in the way it affects the senses of the audience; it is the opposite of harmony; it has something harsh and roughly polished,

aspera et dura et dissoluta et hians oratio.　　(VIII.6.62)

This is like the quality Du Bellay mentioned in his *Deffence et Illustration de la langue française* (ed. Chamard, p. 293) – 'rien dur, hyulque ou redundant' suggested his disapproval of the poverty and harshness of sound.[1] This is suggestive for Scève's lack of musicality. Indeed Odette de Mourgues has called him rather 'unfrench' at times and one must admit that there are a number of lines which almost seem, perversely, to aim at 'hard' unmusical effects.[2]

Secondly, 'durus' was a term denoting a genre or style. Roman practical criticism as it came to maturity substantiates the points made in rhetoric as regards genre, style and finally sound. For instance, Catullus represents a totally new poetic creed – let poets ignore Ennius and other Latin epic poets and rather write according to the canons of more recent Greek poetry. His dedication to Cornelius Nepos

Cui dono lepidum novum libellum
arida modo pumice expolitum?

[1] Cf. Quintilian, XI.3.35 when it is applied to harsh-sounding consonants; or XII.10.30 – to syllables, or VIII.3.32 – to words.

[2] Op. cit., p. 22. 'Although his verse never aims at musical effects or at loveliness for loveliness' sake, its roughness, abruptness at times, is not that of the spoken language.' There may be a connection between Scève and the English Metaphysical poets here. Thomas Carew wrote in his *Elegie upon the death of the Deane of Pauls, Dr. John Donne* in 1633

Thou hast...open'd Us a Mine
Of rich and pregnant phansie, drawne a line
Of masculine expression...

The context is that of Donne throwing away 'servile imitation' and planting 'fresh invention'. The metaphor is that of an exchequer paying the debts 'of our penurious bankrupt age'. Underlying this *masculinity* was the sense of difficulty not only in the style but also in the thought. The whole elegy is written in 'strong lines' – forcing the rhythm across the line break, and making the speech rhythm contest the prosodic paradigm. In the Metaphysical poets this preference for 'strong lines' suggests not only density but also tough 'obscurity' and harshness. J. J. Denonain, *Thèmes et Formes de la Poésie 'Métaphysique'*, Alger, 1956, pp. 22–7, has a discussion of masculinity and 'strong lines' but he does not go further. I suspect that the *durus/mollis* juxtaposition is at the base of this concept. It would be interesting, in another book, to trace out how Scève in France and Donne in England interpreted the classical theorizing on *durus*.

means that the *pumice* is dry, light and hard. (Cf. the Elder Pliny, *N.H.*, 36.154, speaks of its smoothing properties.) Catullus uses it here with the same connotations as Propertius, III.1.8. 'Exactus tenui pumice versus est', and metaphorically one can say it expresses the polish of the poetry itself. (Cf. Martial imitating Catullus in VIII.72.1, with

> Nondum murice cultus asperoque
> morsu pumicis aridi politus.)

It is in fact the opposite of *teneri versus, teneri modi* which apply to elegiac verses and metres specially devoted to love. It is often mentioned as a praiseworthy quality in Augustan love poetry and then is contrasted with the soft, weak style as we have come across it in Quintilian and Cicero's rhetorical terminology.[1]

Lastly, the attitude, the seriousness of the writer of the high style is shown to be demonstrably *durus* by Propertius, who in II.34.41ff epitomises the moral attitude which goes with the higher genres. There is here a resemblance between style and life. The end of the elegy is a justification of erotic poetry: the love poetry of Vergil's Eclogues is not outshadowed by the Georgics even though the style is not as lofty. Finally in I.7

---

[1] It is worth noting Horace's comments on Lucilius' style. In *Sat.*, 1.4.8 he says,

> Hinc omnis pendet Lucilius, hosce secutus
> Mutatis tantum pedibus numerisque, facetus,
> Emunctae naris, durus componere versus.

It is perhaps interesting to note that Valéry used an extreme form of the analogy between poetry and the human body. It is not a casual metaphor but one that embodies the *durus/mollis* antithesis of Roman rhetorical theories,
La forme est le squelette des œuvres; il est des œuvres qui n'en ont point. Toutes les œuvres meurent; mais celles qui avaient un squelette durent bien plus par ce reste que les autres qui n'étaient qu'en parties molles.
(Tel Quel, II., Autres Rhumbs, Paris, Gallimard, p. 130)

Pejorative associations must be implied here; Horace liked Lucilius but admits that he was a harsh composer, meaning that he did not pay enough attention to form, style and sound. Again, in *Sat.*, 1.10.57, Horace implies that Ennius in writing epic has something *durus*, that is a difficult subject, in his hands. The contrast is with writers of *uersiculos...euntis/mollius* to write on. In the *Ars poetica*, 445-6 Horace comes out strongly against *durus*

> Vir bonus et prudens versus reprehendet inertes
> Culpabit duros...

the wise man will cut out and condemn a hard line. The association of *durus* here with *inertes* and *incompti* is pejorative.

Propertius relies on an extension of the literary criticism of *tristis* (like *durus*) and *mollis*.[1]

The connotations of *durus* that we have seen in Roman writers could equally well be seen in Dante and Petrarch. The *facilità* and *dolcezza* that Petrarch had in writing lyric poetry stands at the opposite pole from Scève's *durs Epygrammes*. But here perhaps one recalls *Rime*, 125, where Petrarch states that because of the nature of his passion he cannot always write *dolci rime*,

> Però ch'Amor mi sforza
> E di saver mi spoglia,
> Parlo in rim'aspre e di dolcezza ignude...

He compares the *dolci rime* he used on falling in love with those he uses now,

> Dolci rime leggiadre
> Che nel primiero assalto
> D'Amor usai quand'io non ebbi altr'arme,
> Chi verrà mai che squadre
> Questo mio cor di smalto,
> Ch'almen, com'io solea, possa sfogarme?

Even so, his reputation in the sixteenth century was firmly based on his *dolcezza* as this passage from Lorenzo de Medici implies:

Dante, il Petrarca, il Boccaccio...hanno ne' gravi et dolcissimi versi et orationi loro mostro assai chiaramente, con molta facilità potersi in questa lingua esprimere ogni senso...Chi negherà nel Petrarca trovarsi uno stile grave, lepido et dolce et queste cose amorose con tanta gravità et venustà trattate, quante senza dubbio non si trova in Ovidio, in Tibullo, in Catullo, in Propertio, o in alcun'altro Latino...[2]

And so by being *dur* Scève was deliberately turning away from the *dolcezza* of Petrarch and the petrarchists, and using the Roman term to mean the seriousness of the poet of high-style love. There is obviously a danger in this kind of writing and Scève realises that there will be *mainte erreur* in his poetry.

[1] Quintilian, x.1.93 has this to say on Ovid,

> Ovidius utroque lascivior, sicut durior Gallus.

The antithesis given here lies again in the *durior* ('more masculine') as opposed to *lascivior*.

[2] *Commento sopra alcuni de'suoi sonetti*, ed. Venice, 1554, fol. 119ro.

Sometimes he will wrest words from a different language (in his case Italian or Latin) and will force them to carry specialised associations and meanings which can only be explained in terms of the dizain in question. It is in this dedication that he sets himself in the tradition which he had learnt, using Latin poetry as a model, in his early Neo-Latin poetry. His poetry will be hard and rough, not blurred or indefinite. It will not flow smoothly as Petrarch's does. Since 'hard' and 'rough' suggest the fabrication of a syntax that is highly-wrought and dense, Scève's poetry will perhaps strike the reader (Délie, in this case, for she is the person to whom the book is dedicated) as unpolished, but actually it is careful and difficult because his love and the problems he is going to treat are difficult. But we have not explained the second member of the phrase *durs Epygrammes*.

In Sébillet's *Art Poétique* (1548) we find a generic title given to epigrams,

Le sonnet suit l'epigramme de bien près et de matiere et de mesure; et quand tout est dit, le sonnet n'est autre chose que le parfait epigramme de l'Italien comme le dizain du françois.      (ed. Gaiffe, II, 2, p. 115.)

It is clear that the epigram was of Greek origin. To quote Curtius,

its original definition (an inscription for the dead, for sacrificial offerings etc.). The epigram became the vessel of a judicious or ingenious idea. In itself this is not incompatible with a true poetic statement.[1]

It is also clear that as regards form and content the Greek epigram, the Italian *strambotto*, the dizain and the sonnet are closely connected.[2]

The epigram as a literary term in France derives from the quasi-translation of the neo-Latin poet Angeriano by Michel d'Amboise (*Les Cent Epigrammes*, 1532) and then from Jean Bouchet and Marot, who used the word first in the 1538 edition

---

[1] *European Literature and the Latin Middle Ages*, translated from the German by Willard R. Trask, London, 1953, p. 292. Curtius gives references to Stephen Gaselle's study of a theme in epigrammatic literature, in 'The soul in the kiss', *Criterion*, II, 349ff. (April, 1924) and to the origins of the epigram in P. Friedländer, *Epigrammata. Greek Inscriptions in Verse from the Beginnings to the Persian Wars*, University of California Press, 1948.

[2] See on this question E. Guidici, *Le opere minori di Maurice Scève*, Parma, 1957, Ch. 2. on the *blasons*.

of his *Œuvres*.[1] Saulnier (op. cit., t. I, p. 104) has shown how Lyon in particular was absorbed in writing epigrams until 1536 – partly because the neo-Latin poets like Dolet were experimenting with model epigrams from the *Planudean Anthology* and partly because people like Alamanni and Bouchet and Marot were trying epigrams in the vernacular.

But Marot in his epigrams, while exploiting the same stock-in-trade as Scève in his dizains, was in fact using them in a very different manner to Scève. Take the familiar theme of the light of a mistress's eye (we remember to what kind of poem this led Scève in dizain 1) being sunlight to the lover, darkness everywhere else; and this being transformed into equivalences of presence and absence. Marot turns this theme into a physical point by introducing a witty and typical conclusion,

> Quand je vy ma maitresse,
> Le clair soleil me luict
> S'ailleurs mon oeil s'adresse,
> Ce m'est obscure nuict.

Marot seems to be serious here, and his attitude could be paralleled by any poet within the petrarchist tradition. But he goes on

> Et croy que sans chandelle
> A son lict à minuit
> Je verrois avec elle.

He has introduced a touch of gauloiserie and an enjoyment of a witty and erotic conclusion to a well-known theme. Here we have a clear awareness of the model – Petrarch, but the cleverness and the sensuality of an individual poet – Marot. Many of the epigrams are rather dull, though clear and neat, with some amusement always present in the tongue-in-cheek attitude.

The form of the *epygrammes* that Scève uses is worth looking at in slightly closer detail. Donne in one of his sermons remarks that the full force of a poem lies in its close,

In all Metricall compositions,…the force of the whole piece is for the most part left to the shutting up; the whole frame of the Poem is a

---

[1] Professor C. A. Mayer and Dr P. M. Smith in their article, 'La première épigramme française: Clément Marot, Jean Bouchet et Michel d'Amboise. Définition, source, antériorité', *BHR*, xxxii, 1970, pp. 579–602, state that Michel d'Amboise's *épigrammes* are not epigrammatic, so that, although they were published before Marot's use of the term, it is clear that Marot had been writing epigrams without using the term. 'C'est à Marot, bien que le titre d'épigramme ait été employé avant lui, que revient cet honneur.'

beating out of a piece of gold, but the last clause is as the impression of the stamp and that is that makes it current.[1]

This echoes the last two lines of Scève's preliminary poem: Love has passed them through the fire, so that they will emerge like gold, hardened by the heat and polished to perfection. (This is a commonplace image for love and for the composition of verses.) The dizain is a difficult form since it is short and compressed, mid-way between the huitain and the sonnet, avoiding the maxim-like quality of the former but lacking the amplitude and possibilities of symmetry and contrast of the latter. McFarlane concludes rightly (p. 43) that Scève did not experiment with metrical forms and did not risk the sonnet, although Marot's and Saint-Gelais' few sonnets were already published in France. In other words Scève carried on with a form that was already in use, as a court poet, a précieux poet would do.[2] Scève's unobtrusive indebtedness to tradition is quieter but no less great than the showy experimentation with tradition that the Pléiade were to present in the early 1550s. It is far closer to the adaptation of classical themes that Marot showed in the 1530s. But he differs from Marot in the *durs* aspects of his poetic technique.

The literary allusiveness of Scève resembles that of the Augustan poets in Rome. We have seen how the one word *durus* in the preliminary huitain opens up a whole field of associations and this dovetails with the close feeling of Propertius and Scève in the *innamoramento* which we saw in Ch. 2. Furthermore, it reveals one characteristic of Scève's art: by using a single word or phrase, such as *erreurs* in dizain 1 or *durs* in the huitain Scève can fix himself in the classical and petrarchist tradition. The one word may be intended to strike a chord in the reader's memory and evoke rich associations of its previous context. The handling of borrowed material is important in every sixteenth-century poet and the form it takes in Scève is one of the aspects of his work that sets him apart from the French past.

[1] Cited by H. Gardner, *The Business of Criticism*, Oxford, 1959, p. 70.
[2] This concept of précieux poet will be defined in the next chapter.

# 4

## SCÈVE: COMPOSER OF 'IMPRESE AMOROSE'

We are hampered in our understanding of *Délie* not only by the wider perspective of tradition but also by topical and fashionable conventions from which Scève borrowed certain elements, transforming them into a part of his poetic technique. The most difficult question is still the inclusion of woodcuts and mottoes in *Délie*. In spite of recent attempts[1] to explain their presence in the love *canzoniere*, there is no external evidence that Scève commissioned them for his work. We do not know who the designer was or whether they had been used in any book before 1544. The woodcuts in this first edition of *Délie* are rough and crude in design, and in several cases difficult to decipher. They compare unfavourably with the designs of woodcuts appearing from Lyon presses in the 1540s and even with the Augsburg and Paris editions of Alciati's *Emblematum liber* in the 1530s. The outer frames of the pictures are heavy and elaborate and might be compared with those used by Macé Bonhomme and Rovillius in the 1540s and 1550s. But the designs of the figures in *Délie*, unaccompanied by a background scene, seem much earlier in date than those of the two Lyonnais printers. Until more evidence is forthcoming, any conclusion about the actual woodcuts must remain purely speculative.

Alciati's first edition in 1531 (from the press of Steyner in Augsburg) contains an address to the reader which suggests that Alciati, having composed the verses, went to the publisher's press to look for suitable pictures which would illustrate them. Alciati has to apologise for the crude nature of the woodcuts, the *tabellae quae huic operae adiectae sunt* – indicating clearly that the verses and the pictures in his emblem book were separately

---

[1] For an examination of hypotheses concerning the woodcuts one must still take V. L. Saulnier, *Maurice Scève*, op. cit., t. I, pp. 210–13, as the starting point. Recent work on the woodcuts include Dorothy Coleman, 'Les Emblesmes dans la "Délie" de Maurice Scève', *SF*, VIII, 1964, pp. 1–15, Enzo Giudici, *Maurice Scève, poeta della Délie*, Rome, 1965, pp. 171–356, Ruth Mulhauser, 'The Poetic Function of the Emblems in the "Délie"', in *L'esprit créateur*, 1965, V, pp. 80–9 and Donald Stone, 'Scève's Emblems', in *Romanic Review*, 1969, LX, pp. 96–104.

manufactured. Given that the publisher is the important figure throughout the sixteenth century – controlling the pictures, reprinting them, retouching the worn cuts or plates, employing other wood-engravers and printmakers to copy and reproduce some of the most successful pictures – the hypothesis that Scève found his pictures in the publisher's stock carries some weight. Furthermore, this would explain the difference between the 1544 and 1564 editions of *Délie*: the design of the figures in the later edition is clearer, more carefully executed, and a surrounding border is added – all of which suggests that a more skilled wood-engraver had been called in by the Paris publisher. Also, as will be relevant in a later part of this argument, the reproduction of the pictures was regarded as important in 1564.

The definition of *emblesme* in the *priuilege* seems to apply to the picture or woodcut, while the list at the end of the book – *L'Ordre des Figures & Emblemes* seems to imply that the *emblesmes* are only the mottoes. I am using here the word *emblesme* which appears in the *priuilege* in preference to the English word 'emblem', as the latter begs the question whether the *emblesmes* are in fact 'emblems'. Thus until I have established the real nature of the *emblesmes* the English word is confusing.

Jean de Vauzelles writing to Aretino in 1551 (see Saulnier, op. cit., t. I, p. 307) makes a point of distinguishing Scève's *emblesmes* from those of Alciati:

Si vous compreniez notre langue comme je comprends la vôtre, je vous enverrais certains vers qu'un mien frère a composés à la louange de sa Délie; ils sont accompagnés d'emblèmes mieux appropriés et plus spirituels que ceux d'Alciat; et je pense que vous ne les placeriez pas, quant à l'élégance, à l'invention et au langage, au-dessous de beaucoup de vos écrits anciens et modernes.

Why are they *plus spirituels* and *mieux appropriés* in *Délie* than in Alciati? There is a historical context to this question: where can one put Scève in the framework of the two para-literary genres – emblems and devices (or more accurately, *imprese*) – that were so fashionable in the sixteenth century? In McFarlane's introduction and commentary there are certain puzzling features about the treatment of the *emblesmes*: for example, although he follows Saulnier in his tracing of the history of the emblem (e.g. pp. 18–19) his notes on individual woodcuts (e.g. IV, VII, XI, XV, XVI, XVII) are often dependent on Coleman's findings; but Coleman seemed to imply that they were *imprese amorose*. There is an imprecision in the terminology here, an imprecision that accompanied the appearance of emblems and devices throughout the sixteenth and seventeenth centuries. One might think of the delightful commentary on *imprese* by Ercole Tasso at the beginning of the seventeenth century which takes to task all the critics of the sixteenth century and then states his own view of the differences between hieroglyphics, enigmas, emblems, fables, parabolas, symbols, blasons and *imprese*.[1] Professor Enzo Giudici in his book on *Délie*[2] reviews rather ponderously the views of other critics, rejects most of the interpretations of Coleman, repeats what Professor Mario Praz stated, especially about the plagiarising of Scève[3] and comes to the conclusion that the *emblesmes* are neither emblems nor *imprese* but something in between both genres – without really seeing the *function* of these *emblesmes* in *Délie*. And it is precisely their function that one must examine.

In fact, emblems and *imprese* are socially very far apart from the beginning. Where the emblems are a moralising, didactic and commonplace genre, the *imprese* are personal, individual and non-didactic. Moralising has a far wider audience in any country than an individual's thoughts or feelings, and this factor forces them apart. In emblem books there is a great variety of moral lessons which the reader can apply. Sometimes the moral lesson provides him with general maxims of life: for example, in Alciati we read lessons like 'never miss a chance', 'cast away sloth', 'abstain from wine', 'cast away ignorance'. Sometimes there are general conclusions about the nature of life – 'misfortune is always round the corner'. Sometimes the moral lesson gives advice for the successful living of domestic life: for instance, the importance of parental love, the gratitude that children ought to show their parents or the role of reverence in marriage. Sometimes, one has moralisations about love: the pitfalls awaiting the lover, the snares set by Cupid, the irremediable harm he can wreak, the insatiable lust and dangerously unreliable and unfaithful nature of women. One example will serve to pinpoint the differences between an emblem book and a collection of

[1] *Della realtà e perfettione delle Imprese di Hercole Tasso. Con l'Essamine di tutte le opinioni infino a qui scritte sopra tal'Arte*, Bergamo, 1614 (second edition).
[2] Op. cit., pp. 180ff.
[3] *Studies in Seventeenth-century Imagery*, London, 1939, vol. i, pp. 80–8.

*imprese*: in the late sixteenth century authors like Camerarius and Taurellus used emblem books almost as a substitute for textbooks. Between 1590 and 1604 Camerarius brought out four parts of his *Symbola*: the division into four books corresponds to a division of the natural world into plants, animals, birds and fish. It is almost a natural-history encyclopaedia, but it employs the method of an emblem writer: it expounds the nature, behaviour and symbolic significance of plants and animals and draws moral lessons from these observations. Many of Camerarius' emblems derive from sixteenth-century *imprese*; for instance, the sunflower and the sun with a title *Non inferiora secutus* – which is the *impresa* of Marguerite de Navarre. But, and this is the crucial difference which makes the picture and title an emblem in Camerarius' book, the accompanying poem and commentary are closely linked, in a didactic, moralising, emblematic way, to the picture. Where a poem on the *impresa* would show how apt it was to express the character and conduct of Marguerite de Navarre and praise her virtues, Camerarius is concerned with the *documento universale* of the picture and title.

Since pictures are like images or metaphors in that they may be drawn from any field, classification by source or by affinities with other pictures in other books does not guide us towards their precise function in any given artistic unit. The woodcuts may be classified in *Délie* according to whether they are drawn from Classical mythology, like those on Dido, Acteon, Narcissus or Leda; from natural history and the realm of fable, like the viper; from books of hieroglyphics, from scenes of everyday life, like that of the two young men and a stool; or from the world of alchemy, like the alembic. All this, however, tells us nothing about how they operate in *Délie* for they share this heterogeneous content with dozens of other images in poetry, figures in emblem books and pictures in illustrated books. The nature and function of woodcuts such as those in *Délie* may vary considerably according to whether they appear in an emblem book, in a collection of *imprese*, in an account of a Court festival or funeral or the entry of the King into some town, in a dictionary of conceits or in a cycle of love poems like *Délie*. This is where scholars such as Giudici err; for it is precisely the function of the woodcuts in the work that offers us clues for classifying them.

For the courtly, élite audience of *impresa*-making we need to go back to Italy and not to the moralising verses that Corrozet, La Perrière and Alciati devised. The following remarks will serve as the starting point of my argument:

Le caractère personnel de l'*impresa*, son origine italienne, la vogue qu'elle connut chez les poètes pétrarquisants de l'Italie, tout nous permet de voir dans les emblesmes de la *Délie* des *imprese amorose* richement utilisées par un poète qui était au courant de tous les développements récents dans l'art et dans la littérature, pour qui l'Italie fut une inspiratrice infiniment chère, mais qui sut dépasser à la fois et le genre des *imprese* et les poètes pétrarquisants.

(p. 15 of Coleman, art. cit.)

It is through Scève's use of *imprese amorose* that one can see the fashionable, the topical, the light, the petrarchist and the précieux side of his art. A précieux poet, as defined by Odette de Mourgues[1] writes

a kind of poetry in which the use of a very refined language, of elaborate imagery, and of clever conceits has no other aim than to afford a delicate intellectual pleasure to a certain number of over-sophisticated people of a definite period, and the intellectual pleasure derived from it will depend much upon the code of behaviour, the tastes, and the degree of culture of a particular set of people.

This definition suggests a re-orientation in our view of Scève.

The first part of the re-orientation will be strictly historical: where would Scève find an audience which is sophisticated and cultured? And where would he find *imprese* accompanied by précieux poems as models? The second part, which will be the subject of the next chapter, is the way Scève exploits the technique of précieux poetry. Both are important, and, following Odette de Mourgues' rejection of petrarchist convention as a defining factor (for the reason that a petrarchist is not always a précieux) it is reasonable to call Scève a précieux poet in all those poems in which he does not appear to be going beyond the limits suggested by this label. Of course, in his best dizains he may well be petrarchist while breaking away from the précieux milieu completely. It is only in the light of this re-orientation that we can see Scève in the right perspective.

Most critics of Scève tend to take every word he wrote *au grand sérieux*, but it is precisely the use of *imprese* that can enable us to

---

[1] *Metaphysical, Baroque and Précieux Poetry*, op. cit., p. 108.

see how this poet, not sure of his own poetic technique, not sure of imitating Petrarch well, experimented with over-refined language, over-subtle images, over-abstract concepts in the fashionable Italian manner. The précieux poet pirouettes in language that is refined; conceits (that were no longer unexpected) dazzlingly brought in at the end of a poem, imagery that had become materialistically elaborate, metaphors that had lost their power of evocation and had become dead metaphors, antitheses, hyperboles and periphrases – these were the stock-in-trade of people like Serafino dall'Aquila (1465–1500), Antonio Tebaldeo (1463–1537), Il Cariteo (?1450–1514), Panfilo Sasso (?1454–1537), Pietro Bembo (1470–1547) and others.

*Imprese* in the form of a picture and a motto which complement each other and together express a personal thought are a much older genre than emblems and were born in the courtly societies in the different towns of Italy in the fifteenth century. From the correspondence of poets and artists we learn of the invention and composition of *imprese*, and of requests received from princes, courtiers and the ecclesiastical aristocracy for *imprese* for personal or family use. Salza, in his book on Luca Contile[1] asserts that the composing of devices in the fifteenth century became one of the important duties of a courtier, who was expected to invent *imprese* for his patron. Salza cites many instances of their use in tournaments and jousts: for example, in the 1469 jousts Lorenzo de Medici is known to have worn an *impresa* which declared his love for Lucrezia Donati. Or we find Serafino dall'Aquila composing a sonnet around one of the *imprese* of Isabella d'Este Gonzaga; a labyrinth which he entitled 'Come alma assai bramosa e poco accorta'. (In the Rome edition in 1503 the sonnet bears the title 'Sopra un laberintho che portava la Marchesana de Mantova per impresa' – so suggesting that *imprese* were not uniquely attached to one person for life.) The poet's task was principally to devise a metaphor or symbol, to choose a concrete object or group of objects which could suggest something about the character or intention of the person for whom the *impresa* was made. He had to perceive an apt relationship between the object and the person. Thus he was really inventing or formulating metaphors based on common qualities, substance or origin, and suggesting the design of the

---

[1] Abd-el-Kader Salza, *Luca Contile, uomo di lettere e di negozi del secolo XVI*, Florence, 1903. There is an appendix on *imprese*.

3-2

picture which the engraver could then execute. The witty pithiness of the brief motto which makes the relationship between the symbol and the person radiantly clear is admired for its ingeniousness. It avoids the over-obvious and reveals itself only to a select few. It is certain that as the genre developed, aristocrats wished to have *imprese* not only to express their character or intention on various important occasions but a host of different devices to express their various thoughts on and attachments to various ladies.

The two elements that make up the *impresa* – the picture and the motto – were well established in Italy in the fifteenth century but it was not until after 1544 that the genre was codified and formalised. There was a two-fold development: on the one hand, collections of *imprese* began to be published in book form and on the other hand, theorists set out to justify the genre, give its sources (which were assumed to be French) and history, and draw up rules for its composition. Treatises on the genre appeared first without any illustrations – similar in form to *Arts of Poetry* or other aesthetic treatises. Thus, for example, the first two editions of Giovio's *Dialogo* in 1555 and 1556 were issued without any figures, whilst Claude Paradin's *Devises Heroiques*, published in Lyon in 1551, had no theorising or explanatory text. The pictures in the *Devises Heroiques* are very simple: for instance, a single object may be the symbol, and the exact application or significance is revealed in the title or motto. In the 1557 edition there are well-designed pictures, showing some complexity, but with no grouped tableaux or narrative at all; mostly one or two objects done with scrupulous care for detail. Thus one finds the salamander with a royal crown on his head and surrounded by flames, the phoenix, a spider's web, the sunflower and the sun, a cat, a frog etc.

The main source of inspiration for *imprese amorose* was love poetry, and particularly Petrarch. This helps to explain the unmistakably Italian character of sixteenth-century books of *imprese*, and it explains too why Scève should have been so attracted to them. We shall come back to this point later. As Professor Mario Praz pointed out in 1939 (op. cit., vol. i, Ch. 2) the verses of Petrarch are studded with metaphors and conceits which are potential *imprese:* the *imprese amorose* are merely crystallisations of these love conceits which is why Professor Stone (art. cit.) was able to argue that all the mottoes of Scève are simply the clichés of banal Petrarchan psychology. But when Ruscelli,[1] whom we may take as a typical theorist in the mid-sixteenth century, is explaining how to invent *imprese* we find that he states what the figures represent, for whom they were designed and what the source was: for instance, the sun and the moon with the motto 'Iam feliciter omnia' was made for Isabella Valesia, Queen of Spain, and he expounds a commentary on the device by means of a tercet of a sonnet. Or the crescent moon, made for Henri II, where he cites Ariosto on the triple role of Diana. Or a stag, with a serpent on his back rushing towards a fountain, with the motto *Una salus*, which he explains as an allegory of Christ, noting that poets 'abbian fatto qualche memoria o ricordo dell'acque, come il Petrarca in quel Sonetto,

> Una candida Cerva sopra l'erba
> Verde, m'apparve con due corna d'oro,
> Fra due riviere à l'ombra d'un Alloro.'

Ruscelli was codifying the principles that had been established in the last three decades of the fifteenth century: he makes it quite clear that it was a poet's function to invent the similitude, consult Dante, Petrarch, Vergil, Homer, Ariosto – all poets of great authority in Italy at the time – express the motto through a metaphor from one of the ancient poets or in a half-line from Petrarch or petrarchists and take it to the engraver who then designed the picture. The way conceits were transformed into *imprese* is most clearly expressed by Ercole Tasso:

Quando il Motto è in prima persona, il facitore dell'Impresa quello si fa, che è in lei, quando nella seconda, riguardasi la cosa che è nell'Impresa, con rispetto a se stesso, o ad altri; quando nella terza fa se medesimo corpo dell'Impresa, overo prende quella qualità: Et se impersonale, od assoluto è il motto, il più delle volte si rimovono quelle cose, che sono contrarie all'affetto dell animo del facitore dell'Impresa, e alle volte chiaramente si esprimono.[2]

As was made clear by Coleman's brief analyses of Scève's *imprese*[3] this was how Scève gave a personal meaning to the conceit in the woodcut: either he uses a *je* or a *te* or else the motto expresses something about the poet and his mistress. And as

---

[1] *Le Imprese illustri*, Venice, 1572, Bk 2, pp. 17–20; pp. 28–30^vo; pp. 46^vo–51.
[2] *Della realtà*, op. cit. p. 218.
[3] Art. cit.

was only implicitly suggested all the theorists insist that it should be a poet who devises an *impresa*. All the *imprese amorose* of Scève are, as Stone has shown,[1] dependent on petrarchistic psychology: 'pétrarquiser – faire de l'amoureux transi, comme Pétrarque' as Muret explained in his commentary on the *Amours* of Ronsard.[2]

All the basic paradoxes in Petrarch were taken over without the inner seriousness found in the original. Even serious things could be played with; for example, *per voi moro* is described by Giovio in his *Dialogo dell'Imprese Militari et Amorose* (Roma, 1555) as a witty *impresa* because it pinpoints the element of intellectual pleasure and divine participation of the intellect: ratiocination without the serious. This kind of argumentation is an activity which clearly gave Scève pleasure before he turned it into something personal, serious and original.

The general rules for inventing *imprese*, as described by Giovio in the same treatise, bring *préciosité* to the foreground: among the five conditions that an *impresa* has to fulfil before it can be called 'perfect' he notes that it must not be too obscure,

ch'ella non sia oscura, di sorte, c'habbia mestiero della Sibilla per interprete à volerla intendere; nè tanto chiara ch'ogni plebeo l'intenda. Terza, che sopra tutto habbia nella vista, la quale si fa riuscire molto allegra, entrandovi stelle, soli, lune, fuoco, acqua, arbori verdeggianti, istrumenti mecanici, animali bizzari & uccelli fantastichi.[3]

Now as Odette de Mourgues says à propos of seventeenth-century preciosity, it needs to be 'sufficiently obscure to be appreciated only by his group and yet clear enough not to puzzle unpleasantly anyone in the group'.[4] The erudite seventeenth-century pedants like Menestrier or Le Moyne could see this side of Scève very well, precisely because *imprese amorose* were part of the conventions of *précieux* poetry. One of the joys of a narrow circle of educated people is that of intimate exclusion of the outside world, of the *profanum vulgus* and therefore any *impresa* which brought together subtly two things in a way unexpected

---

[1] Art. cit.
[2] *Œuvres de Pierre de Ronsard Gentilhomme Vandosmois Prince des Poetes François.* Paris, 1617, *Preface de Marc Antoine Muret sur ses Commentaires.*
[3] The edition of Giovio which I have used is the *Ragionamento di Monsignor Paulo Giovio sopra i motti, et disegni d'Arme, et d'Amore che communemente chiamano Imprese con un discorso di Girolamo Ruscelli, intorno allo stesso soggetto.* Venice, 1560, p. 6.
[4] Op. cit. p. 114.

by people excluded from the circle but thoroughly expected by those inside was part of an intellectually delightful game. Le père Menestrier mentions Scève in exactly this social courtly intellectual circle when he imagines a scene of *sçavans* discussing who could devise the *Arcs Triomphaux* for the marriage of Charles Emmanuel II Duc de Savoye and Marie Jeanne Baptiste de Savoye. They argue about who is the best writer of devices.

Quand les faiseurs de devises oüirent parler de Carrousel, ils se levaient tous en tumulte pour s'offrir à faire celles des Cavaliers qui composeroient les quadrilles. Paul Jove crût qu'on n'oserait pas luy contester cet avantage puisqu'il estoit reconnu universellement de tous pour premier maistre de cet art: mais Bargagli luy dit, que quoy qu'on luy en dût les principes, il avoit porté plus avant que luy, et qu'il en feroit de plus justes. Aresi vouloit s'avancer pour faire savoir ses *Imprese Sacre* mais Ferro qui conservoit encore du ressentiment contre luy, dit tout haut qu'il ne s'agissoit pas icy de precher et le renvoya à son Breviaire et à sa Bible pour y chercher les mots de ses devises, quand celuy-cy le menaça de sa *pena reaffilata* faisant mine de ne pas beaucoup craindre ses *ombres* et ses *apparences* dont il le vouloit encore noircir.

Amboise et Boissière craignirent que la faction française ne fut pas assez forte pour eux contre les Italiens, quoyque Malle-Ville leur offrit le secours de quelques devises redoublées: mais lors qu'on y pensoit le moins le sort tomba sur Maurice Sève Lyonnais à qui tout le monde donna sa voix non seulement par ce que l'assemblée se tenoit dans son pays (à Bellecourt) mais encor parce qu'il estoit originaire du Piedmont dont Alpin est le Souverain et qu'il avoit esté le premier qui eut écrit ses amours en vers et en devises pour *Délie* et le premier qui en avoit fait de Françoises estimant que nostre langue n'estoit pas moins belle que l'Italienne et l'Espagnole pour exprimer de pareils sentimens.[1]

This fictional scene shows that Scève was regarded as the first French writer of *imprese*. Other writers make the same point in the seventeenth century: for instance, Adrian d'Amboise, *Discours ou Traicté des Devises*, Paris, 1620, mentions Scève as an *impresa*-maker

l'usage (of *imprese*) appliquant ce mot à des epigrammes mis au bas de quelques images ou peintures, dont on peut tirer quelques avis Politiques ou sentences morales, comme on en void dans Adrian le jeune, Iean Soreau, Achilles Bocchep (*sic*), Barthelemy Anneau, Maurice Scève, et dans nôtre Andre Alciat Milanois.          (p. 118)

The important theorists of the *impresa* genre in the sixteenth century were all Italian, for example, Giovio, Ruscelli, Scipio

---

[1] *L'Assemblée des sçavans et les presens des Muses*, Lyon, 1665, pp. 14–15.

Ammirato, Scipio Bargagli, Caburacci, Contile, Lodovicho Domenichi, Giovanni Palazzi, Torquato Tasso and Ercole Tasso. In
the seventeenth century the important theorists were French,
for example, Menestrier in *La Devise du Roy*, (1679), *Devises des
Princes* (1683), *La Philosophie des Images* (1682) and *La Science et
l'Art des Devises* (1686), Adrian d'Amboise, in *Discours, ou Traicté
des Devises* (1620), Henri Estienne, *L'Art de faire les Devises*, (1645)
and le père Bouhours, *Les Entretiens d'Ariste* (1671). This
suggests that petrarchism as a précieux phenomenon had
shifted from Italy to France (and other parts of Europe) and
that *imprese*, being a distinguishing feature of this phenomenon,
had gone along with it.

It is in the light of the Italian game – which was petrarchist,
elegant, noble and précieux – that Scève must be seen. He
borrows this fashion from the Italian poets. It is in this light too
that we must see the contribution of the petrarchists to Scève's
poetry. Serafino was a person to whom Scève was heavily in-
debted not only for the parallels between his *strambotti* and the
dizains of Scève (e.g. dizains 98, 100, 132, 139, 206, 334, 355)
but also because he copied the idea of producing *imprese*
verses. A recent study of petrarchism by Professor Leonard
Forster[1] makes the valuable point that petrarchism as a style
was the perfect instrument for poets intent on producing in the
vernacular what had been done in Latin for fifty years. Forster
provides an excellent *mise en position* of Serafino's role in writing
poetry that was light, intellectual and witty. He plays with
conceits in writing courtly sonnets for the Duchess of Urbino or
a sonnet for a Borgia and he elaborates his highly refined
imagery until it almost disappears like the smoke from a
Sobranie cigarette.

In order to place Scève as a précieux poet one must go back
to 1533 and to his 'discovery' of Laura's tomb at Avignon. The
role of Avignon during the fifteenth century has been so
excellently demonstrated by Professor Franco Simone[2] (and in
particular the very formative influence of Petrarch's sojourn
there) that it is no surprise to find Scève, imbued with the Italian
*canzoniere*, taking a leading part, probably at the request of

[1] *The Icy Fire*, C.U.P., 1969.
[2] *The French Renaissance. Medieval Tradition and Italian influence in shaping the
Renaissance in France.* Translated from the Italian by H. Gaston Hall, London,
1969.

François Ier, to find out where Laura was buried. In the early 1530s François Ier had commissioned Marot to translate six sonnets of Petrarch and they were called *Les Visions de Petrarque*.[1] In 1532 there was published the *Opere Toscane* of Luigi Alamanni which opened the doors for Lyonnais italianism. (Later Alamanni translated Scève's *blason, Le Sourcil* into Italian.) That Alamanni was important as an exile caught up with the French court is implicit in the epistle which formed the preface to Jean de Tournes' edition of Petrarch in 1545, 'les divines oeuvres de M. Luigi Alamanni, gentilhomme à qui la France donne autant d'honneur que l'Italie de gloire...' (Saulnier, op. cit., t. I, p. 40).

In the years between 1532 and the *Affaire des Placards* 1534 Marot was at the height of his renown, both as a popular poet and, what is more relevant to us, as a précieux court poet. Recent studies[2] have shown that petrarchism started in France towards the end of the fifteenth century and was the principal source of inspiration during Marot's youth and before he went to Italy in exile. The 1530s saw the flourishing of François Ier's court and, what is more important, are a period when petrarchism informed the code of communication between literati.

*Impresa*-making was a metaphorical mode of communication; according to the social code all the objects in an *impresa* were borrowed either from love poetry or, if the *imprese* were military, they could come from fencing, battles, playing-cards etc. They were the lowest common denominator of the tastes in a given period. That the court of François Ier was such a circle is a commonplace, and the slavishness of the group as regards the stylish features of dress, of ornament, of entertainments, pageants, masquerades and *objets d'art* plus the exchanging of elegant courtesies in verse are well-known.[3]

If we see Scève in this light it is surely much easier to understand why he joined the *blasons* match started by Marot –

---

[1] This was published, called *Le dict Autheur introduysant ung amoureux declairant six visions siennes* in 1534 in L. B. Alberti's *Hecatomphila*.

[2] C. A. Mayer and D. Bentley-Cranch, 'Clément Marot, poète pétrarquiste, Jean Marot', *BHR*, t. XXVII, 1965, pp. 183–5, and M. White, 'Petrarchism in the French Rondeau before 1527', *FS*, vol. XXII, October 1968, no. 4, pp. 287–95, and the whole work that Professor Mayer has done in preparing the editions of the *Epigrammes* and *rondeaux* in his standard edition of Marot, London, The Athlone Press, 1958–1973.

[3] The most recent book which brings out the milieu and the court of François Ier is Pauline Smith, *Clément Marot, Poet of the French Renaissance*, London, 1970.

he was following the guide of courtly *préciosité* and making himself known to the Court and to Marot. Marot in exile in Ferrara composed in 1535 and published in 1536 a delightful *blason* (a poem describing one part of a woman's body) on the beautiful breasts of a woman, and it knew a *succès de scandale* in France very quickly, with every poet joining in and writing poems on a woman's eyes, forehead, her tears, her smile, her hair, ear, nose, cheek, voice, teeth, sigh and even her nails. Marot's *blason Du beau Tetin* shows several features of sixteenth-century poetry,

> Tetin refect, plus blanc qu'un oeuf,
> Tetin de satin blanc tout neuf,
> Tetin qui fais honte à la Rose,
> Tetin plus beau que nulle chose,
> Tetin dur, non pas Tetin, voyre,
> Mais petite boule d'Ivoyre
> Au milieu duquel est assise
> Une Fraize ou une Cerise
> Que nul ne voit ne touche aussi,
> Mais je gage qu'il est ainsi;
> Tetin doncq au petit bout rouge,
> Tetin qui jamais ne se bouge,
> Soit pour venir, soit pour aller,
> Soit pour courir, soit pour baller;
> Tetin gaulche, Tetin mignon,
> Tousjours loing de son compaignon;
> Tetin qui portes tesmoignage
> Du demourant du personnage;
> Quant on te voit, il vient à mainctz
> Une envie dedans les mains
> De te taster, de te tenir;
> Mais il se fault bien contenir
> D'en approcher, bon gré, ma vie,
> Car il viendroit une aultre envie.
> O Tetin, ne grand, ne petit,
> Tetin meur, Tetin d'appetit,
> Tetin qui nuict & jour criez:
> Mariez moy tost, mariez!
> Tetin qui t'enfles & repoulses
> Ton Gorgerin de deux bons poulses;
> A bon droict heureux on dira
> Celluy qui de laict t'emplira,
> Faisant d'ung Tetin de pucelle
> Tetin de femme entiere & belle.[1]

[1] *Les Epigrammes*, p. 156–7, ed. Mayer, op. cit.

Now the fact that the French court lapped up this sweet little précieux poem is significant. There is a sensual current underlying Marot, Scève and the whole of the Pléiade, although it never assumes the same proportions of eroticism in Scève as in Marot; nonetheless it is a grave error to pretend that there is nothing sensual or carnal about Scève's view of love.[1] Secondly, it demonstrates that the petrarchist convention had reached France but that it had changed slightly in that Marot could be petrarchist but still have a native tradition and audience to which he addresses a poem like *Du beau Tetin*. And lastly, the Lyonnais circle was noble, looked towards Italy and counted among its élite poets like Marot, Saint-Gelais, Dolet and Scève. Both Marot and Scève were précieux in so far as they treated subjects that were much discussed in François Ier's court circles but not précieux in that they freed themselves from convention, Scève by achieving in his best poems a psychological and metaphysical type of poetry, and Marot through his wit.

Scève's imitation of petrarchists in making *imprese amorose* and in writing a host of précieux poems demonstrates two things: he sought for and found a means of creating poetry through a poetic diction and a style which was imitable; but secondly he went much further than the minor poets of petrarchist poetry in that he sought intrinsic value in a love experience which placed him apart from other French or Italian poets who were contemporary with him.

Professor Stone[2] has shown how the mottoes of the *imprese* are steeped in petrarchist psychology and has demonstrated how the companion dizains (or at least some of them) can be understood if seen from the petrarchist point of view. But there are other factors to take into account. We need first to see how Scève, the user and writer of *imprese*, fits into the para-literary and social genre of *imprese* in the sixteenth and seventeenth centuries before looking at his poetic technique.

In the 1544 edition the *priuilege* allowed Antoine Constantin

de imprimer, ou faire imprimer...ce present Liure traictant d'Amours, intitulé DELIE, soit auec Emblesmes, ou sans Emblesmes...

and forbade any other printer,

de ne le imprimer ne faire imprimer uendre ne distribuer, soit auec lesdictz Emblesmes ou sans Emblesmes...

---

[1] This will be discussed in the next chapters.  [2] Art. cit.

This was a safeguard to the printer against the possibility of slightly altered versions of the book being put out by other printers. The wording of the privilege in *La Magnificence de la superbe et triumphante entrée de la noble et antique Cité de Lyon faicte au treschrestien Roy de France Henry deuxiesme*...Lyon, 1549, states the same; the publisher

est permis d'exposer en vente sans que autre que luy... puisse imprimer ou faire imprimer soyt avec figures ou sans figures, petite ou grande marge tant en Italien que Françoys...

Thus it is misleading to argue as Professor Stone did (art. cit., p. 102)

what better explanation of the fact that the original *Privilege* provided the (sic) *Délie* could be published with or without the emblems; in general Scève had been indifferent to them.

The 1564 edition is an improvement on the 1544 edition but the text remains unaltered apart from typographical slips which are sometimes corrected. The figures in the woodcuts are much clearer; for instance *L'Hyerre & la Muraille* (no. 17): the 1544 woodcut is very rough whilst the 1564 woodcut shows a magnificent building on a hillside with ivy creeping along the right side of the edifice; not only is this a more elaborate design but the point of the motto is greatly reinforced by the fact that this building is being *attacked* by ivy. In all pictures where the human figure occurs, the costume, the jewellery and the lines of the body reflect the change in taste and fashion. We step out of a world of simple peasant clothing into a world where the Italian influence is marked. For instance, the women are dressed in flowing garments and bedecked with necklaces: in no. 1 the virgin is drawn in profile, her hairstyle is more elaborate and she is wearing jewellery (cf. *emblesmes* nos. 12 and 38). The male figures reflect the same trend: for instance, *L'homme & le Boeuf* (no. 4) changes from a simply clad figure to a fully clothed one with a hat and a cloak (cf. nos. 7, 19, 25). Other changes reflect the Renaissance: for instance Orpheus (no. 20); in the 1544 woodcut he is playing a stringed instrument whereas in the later woodcut he is a handsome young man playing a lute (cf. the rising importance of music and the link between poetry and music by the Pléiade). Very little background was given in the 1544 woodcuts while in the later edition great attention is paid to landscape scenes, cliffs, stretches of water, rocks and in certain cases (e.g. no. 25) the scene is set indoors. One has the impression that the designer of the woodcuts knew the companion dizains: for instance, in no. 3 the motto is changed to *t'adorer* (1544 *te adorer*) to correspond with the last line of the dizain which also has *t'adorer*. Or in no. 9: there is now a more elaborate shield, with a figure-head in the centre with flowing hair, and an arrow entering the mouth of the figure. Alberti's *Deiphire*, 1534, had lines which fit this *impresa* exactly,

interviene a miseri amanti come alla targa, quanto lo strale la trova più doppia e dura, tanto più vi si ferma et affigge e con più fatica si sficca, così lo amore, quanto più trova l'animo fermo e ostinato a repugnarli, tanto più ivi assiede e insiste.                    (p. 20)

You must obey love and not resist or fight it otherwise you make the wound deeper; another piece of petrarchist psychology which applies to the motto and the picture.

There is no doubt that *Délie* was reprinted in 1564 partly because of the *imprese*. Even during the first sixty years of the sixteenth century Lyon knew its first salons; for example, those of Marie-Catherine de Pierre-Vive or Madame du Perron, the Maréchale de Retz.[1] We have the manuscript of an Album made for the wife of Albert de Gondi, Claude-Catherine de Clermont.[2] And Lavaud and Giudici have described the love *imprese* in this manuscript. Scève is the most often-quoted poet and there are several dizains as well as *imprese* from *Délie* included. Lavaud states that,

Beaucoup de grandes dames de ce temps... devaient posséder de semblables livrets et les poètes, illustres ou non, s'ingéniaient à en commenter les figures.                    (art. cit., p. 422)

Furthermore, Giudici has uncovered one or two mottoes and pictures in Lyon which are identical to Scève's *imprese*: for instance *La Girouette* (*impresa* no. 15),

l'*emblema* e il motto sceviani sono identici (solo la disposizione grafica delle parole è diversa) a uno di quelli affrescati su un soffitto dell'attuale

---

[1] See Saulnier, op. cit., t. I, pp. 17–112, for a detailed examination of Lyon salon life.
[2] *Album pour la Maréchale de Retz, qui est un recueil manuscrit appartenant à Fr. Chandon de Briailles. L'album fut composé pour Claude-Catherine de Clermont, épouse de Albert de Gondi.* Dates for which have been suggested as 1575–6. See also, J. Lavaud, 'Note sur un Recueil Manuscrit d'Emblemes composé pour la Maréchale de Retz', *Hum. et Ren.* 1937, t. III, pp. 421ff. And E. Giudici, op. cit., figs. 4–26.

Hôpital Jules-Caumont presso Lione. Dobbiamo concluderne che lo avere Scève utilizzato in parte gli *emblemi* del castello del Perron non implica necessariamente che egli abbia composte espressamente dei *dizains* e che anche in questo caso egli può essersi limitato all' accoppiamente dell'*emblema* con versi già pronti?[1]

It was *imprese amorose* which became particularly popular in social salons and this may be compared with other pastimes such as writing madrigals and sonnets to please the habitués of an inner circle. The potentialities of the *impresa* can be seen in the famous embroideries of Mary Stuart. A full description of them is given by William Drummond of Hawthornden:

> for all inscriptions I have been curious to find out for you, the Impressaes and Emblemes on a Bed of State wrought by the late Queen Mary mother to our sacred sovereign, which will embellish greatly some pages of your book, and is worthy of your remembrance; the first is the Loadstone turning towards the pole, the word her Majesties name turned in an anagram, Maria Stuart, sa vertu m'attire, which is not much inferior to Veritas armata...[2]

Drummond describes all the *imprese* on the embroidered quilt – most of them culled from French device books of the middle of the sixteenth century. It is clear that Mary Stuart was attracted to the genre while she was resident at the French Court and took the custom home with her to Scotland. But in fact few poems written around *imprese* rise above the flattery of précieux poetry. Scève's case in a few companion dizains is an isolated example.

At the turn of the sixteenth century Dutch engravers were the most proficient in the art of making emblems and devices: for instance, the work of Otho Vaenius, of Daniel Heinsius, the Wierix brothers and the schools of engravers working with various publishing houses in Amsterdam and Antwerp. It is exceedingly difficult to trace Scève's *imprese* through Europe, but one thing is certain: that various of his pictures and mottoes were available to Heinsius (as Praz pointed out, vol. 1, p. 81). Otho Vaenius' *Amorum Emblemata* and *Amoris Divini Emblemata*, published in Antwerp in 1608 and 1615 respectively, wielded considerable influence on making pictures throughout the century and it is believed that Scève's *imprese* were among the thousands that passed through his hands. The curious problem

[1] Op. cit., p. 214.
[2] W. Drummond, *History of Scotland*, London 1655, Letter to his worthy friend Master Benjamin Johnson, dated July 1, 1619.

of Menestrier's sources for Scève's *imprese* has not been solved. Some of his remarks would suggest that he had read Scève in a collection of *imprese* which had multiplied through Europe and was translated from language to language. In his *Devises des Princes*, Paris, 1683, p. 101 he comments on one of Scève's *imprese* in this way: 'C'est une des Devises de Maurice Seve [sic], qu'on a traduite ou imitée en diverses Langues', and later on p. 207 he talks of 'Un coq battant de ses ailes sur un feu. Plus je l'éteins et plus fort je l'allume' followed by this remark, 'Cette Devise est une des cinquante de Maurice Seve [sic], les deux derniers vers du *Huitain* [sic] qu'il employe pour l'expliquer sont ceux-cy,

> Voulant ma flâme éteindre aucunement,
> Plus je l'éteins, & plus fort je l'allume.

The fact that Menestrier does not seem to know that Scève wrote *Délie* consistently in dizains suggests that neither the 1544 nor the 1564 editions of *Délie* were known to him and that knowledge of Scève's *imprese* comes from an anthology of devices or through theoreticians of the genre. But it is the second edition of his *Art des Emblemes* (first edition 1662) which appeared in 1684 that makes this quite clear. A few examples of Menestrier's misreading of the *imprese* will suffice to demonstrate this. He takes the last *impresa* (no. 50) and comments,

Maurice Seve en sa Delie 'Objet de plus haute vertu' pour se plaindre de la dureté de la personne qu'il aimoit, s'est fait peindre étendu auprés d'un tombeau où brûlent des flambeaux allumez, avec un grand bässin d'eau semblable à ceux dont se servaient les Anciens pour les aspersions ou lustrations des cadavres devant que de les brûler, et il a expliqué cet Emblême par ces Vers...                                        (p. 160)

And Menestrier reproduces the companion dizain *in toto*. He modernises the spelling, for instance

1.2. L'on auroit mis deux élemens contraires
1.3. vois
1.4. Entre élemens
1.5. Je t'avertis qu'ils sont tres necessaires
1.6. Pour te montrer par signes évidens
1.7. residens
1.8. aprement
1.9. Qu'après ma mort encore cy-dedans.

and reproduces a totally different woodcut from the two editions of *Délie*: the picture in Menestrier shows a tomb and large candles burning on the left, a corpse on the floor in front of them and on the right a large bowl of water and a maiden naked to the waist who is scattering water on the corpse. Sometimes Menestrier does not produce the companion dizain (p. 161), and sometimes (p. 164) he reproduces dizains which are without *imprese*. Thus Menestrier comments, 'Tantost il se plaint que voulant suivre raison, elle l'engage à suivre l'amour...' and quotes dizain 179 and the first four lines of dizain 180 without a break. This is accompanied by a woodcut showing a man in armour, seemingly holding a conversation with a woman and Cupid; she is pointing in one direction and the man holds up his shield with his left hand. This is to mean that he follows love rather than his reason or his duty.

Both the woodcuts and the number of dizains (or indeed huitains or sonnets!) must have been circulating somewhere in the seventeenth century but given the present state of research we cannot say where Menestrier could have come across them.

What we can say is that the demonstration in historical terms has proved fairly clearly that Scève was using *imprese amorose* in a well-established contemporary Italian tradition, although the theoreticians appear on the stage after 1544. He was well-known enough by the 1570s to be popular precisely as a writer of *imprese* and to be used in albums designed to be the précieux source of much entertainment in Lyon. There remains the question of his use of them, as a précieux poet, or not.

# 5

## PRÉCIEUX POET

Whether Scève chose the fifty *imprese amorose* or not (and this can only be a matter of speculation) there are a number of important points raised by them. These woodcuts determine the typographical layout of the book: 5 poems precede the first *impresa*, then there are 49 groups of 9 poems separated off from one another by *imprese* and 3 final poems. One is moved to ask whether the formula,

$$5+(3^2 \times 7^2)+3 = 449$$

means anything? Brunetière's fantastic cabbalistic account is arbitrary and to be dismissed on the grounds that the first edition of *Délie* came out with faulty numbering of dizains. Schmidt's account is further removed from the text; giving a hermetic interpretation of the figures I have just mentioned, he is led to say,

*Délie* retrace les aventures initiatiques d'une âme incarnée, mais déjà épanouie dans la 'Rose trémière' des mystères, où 'Quintefeuille' (5), qui se dirige vers la réintégration finale (9) en gravissant tous les échelons de la 'Haute Science' (49) dans l'espoir de passer la porte de l'illumination suprême (50) pour participer substantiellement à l'oeuvre d'une 'Déité' éternellement active et créatrice. (3)[1]

This is an intellectual game where any number can mean what the author wants it to mean and there is no 'proof' in human reasoning to discredit this poetic fantasy. The answer to the question of meaning in this dazzling formula is probably no. The woodcuts do not follow each other in any systematic order apart from the first, which is the *innamoramento*, and the last one which affirms that the passion and suffering of the lover will outlive death. Beyond this, one cannot point to any pattern in the succession of *imprese amorose* and furthermore the groups of nine dizains do not contain a thematic unit (for a discussion of this see McFarlane, p. 22).

[1] A. M. Schmidt, 'Haute Science et poésie française au XVIe siècle: La gnose de Maurice Scève', in *Les Cahiers d'Hermes*, no. 1, Paris, 1947, pp. 14–15.

Yet the *imprese* do serve two functions: they imprint upon our minds many of the petrarchist leit-motifs which run through the collection. And secondly, they bring into play the physical, even carnal aspect of Scève's love. This second point needs some elaboration. The notion current in the sixteenth century that a picture can present the intelligible by means of the visible, using the particular to point to the universal or to the essence of something, is a basic one for the understanding of Renaissance poetics and, coupled with the Neo-Platonic idea that the eye is the highest and noblest sense organ in man, could well have been one of the considerations which led Scève to make use of woodcuts in *Délie*. Moreover, as Scève is constantly returning to the *innamoramento*, depicted as the meeting of two pairs of eyes, there is something almost obsessive about the visible throughout his poetry. The visible and the symbolic are prime features in his organization of the love experience, yet he did not moralise, he did not symbolise allegorically nor work out comparisons in the fashionable manner. Claude Paradin gives expression to the symbolic elements of pictorial woodcuts when he marries Poetry and Painting together in this way:

Et à la verité l'une & l'autre [Poetry and Painting] ont quasi un mesme effect & proprieté. Attendu que toutes deux resjouissent, repaissent, consolent & *animent l'esperit à choses vertueuses:* & d'avantage peuvent esmouvoir les passions & affections, avec si grande vehemence, qu'il est impossible de pouvoir trouver plus ardans & affectionez aguillons, que ceux qui *incitent à la mort.*[1]    [The italics are mine]

Scève can use *mort* with its usual meaning – either simply that state which leads to nothingness or the rewards and punishments of the after life – or as a personification of the Goddess Death. Or he can use *mort* in the petrarchist sense – a state of mind where death and life are interchangeable states, dependent on the power of the mistress to deal out death or life every minute of the day with the plural *mortz* referring to the passions and sufferings which are his normal state of life. (Perhaps too there is an ambiguous play with *la petite mort*, meaning orgasm.) *Vertu* is a combination of *virtus*, where the components are moral force and active *élan*, and virtue a rather more general quality, comprising her unusual worth and superiority as a person. Menestrier declared that

[1] C. Paradin, address to Dame Jeanne de la Rochefoucauld in the *Quadrins historiques de la Bible*, Lyon, 1553, p. A2.

elles [Scève's *devises* = *imprese*] sont autant de peintures de ses amours, mais peintures ou [sic] tout est tellement honnête, que c'est la vertu de la personne qu'il aimoit, qu'il se propose en ces Vers & en ces Devises, sous ce titre, DELIE OBJET DES PLUS HAUTES VERTUS.[1]

[The plural of *vertu* is Menestrier's own.]

Now this statement proposes a half-truth about the *imprese*. It would explain, for instance, the inclusion of nos. 2, 3, 5, 6, 8, 9, 14, 24, 28, 29, 32, 33, 34, 35, 39, 43 and possibly 47. In other cases the sensual aspect makes an immediate impact on the reader's senses and thus gains entrance to his understanding. Admittedly, the modern reader of *Délie* may not be familiar with the significance attached to the figures in the picture; he may not know what associations would be awakened by the pictorial representation of the bat or the fly (no. 42 and no. 48). The bat is a creature of evil omen, an emblem of melancholy, because of its nocturnal activities when all other living things are asleep.[2] The fly is a symbol of *indocilitas* and *rusticitas* (as we saw in Ch. 2) so it is an apt parallel for the virgin who cannot be 'tamed' by the lover. These animals mean very little to the modern reader whose mind is not conditioned to recognise even the presence of fixed attributes in animals, let alone identify them correctly. But he may recall the Proust quotation used earlier (*Introduction*, p. 17) in which the unicorn was used as an analogy to describe Swann in love. If he looks up the first *impresa*, he will see that it shows a unicorn, wounded by an arrow and dying in the lap of a maiden. If he then reads the motto: *Pour te* (the *te* is unclear, but comparison of the *t* with the *l* of *la*, makes the reading pretty certain; besides which the sense requires *te* not *le*) *veoir ie pers la vie*, the whole significance of the legend will surely become clear. Shepard (*The Lore of the Unicorn*, London, 1930) points out the underlying sexual connotations of the story: the unicorn represents the wild and ferocious male who is attracted to the pure maiden. It is almost an archetype of male submission at the hands of woman. And he may well think of lovers longing to 'die in their lady's lap' when he gazes at the picture with the unicorn's head being just in the right position to suggest sexual connotations. Then he reads the dizain:

> Libre viuois en l'Auril de mon aage,
> De cure exempt soubz celle adolescence,

---

[1] *Devises des Princes*, op. cit., p. 250.
[2] L. Réau, *Iconographie de l'art chrétien*, Paris, 1955–9, t. 1. p. 108.

Ou l'oeil, encor non expert de dommage,
Se veit surpris de la doulce presence,
Qui par sa haulte & diuine excellence
M'estonna l'Ame & le sens tellement,
Que de ses yeulx l'archier tout bellement
Ma liberté luy à toute asseruie:
Et des ce iour continuellement
En sa beaulté gist ma mort, & ma vie.

In the poem the unicorn = poet loses both his liberty and his life: but it is *continuellement*, and so clearly suggests the Neo-Platonic idea of losing one's identity in the mistress's presence and also the *piccola morte* – the extreme point of passion. The reader may further recall that *impresa* no. 26 uses a unicorn quite differently, with the motto 'De moy je m'espovante', and where a metamorphosis is clearly implied. (We shall examine this *impresa* in the next chapter.)

Let us look next at no. 4 *L'Homme & le Boeuf*, with the motto *Plus l'attire plus m'entraine* and read the companion dizain;

Tant est Nature en volenté puissante,
Et volenteuse en son foible pouoir,
Que bien souuent a son vueil blandissante,
Se voit par soy grandement deceuoir.
    A mon instinct ie laisse conceuoir
Vn doulx souhait, qui, non encor bien né,
Est de plaisirs nourry, & gouuerné,
Se paissant puis de chose plus haultaine.
    Lors estant creu en desir effrené,
Plus ie l'attire & plus a soy m'entraine.

This dizain stresses the uncontrollable nature of desire and emphasises the physical nature of the passion – so refuting the theory that spirituality and Neo-Platonic conceptions are the sole ingredients of Scève's love. Commenting on the meaning of this woodcut Menestrier (*Art des Emblemes*, op. cit., p. 161) says

pour exprimer qu'il n'estoit plus maitre de sa passion, il peignit un de ces chars des jeux Olympiques où le cocher faisoit tous ses efforts pour retenir ses chevaux quand ils sont au bout de la carrière, ne sçauroit plus les retenir dans le mouvement impetueux qu'ils ont pris.

Menestrier's description of the driver and the two horses is rather far from Scève's woodcut (in 1544 and 1564) but it is close to its meaning in terms of the poet's carnal passion. Does it not perhaps recall the analogy used by Plato (*Phaedrus*, 245, 246 and 254)? The judgement as driver, controls the two horses which drive the chariot of the soul, the one good, the other bad, being honour and appetite respectively. The behaviour of the bad, black horse is uncontrollable; he knows only physical lustful pleasure. Or again no. 40 *Le Coq qui se brusle* with its motto *Plus l'estains plus l'allume* where the poet's love is so intense that the more he tries to quell it, the stronger it becomes. A possible explanation of this bird is in the writer Horapollo.[1] He describes the behaviour of a pelican when it returns and finds its nest in flame. The words are

Fumum vero ex inde provenientem Pelicanus videns ac propriis aliis ignem extinguere affectans, alias vehementer quatit eoque ipso motu ignem magis imprudenter satis excitat.

In the *Hieroglyphica* the picture is used *dementem indicare* and it is significant that the amorous *impresa* here is followed by a dizain which is concerned with the 'madness' of the lover.

In other words, Scève could use these pictures as implicit reminders of the physical desire which was part of his experience in love. Furthermore the identification or the non-identification with mythological figures established the poet within the universal line of tragic love. Let us take one figure as an example (we shall look at several others in the next chapter). In both literary and iconographical sources of the Renaissance, Narcissus (no. 6) is the figure punished by Eros for spurning the love of the nymphs, particularly that of Echo, and he dies at the hands of Venus or Eros.[2] The emphasis was not simply laid on the *philautia* aspect of the legend but, more significantly, on the punishment inflicted by the God of Love. Without these associations the companion dizain (no. 60), in which the poet constructs his argument around the points of contrast and comparison between himself and Narcissus, is obscure and tortuous. When one sees first the pictorial representation of Narcissus the dizain is not so obscure but it is still tortured:

> Si c'est Amour, pourquoy m'occit il doncques,
> Qui tant aymay, & onq ne sceuz hair?
> Ie ne m'en puis non asses esbahir,
> Et mesmement que ne l'offençay oncques:

[1] *Hieroglyphica*, Paris, 1517, Cap. 54.
[2] See D. Panofsky, 'Narcissus and Echo: Notes on Poussin's "Birth of Bacchus" in the Fogg Museum of Art', *Art Bulletin*, XXXI, 1949, pp. 111–20.

Mais souffre encor, sans complainctes quelconques,
Qu'il me consume, ainsi qu'au feu la Cyre.
Et me tuant, a viure il me desire,
Affin qu'aymant aultruy, je me desayme.
    Qu'est il besoing de plus oultre m'occire,
Veu qu'asses meurt, qui trop vainement ayme?

There is their common situation in love – both loving some object
which either cannot or does not return that love – and this
suffering leads them both to death. Frappier has pointed out
how closely the theme of the mirror and that of Narcissus were
interwoven in the Middle Ages and how a lover's desperate
passion was often compared to Narcissus' anguished love for
himself.[1] But one is forced to remark the differences that
separate the two figures. Narcissus fell in love with his own image
while Scève's love is directed towards Délie. How then does Scève
make use of the metaphor in the dizain and how does he try
and convince the reader of its appropriateness? Let us look at
the argument of the poem. One could restate it in this way:
'Why does Love persecute me, who has never known hatred?
His attack on me is particularly surprising as I have never
offended him. And yet he makes me suffer and urges me to love
another and move away from love of self. This is totally
unnecessary seeing that I love another and am thus already dead
in and to myself.' Narcissus was sentenced to fall in love with
himself in the first place because he had offended the God of
Love in rejecting Echo. This is the basic difference between
Narcissus and Scève and the latter uses it as the basis of the
argument. The way he does this perhaps may recall the
evocation of the Dictynna–Minos myth in dizain 353 (which we
shall look at later) where in the last two lines he calls up the
legend and obliterates it at the same time,

Ie ne suis poinct pour ressembler Minos,
Pourquoy ainsi, Dictymne, me fuis tu?

Basically, it is the same technique as the introduction of startling
images as a *pointe* to a dizain but whereas, as we shall see later
on, these astonishing images compel the reader to re-read the
dizain, I think that in this Narcissus dizain the allusion to the

[1] J. Frappier, 'Variations sur le thème du miroir de Bernard de Ventadour à
Maurice Scève' in *Cahiers de l'Association Internationale des Etudes Françaises*,
mai 1950, no. 11, pp. 134–59.

*impresa* is used tortuously and obscurely. It is as if we are watching the working out of some aspects of Scève's technique in companion dizains where it does not quite come off: a failure as a précieux poem and a failure as poetry.

The suggestions of the Heliotropic legend of Clytia (no. 16) establishes his total and continual dependence upon Délie – a leit-motif of the whole cycle brilliantly brought out in dizain 216

> En diuers temps, plusieurs iours, maintes heures,
> D'heure en moment, de moment a tousiours
> Dedans mon Ame, ô Dame, tu demeures
> Toute occupée en contraires seiours.
> Car tu y vis & mes nuictz, & mes iours...

But whereas the language, the control of the sentence, the repetitions and the lingering pause on *ô Dame* make this a fine statement, the companion poem (dizain 141) plays around with a simple image, several elaborations and ends on a banal equivocation.

> Parquoy de rien ne me nuyt son absence,
> Veu qu'en tous lieux, maulgré moy, ie la suys.

It would be tedious to go through all the *imprese* that present physical love or some aspect of a physical experience that emanates from his feelings.[1] Suffice it to state that they are either leit-motifs of petrarchist psychology or of human love.

In fact Scève has used the set of fifty woodcuts as part of his poetic technique. They function as ordinary metaphors and provide a visible second term of comparison which makes the tenor in the companion dizain more easily intelligible. By using figures, myths and legends whose significance were known to the sixteenth-century reader Scève could dispense with explicit statement in the dizains. He seems to be the only sixteenth-century poet to do this – to incorporate *imprese* into a serious work on love. Italian academies did publish *imprese* together with the verses of their members towards the end of the sixteenth century, for instance *Rime degli Accademici Occulti con le loro Imprese e Discorsi* (Brescia, 1568) and B. Percivallo, *Rime e*

---

[1] Let me list some of the obvious ones which readers may follow up in *Délie*: nos. 15, 17, 18, 21, 27, 36, 38, 41 and 49. Others like Dido (no. 13), Acteon (no. 19), the unicorn looking at itself (no. 26) and Cleopatra (no. 30) I shall be dealing with in the next chapter.

*Imprese* (Ferrara, 1588); but none have the underlying unity of theme or complete integration of *imprese* and companion dizains within a single work that we find in *Délie*. Rosemary Freeman in her *English Emblem Books* (London, 1948, pp. 52–3) gives examples of isolated emblems inserted in a work: for instance the three emblems in Gascoigne's *Hermit's Tale*, but adds that 'they bear no immediate relation to the story and were obviously intended to be an additional attraction to catch the eye of the Queen'. The tradition of adding either a poem or a commentary or both by way of exegesis was firmly established by the beginning of the seventeenth century, and it would be difficult to match the fire and fervour of some of Villava's poems in his *Empresas espirituales y morales* (Baeça, 1613); for instance his appeal to Christ the Phoenix showing a phoenix seated amid flames, with the attached motto *Del Embidioso* and the following poem;

> Dime Phenix hermoso,
> Como entre tanto olor qual da pon censo
> La rica Arabia, que a su honor si inclina,
> Te mueres, sin que en nido tan precioso
> Pueda esforçante el religioso encienso,
> La Casia, el Nardo, y la Canela fina.
> Mira que se imagina,
> Que das exemplo al suelo
> De lo que haze el embidioso en tanto
> Que entre agenas virtudes se possea.
> Pues el olor del Cielo
> Que arroja el bien de Dios perfumo sancto,
> Con que se adquiere vida,
> La muerte se acarrea,
> De culpa tan forz pena denida                        (pt. ii, p. 19)

The free verse found in this example shows that the form of the poems is elastic and can stretch to contain any amount of lyricism, but few writers took advantage of the liberating opportunities offered by the *imprese* and brought instead its functions closely in line with that of emblems. From the private expression of one individual's thought, or the representation of a personal religious, political or moral problem the *impresa* was extended to become the general mirror of a public problem. Thus Villava was carried away by his religious convictions to turn his book into an apology for the Spanish Inquisition and the character of his poems changes accordingly. It is true that the indirect appeal to the senses in the pictorial genre (mainly emblems) was exploited in the late sixteenth century and throughout the seventeenth century (e.g. Herbert's incorporation of non-pictorial emblems into his religious poetry) but the best ones used non-pictorial emblems to provide a starting point for a personal analysis of serious and complex relationships. But as far as we can see, Scève's *Délie* was the first and the finest use of *imprese* in love poetry.

The relationship between the picture and the accompanying verses is crucial for an understanding of emblems and *imprese*. In Alciati, for example, the verses are without exception concerned with explaining the picture. They take up, point by point, all the elements in the picture and clarify their significance. Thus the picture or symbol is in a way separated from its meaning, which only emerges in the companion verse. As the emblem fashion develops, the commentary separates itself from the verses proper and becomes more and more elaborate until with Claude Mignault it reaches the point where it completely overshadows the actual emblem (picture and verse). The analysis of one example will clarify my remarks here. Inside his emblem picture entitled 'Fidei Symbolum' Alciati shows three figures which are allegorical representations of Truth, Honour and Love.[1] Truth and Honour face each other and join hands while the boy Cupid, representing Love, stands between them and touches both of them with his hands. In the accompanying verse Alciati first describes the scene,

> Stet depictus Honor tyrio velatus amictu
> Eiusque iungat nuda dextram Veritas.
> Sitque Amor in medio castus, cui tempora circum
> Rosa it, Diones pulchrior Cupidine...

in order that we may recognise the individual figures in the picture for what they are meant to be. Then he explains their pose and the significance of the picture,

> Constituunt haec signa Fidem, Reverentia Honoris
> Quam fovet, alit Amor, parturitque Veritas,

so the reader is left in no doubt as to the purport of the picture as a whole.

Now when Menestrier summarises the positions of the theoreticians of emblems and *imprese* he stops at the great work of

---

[1] *Emblematum liber*, Augsburg, 1531, fol. E7, emblem no. 92.

Emanuel Tesoro – *Il Canochiale Aristotelico*.[1] Urged by profound admiration for this work he says, 'Tout brille d'esprit dans cet ouvrage comme dans tous les autres que cet Autheur nous a donnez, mais il demande des lecteurs sçavans.' The first condition of an *impresa*, according to Tesoro, is that 'la parfaite Devise est une Metaphore'. Menestrier adds later that for an *impresa* to be a proper metaphor it is essential to have both figure and motto together. It is only when we have both elements present that the connection between the two terms becomes intelligible, the figure in the picture being identified with the *je* of the motto. But this connection is not grammatically stated, that is, it is not explicit, as in a simile or emblem. The second condition that Tesoro gives is that 'elle est une Metaphore de proportion'. This is of course a fundamental criterion for any type of comparison but it is the poet's responsibility to convince the reader of the resemblance of two different things.

There is only one companion dizain in *Délie* where Scève refers explicitly to the objects in the picture and then proceeds like Alciati to comment on their significance. This is the last *emblesme* of the book, *Le Tumbeau & les chandeliers* which shows a tomb flanked by two candles and in front of which is a pail of water. Scève sets out in the dizain to explain what each of these objects signify. The pail of water and the candles are the two warring elements in the poet's heart, and the tomb symbolizes his death. By putting together all the objects we can 'read' the motto in words – 'Apres la mort ma guerre encor me suyt'. The objects are separated from their significance; that is to say their significance does not emerge until it is explained by the companion dizain:

> Si tu t'enquiers pourquoy sur mon tombeau
> Lon auroit mys deux elementz contraires,
> Comme tu voys estre le feu, & l'eau
> Entre elementz les deux plus aduersaires:
> Ie t'aduertis, qu'ilz sont tresnecessaires
> Pour te monstrer par signes euidentz,
> Que si en moy ont esté residentz
> Larmes & feu, bataille asprement rude:
> Qu'apres ma mort encores cy dedens
> Ie pleure, & ars pour ton ingratitude.

There is no fusion between the symbol and what it symbolises, therefore the likenesses have to be established point by point.

[1] *La Philosophie des Images*, Paris, 1682, p. 65.

And since the *impresa* is rather trite, so is the dizain: line 4 expands what lines 1–3 said – 'Ie t'aduertis qu'ilz sont tresnecessaires' – and line 5 prepares to explain why they are necessary; the last four lines give the significance of the objects in the picture. Ruscelli (as we saw in the preceding chapter) can give us many examples of poems written around an *impresa*: for example the sonnet written for Ferrante Carrafa on a lotus flower and the sun:[1]

> Nascendo il Sol dal mar, s'erge sù l'onde
> D'Eufrate, un'erba, che quel mira ogn'hora,
> E quando è al mezo Ciel, tutta s'infiora
> Dal raggio ond'han vigor fior, frutti e fronde.
>   Poi che nel Oceano il carro asconde,
> Tosto quel bel, ch'ella mostrava fuora,
> Nel sen umido attuffa e discolora
> I fiori, e le sue foglie alte, e feconde.
>   Cosí al vostro apparir, mio vivo Sole,
> Fiorisce quest'ingegno; e l'alma gode
> Sovra il gran mar de la sua certe speme;
>   A lo sparir, nel pianto, e ne le pene
> Proprie s'immerge, e'l cor s'imbruna e rode
> Nel fosco, che altro ben l'alma non vuole.

But is there anything in this sonnet which makes it distinct from a thousand other précieux poems to ladies? The separation of the symbol from what it symbolises is the same as in the Scève dizain and they are both prosaic re-statements of commonplaces of petrarchist poetry.

Of course, Scève's technique in the companion dizains can vary tremendously and the ones which use the metaphor given by the *impresa* in a rich or unusual way will be looked at in the next chapter. But the neutral ones like no. 11 simply produce petrarchist-précieux poems. The legend behind the phoenix in no. 11 is indicated by the words of the motto – *De mort a vie* – the rebirth of the bird from the dead. The companion dizain assumes that the legend is in the reader's mind and proceeds to recount the sharply changing feelings and *état d'âme* of the poet according to Délie's behaviour towards him. Thus lines 1–4 describe the hope engendered by her smile, lines 5–6 the despair when she is cold towards him and lines 7–8 the rebirth of desire when he hears her honeyed speech. In conclusion he addresses Délie with

---

[1]  G. Ruscelli, op. cit., p. 127.

Parquoy tu peulx...
En vn moment me donner vie, & mort.

The poem does not rise above the conventional recital of the woes and vicissitudes suffered by the typical petrarchist lover. The motto and the last line do bring in a whole range of associations, but although potentially rich and intense they merely evoke a surprised smile in the reader because the metaphor is trite and conventional and it has not been knit in with the dizain. Some companion dizains are feeble précieux poems, as for example no. 276. The *impresa* (no. 31, *Le Papillon & la Chandelle*) with the motto *En ma ioye douleur*, illustrates a general statement about the poet's expectations being dashed to nothing and is accompanied by a dizain which wanders from image to image. The first two lines discuss the effects of hope in terms of this parallel,

> Voyez combien l'espoir pour trop promettre
> Nous fait en l'air, comme Corbeaulx, muser...

*Muser* here means *perdre son temps* and the *corbeau* was regarded as an attribute of hope in the sixteenth century. But in the 3rd and 4th lines we have a new image,

> Voyez comment en prison nous vient mettre,
> Cuydantz noz anz en liberté vser...

which leads in turn to the image of bird-lime as figure for 'vn desir trop glueux'. And finally the last line leads us back to the butterfly-picture of the *impresa*. A confused and muddling précieux poem.

Other *imprese* like the alembic (no. 23, *L'Alembic*) are more interesting. Quite clearly (as Praz. op. cit., p. 81, said) the *impresa* comes from one of the most common conceits in love lyrics in the fifteenth, sixteenth and seventeenth centuries. Praz refers us to Petrarch, Serafino, Marot and Pontus de Tyard who used the conceit before it appeared in pictorial form in La Perrière's *Theatre des bons engins* in 1539. These references provide us with the idea contained in the conceit, which in the hands of the above authors should properly be termed the 'distillation' conceit, for it is actually the process of distillation that is alluded to and not the alembic. These poets make no mention of the alembic but by their frequent use of *distillare* or *distiller*, use the process to describe their own heart which in grief distils tears through the eyes.

Petrarch for example uses the comparison thus,

> Per lagrime ch'io spargo a mille a mille
> Conven ch'il duol per gli occhi si distille
> Dal cor c'ha seco le faville e l'esca,
> Non pur qual fu, ma pare a me che cresca.
>
> *(Rime,* 55, lines 7–10)

Here he calls up the whole process and makes an analogy between the heart with its flames and embers of love and the fire heating the alembic, and between the eyes which distil tears of grief and the distilled water which is the end-product of the alembic process. But the picture of an alembic only comes once before *Délie* and La Perrière makes a very different use of it. He demonstrates the dangers of love. After making a general statement on love La Perrière preaches a warning which is universally applicable, and he is able to show the result of foolish love in action:

> Pour folle amour les suppotz de Venus
> Ont des dangers a milliers et a cens:
> Les ungs en sont malheureux devenus,
> Aultres en ont du tout perdu le sens.
> Plusieurs autheurs en termes condecens
> De c'ont escript exemples d'importance,
> Si ne voulons endurer grandz alarmes:
> Car a la fin sous feu de repentance
> Voyez amour distiller eau de larmes.          (no. 19)

Now Scève was clearly attracted to the conceit: it is one of the few that provide the theme of three dizains in the same unit as the *impresa* (nos. 204, 206 and 207). In the companion dizain he establishes a strong personal analogy but materialises the poet's position through the choice of a scientific instrument without linking it more closely to the argument of the poem. The first six lines describe the process of self-deception and deception by Cupid which is part of the poet's life, the building up of false hope, the false expectation, all of which tend to conceal from the poet the fact that he is suffering. 'Et toutesfois' in line 7 heralds the change of tone, the way the poet is undeceived – the appearance of his tears proves that there is a constant fire within him and exposes the falsity of the first six lines. If the poem is worth anything it is because of the quasi-abstract psychological reasoning that hides a banal pet-rarchism. The alembic picture is evoked by the last line and, being without explicit elaboration, it makes the point at only a slightly less ridiculous angle than it would have been if put into words and explained or even exaggerated. The other two poems which use it are similarly quasi-psychological arguments and again the entry of the alembic at the end is too material to go with the abstractions of the poems.

When Saulnier says (op. cit., t. I, p. 305) 'ce qui plut surtout, à l'époque, ce furent les pointes, les effets où le chantre d'un amour complexe rejoint la pure et simple galanterie. Dans ce genre de réussites madrigalesques, Scève suit parfois l'exemple des Pétrarquistes...' I would agree with him but would put *très souvent* for his *parfois*. He picks out isolated lines like

> Comme vn Printemps soubz la maigre Caresme (99)

or the lightness of touch in

> Meritera mon leger demerite
> D'estre puny d'vn plus leger pardon (32)

or the *finesse* in

> Qui la pensée, & l'oeil mettroit sus elle...
> Bien la diroit descendue des Cieulx,
> Tant s'en faillant qu'il ne la dist Déesse,
> S'il la voyoit de l'vn de mes deux yeulx. (44)

I would even go so far as to say that a large number of the dizains are petrarchist-précieux poems and to press quite strongly the analogy with Marot (not as regards the quality of the poetry – for Marot is a much better court poet than Scève – but as regards the quantity of sheer verse-making).

Take the themes Scève uses. They are traditional. The *innamoramento:* 1, 2, 3, 4, 5, 6, 7, 13, 16, 24, 30, 80, 81, 82, 89, 115, 140, 186, 197, 212, 243, 269, 292, 305, 306, 321, 359, 375, 411, 416, 424 and 440 (*innamoramento* and the effect of the eyes upon the poet). Délie as the *chef d'œuvre de la nature:* 2, 4, 13, 97, 149. The lover's conflicting and alternating states: 22, 43, 66, 68, 96, 108, 155, 157, 158, 194, 196, 201, 207, 265, 313, 328, 369, 370, 373. Immortality and praise of Délie: 11, 23, 44, 90, 97, 124, 127, 166, 175, 182, 208, 219, 227, 228, 245, 269, 283, 284, 288, 303, 304, 319, 380, 381, 387, 389, 397, 398, 407,

408, 417, 436 and 439. Sleep/torment/awakening: 11, 79, 98, 106, 111, 125, 152, 153, 164, 174, 187, 188, 189, 190, 203, 212, 232, 238, 239, 260, 300, 334, 355, 356, 357, 378, 384, 396, etc. Not only are the themes commonplace (and there are many more which it would be pointless to go through) but the tones of humility, timidity, compliment, suffering, dying and living, coming and going of torment, metamorphosing himself are all basic features of the petrarchist pattern.

The technique that Scève was copying was petrarchist too. Many of the dizains are marotic *billets de circonstances* like 27, 28, 31, 32 and 70 and some are allegorical tableaux or incidents, e.g. 154, 179, 180 and 181. He does little more than alembicate his *pointe. Impresa* No. 2 *La Lune a deux croiscentz*, with the motto *Entre toutes vne parfaicte,* is one of the most renowned *imprese* and the context is a gallant courtly one. Giovio in his *Dialogo dell' Imprese Militari et Amorose* (Rome, 1555, p. 48) comments on an *impresa* of Hypolito Cardinal de Medici which was not well understood by his contemporaries,

volend'egli esprimere che Donna Giulia di Gonzaga risplendeva di bellezza sopra ogn'altra, come la stella di Venere chiamata vulgarmente la Diana ch'ha i raggi per coda a similitudine di Cometa e riluce fra l'altre stelle, le pose il motto che diceva, *Inter Omnes.*

The contemporary reader of Scève would find no difficulty in recognising this as an amorous *impresa* in praise of the lady – her perfection in comparison to all other ladies. The dizain could be compared to hundreds of other poems written around *imprese*. It elaborates the praise of Délie in terms of her effect and influence on her time and age. Basically the theme is that of the poet's mistress as the wonder of the world, embellishing the age she lives in by virtue of her presence (cf. dizains 97, 194, 228, 319 and Petrarch *passim*). Here her virtue is instrumental in bringing the world closer to virtue, conquering the Monster of Ignorance and thereby changing the world (cf. other examples of Scève merely alembicating a *pointe* are *imprese* nos. 8, 9, 10, 11, 15, 20, 22, 23, 24, 25, 28, 29, 31, 32, 33, 35, 39, 41, 43, 44, 45, 47 and their companion dizains).

Another example is the *impresa* of *L'Oyseau au glus* (no. 12). It derives from a stock image in Italian and French love poetry – the comparison between love's snare and the bird-lime set down to catch birds. Petrarch himself made frequent use of the same image and he is particularly fond of the verb *invescare* and the participial form *invescato* and the noun *visco* (eg. *Rime*, 142, line 29 *gl'invescati rami;* 165 line 5 'Amor che solo i cor leggiadri invesca'; 211 line 11 'Ove soavemente il cor s'invesca'; 99 line 8 'l'animo invescato'.) In one sonnet (*Rime*, 207) he states

> augel in ramo
> Ove men teme ivi più tosto è colto...

which is almost identical to the motto of the *impresa* in Scève – *Ou moins crains plus suis pris.* The companion dizain also has definite reminiscences of another Petrarchan sonnet (*Rime*, 257): for instance Petrarch uses two analogies to describe the way he was 'hooked' by Laura,

> Il cor preso ivi come pesce a l'amo,
>   Onde a ben far per vivo esempio viensi,
>   Al ver non volse li occupati sensi,
>   O come nuovo augello al visco in ramo.

In the dizain Scève uses Petrarch's second image which clinches the whole theme of the surprise *innamoramento*, and again the poem does not move outside the petrarchist convention. Scève remembers Petrarch's first analogy and uses it elaborately in dizain 221 within the framework of an anecdotic, narrative and didactic, poem,

> Cesse: luy dy ie, il fault que ie lamente
> L'heur du Poisson, que n'as sceu attraper,
> Car il est hors de prison vehemente,
> Ou de tes mains ne peuz onc eschapper.

Dizains which have no *impresa* to support them still reveal quite often the inspiration of *imprese*. For example the political dizains 19–21. Giovio mentions the Connétable de Bourbon's *impresa* 'Cervo con l'ali', which represents not only extraordinary swiftness but a speed that overcomes every difficulty. This is the theme in dizains 19–21 – *Le Cerf volant* which could be taking the *impresa* as their starting point. Then dizain 55 takes the eagle *impresa* of the Emperor Charles-Quint and uses it as an extended metaphor or allegory. Scève talks of historical events like the expedition to Tunis (1535) and the invasion of France (1536) in terms of the eagle's flight. Other images throughout *Délie* have affinities with *imprese*: for instance in Adrien d'Amboise *Discours ou Traicté des Devises* (Paris, 1620 but with devices collected by his father François d'Amboise); one finds here *imprese* like the crocodile running after a hunter (p. 120) with the motto' Te fugiente premit, teque premente fugit' which goes well with dizain 329

> Amour, Cocodrille parfaict,
> Que ce fol Monde aueuglément poursuyt,
> Nous suit alors, qu'on le fuyt par effect,
> Et fuyt celluy, qui ardemment le suyt.

Or there is a verse around Narcissus (p. 120) which goes with the *impresa* in Scève,

> En la fontaine se mirant,
> Et de l'amour de soy mourant:
> Quiconque ayme autruy plus que soy,
> Pres la fontaine meurt de soif.

In dizain 243 Scève takes up the most jaded metaphor of the petrarchists' repertory: the mistress's eyes as celestial spheres. It conditions the whole poem:

> Ces tiens, non yeulx, mais estoilles celestes,
> Ont influence & sur l'Ame, & le Corps.

The procedure whereby he introduces the conceit is worn thin: the negative rectification had been used by Petrarch (*Rime,* 161 'O occhi miei, occhi non già, ma fonti') and by his followers in Italy and France, and also by the *imprese* makers. One might compare it to Marot's 'Tetin dur, non pas tetin voyre...' Or we may remember, much later, the development of two quatrains of Laugier de Porchères. They strike us as typically précieux:

> Ce ne sont pas des yeux, ce sont plutost des Dieux,
> Ils ont dessus les rois la puissance absolue:
> Dieux, non ce sont des cieux, ils ont la couleur bleue,
> Et le mouvement prompt comme celuy des Cieux,
> Cieux, non, mais deux Soleils clairement radieux
> Dont les rayons brillans nous offusquent la veue;
> Soleils, non, mais esclairs de puissance incogneue,
> Des foudres de l'amour signes presagieux.

The schematic movement accompanies a fanciful elaboration which can be continued ad infinitum. Scève's elaboration is similar; the ambivalent influence of his mistress's eyes on the one hand causing torment and suffering and a thousand changes in his condition and on the other hand being his guiding stars. Lines 7–10 go on developing the initial conceit by adding more nautical details and parallels. Scève is teasing out in a very précieux manner the description of her effect on him through one part of her face.

A number of précieux dizains make use of the familiar simile between the poet's passion and the flame of a torch. For example no. 130 describes a common experience of lovers – the inability to utter a single word at the crucial moment in the presence of their beloved. In the last four lines Scève uses the torch image – the torch which dies if it is immobile for too long but only needs a touch or a slight fanning to burst into life – to reinforce his point. The image is fully developed, explicit, and evokes a complete picture which might well have figured in emblem and device books,

> Ainsi veoit on la torche en main s'estaindre,
> Si en temps deu on laisse a l'esmouoir,
> Qui, esbranlée vn bien peu, sans se faindre
> Fait son office ardent a son pouoir.

One may compare it to any poem by Serafino, Vaenius or any of the similar ones by Scève himself – e.g. no. 196 where the simile of the wind fanning and extinguishing a flame conveys the various effects of Délie's voice and presence on him, or no. 76. The image of the rose and thorn in no. 251 functions in a similar way and is a cliché of the précieux technique.

The images that we have just seen as part of Scève's précieux technique tend not to open up whole fields of association in a terse sometimes even brutal and rough way like no. 2 'Comme de tous la delectation,/Et de moy seul fatale Pandora' but are more fully expanded and even explained. It is as if they are not images at all, but merely the last stage in an inductive argument which gathers up the truth suggested by the preceding lines.

The inevitable love-casuistry of petrarchism seems to provide Scève with the rhetoric, the antitheses and the periphrases which tame the complex reality of a love experience. Thomas M. Greene in an article 'The Styles of experience in Scève's *Délie*'[1] picks up a point regarding his use of periphrase, 'Scève's periphrases *formalize* the outer world by investing it with an almost heraldic stiffness, a ceremonial majesty, withdrawing it from the commonplace and quotidian, until it becomes almost as artificial as the language that evokes it.' I should accept the formalisation that makes Scève put his experience of love on a totally different footing, from, say, Ronsard's, but Greene, while calling him a précieux poet does not have any criterium for evaluating the

---

[1] In 'Image and symbol in the Renaissance', *Yale French Studies*, no. 47, 1972, pp. 57–75.

whole of the poetry. As we shall see in later chapters there are many poems in which he does not appear to be *precious* even though the formalization (or intellectualisation) of experience is there.

I shall demonstrate these points – the use of the rhetoric and the over-erudite imagery which Scève picked up from the petrarchists – by analysing two poems: the first is no. 373 which ends in a *pointe finale*

> Tout transformé en sel Agringentin

and the second no. 331 which starts with a splendid metaphor

> L'humidité, Hydraule de mes yeulx.

The poem ending with the climactic last image of Agrigentine salt is concerned with the effect of Délie's eyes and presence on the poet – he has to avoid her gaze. The fascination and physiological effect are traced to various regions of his body; for example, in the heat of affection the heart seems to dissolve into tears and the tears seem to 'congeal' him. Cotgrave has an explanation of the verb *congeler* and more particularly of the noun *congelation*.

a congelation, congealing, freezing; also the disease termed *Catalepsis*, viz. a suddain detention or occupation of the bodie and mind; the Patient continuing in the same form, and holding the same posture which he had when he was taken with it.

Is it possible that Scève had in mind such a violent reaction on the part of his body? This would perhaps lead into the image of transformation in the last line. The image conveys the double action of Délie's presence – the salt behaves in heat as other salts do in water: instead of crackling it dissolves and in water it crackles as other salts do in fire. The whole process, laboriously worked out by Scève, not only operates by means of the Agrigentine salt image but also borrows terms from alchemy. We have first the 'dissolving' and then the strong suggestion of mercury in *ruisseau argentin*; and *congeler*, beside its possible medical reference, is a technical term entailing both crystallisation and solidification while the transformation at the end is obviously the end-product of an alchemical process. But all these allusions do not add up to a recognisable and specific process, although Scève does strengthen the evocation of change and transformation by means of these alchemical echoes. When all is said and done, however, the elaboration and excessive materialisation of the metaphor make this a very contrived and unconvincing dizain. One might recall the fine sonnet by Nerval, *El Desdichado* where the alchemical threads are only part of the experience that the poem offers. In Scève the dizain is not a good précieux poem although theoretically its technique is operating well.

In the other dizain – no. 331 – the working out of the initial allusion or metaphor becomes equally complicated and artificial. The first line is splendid, but the rest of the poem is needed to explain the metaphor. The poem does not hold our attention partly because of the totally unconvincing development of the comparison, partly also because of the unredeemed triviality of the tenor – what the poet is actually describing (cf. nos. 13, 155 and 343). One may even wonder if the metaphor does not destroy itself from within through over-elaboration thus producing an almost 'burlesque' effect. There is nothing in poems such as these which bursts out of the conventional mould of love poetry.

Court life was full of courtesies in verse like dizain 26, where the very facility of what is said makes the pattern of the poem easily predictable. The initial statement

Ie voy en moy estre ce Mont Foruiere

offers a comparison which is not immediately clear. And Scève has to develop the correspondences point by point. Each detail of the vehicle is made to correspond to each detail of the tenor so that the poem develops in a see-saw movement: from Mont Fourvière to the poet, with a continual juxtaposition of *moy* and *il, son* and *miens* until the whole dizain culminates in the *pointe* –

Las tousiours i'ars, & point ne me consume.

(Cf. nos. 39, 95, 260 and 360.)

The worn conceit tagged on to a cliché-laden poem is all too frequent in *Délie*. Précieux themes like the fetichistic gloves (169, 198, 272), the ring (347 and 349), the mistress's blue girdle (172 and 173), the mirror (229 and 257), flattery of the King (252 and 253) of Marguerite de Navarre (254 and 255), or description of the salamander (199) are all imbued with a précieux technique. Where the poet is the witness and commentator of the scene one might have had a petrarchist conceit used not so much as a compliment to the lady but as the starting point for the examination of his own situation. But in dizain 335 for instance the conceit is all, the poem nothing; it is a question of mistaken identities, Cupid thinks that it is his mother Venus instead of which it is Délie,

> Hà, dy ie lors, pour ma Dame appaiser,
> Tu pleures bien cest Amour en ces eaux,
> Et si ne plaings le mien, qui pour se ayser,
> Se pert du tout en ces deux miens ruysseaulx.

Mythological games and storm-battered ships are very often nothing but précieux virtuosity; for example 131, or narrative and anecdotic pieces like no. 170. When we read these poems we find hardly any poetry. This is true even when as in the companion dizain to the *impresa* of *L'Horologe* (no. 43, dizain 384) a bold analogy is introduced. Here the tenor and the vehicle of the metaphor are much further apart; the logical basis of the comparison is the ceaseless activity of both poet and clock. The argument of the poem concerns the way the poet hates and condemns himself and feels unworthy of relief in suffering, but as a result paradoxically works all the harder to achieve his goal,

> i'aspire a la merueille
> D'vn si hault bien, que d'vne mesme alaine
> A mon labeur le iour, & la nuict veille.

The juxtaposition of mental activity and mechanical object produced by this *impresa* serves to bring out strongly the regularity, the unceasing nature of the poet's activity. The distance between the two terms of the metaphor does not necessarily betoken a metaphysical conceit comparable, say, to Donne's famous *compass* image which is introduced in order to illuminate how 'our two soules' are one even after separation. After the initial surprise of the comparison Donne proceeds to reveal the similarities and to make us see, *through* the analogy, the unity of lovers and the effects of separation in terms of body and soul. In the case of Scève's clock-image there is no metaphysical investigation or discovery and the analogy rests on one simple likeness.

Scève very rarely succeeds in transmitting the experience of love in these poems; for, as the above poem typically reveals, he

rarely has the emotional élan that Donne or Propertius convey.
Take dizain 144, for instance,

> En toy ie vis, ou que tu sois absente:
> En moy ie meurs, ou que soye present.
> Tant loing sois tu, tousiours tu es presente:
> Pour pres que soye, encore suis ie absent.

It does not fare very well. For, indeed, by dint of repetition, by
juxtaposition of *absent/present* and by mere sound the lines would
be a fine start to a metaphysical poem about separation. Scève
attempts an analysis of the essential relationship between the
two lovers; intellectually we can follow the argument in the last
six lines, worked out in Neo-Platonic and Aristotelian terms of
the qualities which are potential in the lover becoming actualised
only in and through the mistress. But the intellectual abstraction
of love and lady which Scève prolongs in many a poem forms a
pattern of artificiality (in the modern sense of the word) that is
not translated into a pattern of reality or experience. The
excessively abstract vocabulary, the philosophical notions and
the psychological descriptions are there as raw materials but
Scève does not give them the emotional power of actual
experience (cf. no. 299, also 96 where the framework is strong
and the content rather bare).

Saulnier (op. cit., t. I, Ch. 13) has analysed the battery of
allegorical personages and expression found in *Délie* and argues,
quite rightly, that these are part of the stock-in-trade of any poet
in the sixteenth century. The way Scève uses allegory is again
taming reality; taking a medieval framework and schemework
of mental faculties, each with a set place in a hierarchy of human
faculties (e.g. nos. 71 – Dialogue with death, 179 – *Amour/
Raison*, 180 – Poet following Reason, 181, 182, 184 and so on).
Scève seems to start from a pattern (e.g. the battle of feelings,
or the duel between love and reason) but to be unable to break
out of that pattern and reach reality. He tries to intellectualise
and to appeal to the pattern of François Ier's court, and is unable
in many of the dizains to get to the field of actual experience.
The antitheses that produce an automatic response from his
readers, the hyperboles which are not creative, the personification of abstract qualities, the formal logical structure of his
dizains, the cumbersomeness of his syntax – all take him away
from the centre of reality but do not, by way of compensation,
produce first class précieux poetry.

A final word about his language in précieux poems. It is to be expected that none of his neologisms come from précieux dizains. Words like *gruer, girouetter, degluer, serainer, deluger, se paonner, ahontir, apourir, s'enaigrir, encendrir, illusif, pressif, funebreux, encombreux, apollinées, fulminatoire, contrelustrer, neronnerie, abortivement, nuisamment, opulentement, perseueramment* or *vacillamment* are not created to amuse the audience. They occur in poems where Scève says or expresses some things that he has actually experienced or imagined and we will have to examine them later.

We can now move on to his more original poems and see them in perspective, see also how Scève blossoms out of the contemporary and past stereotype of convention.

# 6

## OBLIQUE ART

What we are going to look at in this chapter is very different from the précieux features related to the *imprese* examined in the last chapter. Another side to the *imprese* – and a side which was not put to any use in the dizains already examined – is allusiveness controlled by a firm intellectuality.

A great difference between emblems and *imprese*, commented upon by sixteenth- and seventeenth-century theorists, is the 'open', easily understandable or easily explicable nature of the emblem (as befits a genre whose main function is to instruct its reader) and the 'closed', subtle, half-hermetic quality of the *impresa* which aims to express a personal thought or intention. How this personal and symbolic expression of thoughts and feelings is achieved by the *impresa* is what we must now look at. Let us take as a starting point Alessandro Farra's book, *Settenario dell'humana riduttione*[1] where there is a section on the symbolic meaning of the *imprese* called 'Filosofia simbolica, overe Delle Imprese'. Here an explanation is given of the intellectual character of *imprese*. Without venturing into Farra's whole philosophical background or even taking note of the Neo-Platonic, cabbalistic, Hebraic and Orphic tendencies in his way of thinking there are some aspects of his view of *imprese* which can help us to place Scève.

Farra insists on the intellectual character of *imprese*: for example, on p. 158 he traces them back to the Ancient Jews and to the noble will of God; inevitably they are a 'Nobili operatione dell'Intelletto'. Or again, p. 268, the *impresa* is the most perfect form of human understanding since, 'quanto ch'egli per la simiglianza, che tiene con l'huomo autore, & opefice suo, pùo dirsi huomo ideale, & vera & propria operatione, & impresa dell'intelletto humano'. The aristocracy in Italy in the fifteenth century had returned to the use of symbols, 'percioche gli animi generosi, scegliendo alcuni hieroglifici conformi ne gli occulti

---

[1] I have used the B.N. copy (Z.30.990) which came out in Venice, (appresso Christoforo Zanetti) 1571. The pages are 157–279.

sentimenti ad alcuno virtuoso concetto loro, & ad essi congiun-
gendo simbolo della medesima proportione, n'hanno formato
quel bellissimo componimento simbolico...' (p. 268). Everything
in an *impresa* must appeal intellectually to man and Farra is thus
able to fix five points which it must have: the *concetto o intentione
dell'autor*; the *parole del motto*; the *proportione tra le parole e le figure*;
the *significatione della figura*; the *figura istessa* (p. 271). If all five
are present in an *impresa* then 'cosi nell' impresa tutte le parti
di essa deono servire al concetto'. Both parts, the figure and
the motto, are as perfectly joined together as the mind and body
of man by God. When one of the two parts can stand without
the other, it is an imperfect *impresa*, since either words or motto
would be superfluous. The fact that allusiveness is insisted upon
by Farra is crucial for our understanding of Scève: on p. 277 in
dealing with an allusive *impresa* he says 'sotto questo capo è
difficile riuscire perfettamente, percioche, come vogliono alcuni,
o si fanno miracolose overo s'inciampa nel goffo o nel ridicolo'.
Thus one might want to call the 25th *impresa La Selle, & les deux
hommes*, where one man is pulling away a stool that another is
going to sit on, in *Délie* ridiculous in that it is incongruously
funny in a context where there is no call to be humorous. But
Farra comes to a fine conclusion 'l'imprese potranno perfette,
& nobili farsi, & le ignobili & imperfetti conoscersi, & emendarsi
con quell'arte medesima, con la quale si compongono i veri &
perfetti sillogismi, & onde si scuoprono i sofistici, & gl'imperfetti
alla perfettione si riducono' (p. 277). Along with this evaluation
he says that no doubt many will object to his reasoning but he
cannot satisfy the vulgar and the ignorant who are 'incapaci
de i misteri dell'alte & divine scienze'. In this respect perhaps
one may see another added clue for Scève's use of *imprese*: they
too, like many of his poetic characteristics, are not intended for
the great mass of the public.

In the whole section on the symbolic philosophy of *imprese*
Farra is virtually saying that an *impresa* is closer to a poetic image
than an emblem, a hieroglyphic, Pythagorean symbols, medals,
liveries, shields, ensigns and so on: it is a more complete all-round
statement with moral as well as metaphysical connotations built
into it. And this is partly the allusiveness, partly the intellectualisation and partly the poetic talent of the author. In all these ways
Scève can be seen as the fabricator of some perfect *imprese*.

Every theorist of the seventeenth century makes use of the body/

97

soul image to express the essentiality of there being a figure and a motto in a perfect device: for instance, in *Les Devises de Monsieur de Boissiere. Avec un traitté (sic) des Reigles de la Devise, par le mesme Autheur*, Paris, 1654, we find on the second page, 'Les Devises donc que les Italiens appellent *imprese*, & les Latins *simbola*, sont composees d'un Corps et d'une Ame, le Corps est la chose peinte ou gravee, l'Ame est le mot...' The picture itself is the second term of a comparison whose first term is the author's feelings, state of mind or thoughts. Similarly Henri Estienne provides an example both of the kind of language used and of the intellectual labour involved. He defines a device thus, (after Ruscelli) 'il vaut donc mieux considerer les paroles d'une devise comme la proposition majeure d'un Syllogisme, & la figure comme la mineure, de l'assemblage desquelles resultat la conclusion, qui n'est autre que l'intention de l'Autheur'.[1] He later analyses the 'causes principales qui composent la devise' (pp. 127–53) treating the question according to material, formal, final and efficient cause in good Aristotelian fashion. The 'cause matérielle' is the 'figure des corps ou les instrumens des choses qui se mettent dans la devise'; the formal cause is the 'ressemblances ou comparaisons, lesquelles pour exprimer la pensée de l'Autheur, se rencontrent dans les proprietez naturelles ou artificielles de la figure'; the final cause is the 'signification ou la comparaison souz-entendue, par l'entremise de laquelle nous exprimons plus clairement, avec plus d'efficace & plus de gayeté une conception d'esprit rare et particulière'; the efficient cause is the 'esprit ou l'entendement disposé à cognoistre les rapports, les similitudes & conformitez qui se rencontrent dans les choses figurées'.

Many of the *imprese* in Scève's *Délie* contain an illustrated metaphor which is used intellectually and allusively. As Bou-hours said of a device 'C'est une métaphore peinte et visible qui frappe les yeux, au lieu que celles des Orateurs et des Poetes frappent seulement l'oreille...'.[2] The companion dizain is read in conjunction with the metaphor, the combination forming something that Farra would have regarded as a perfect *impresa*.

---

[1] *L'Art de faire les Devises*, Paris, 1645, p. 100. Menestrier severely criticised the obscure logic-chopping of his predecessors in *L'Assemblée des Sçavans*, Lyon, 1665, pp. 14–15. Aresi, *Imprese Sacre*, Milan, 1625 is a good Italian counterpart to Estienne.

[2] Le père Bouhours, *Les Entretiens d'Ariste et d'Eugene*, Paris, 1671, p. 262.

The tenor of the metaphor is contained in the dizain and the vehicle is the *impresa*. For example, the Acteon *impresa* (no. 19) shows the last stage of the Diana and Acteon story whilst the dizain is concerned with the effect that Délie has on the poet.[1] The hunter Acteon, one of the beautiful rustic youths of Classical mythology, surprises Diana and her nymphs while they are bathing naked in a pool. Ovid gives the story (*Met.*, 3.183ff) of how the Goddess is overcome by shame and ensures that Acteon will not live to tell the tale by transforming him into a stag who is set upon by his own hounds. An important element of the myth is that Acteon still retained his human faculties after his metamorphosis,

> me miserum, dicturus erat: vox nulla secuta est.
> ingemuit: vox illa fuit lacrimaeque per ora
> non sua fluxerunt; *mens tantum pristina mansit.*
> quid faciat? repetatne domum et regalia tecta
> an lateat silvis? timor hoc, pudor inpedit illud.     [my italics]

This account is repeated by Boccaccio and by the sixteenth-century compilers of Classical dictionaries.[2]

Emblem writers were fond of the fable. Alciati had included an emblem picture and verse in his first edition, where the picture is similar to the one in *Délie* but the underlying moral of the fable – that the reader should be on his guard against the people surrounding him, who flatter him now but will eventually turn against him as Acteon's hounds did against their master – is the only thing stressed. The motto surrounding the figure in *Délie* 'Fortune par les miens me chasse' would seem to coincide with the moralising intention of emblem writers but for the personal element which is introduced in the pronouns *me* and *miens*.

This same fable was however just as popular with love poets as with emblem writers and the treatment of it in this context is more illuminating for its meaning in *Délie*. Petrarch for instance, had used the myth (taken direct from Ovid, one assumes) in one *canzone* (*Rime*, 23) where he narrates the story of his love by means of a number of fables of transformation. A brief glance

---

[1] For fuller details of different representations of Acteon in the fifteenth and sixteenth centuries see the article by R. W. Lee, '"Ut Pictura Poesis", the Humanist Theory of Painting', op. cit., p. 197–270.

[2] Boccaccio, *De genealogia*, Bk 5, Ch. 14. R. Estienne in his *Dictionarium propriorum nominum*, Paris, 1541, gives other sources of the story but adds that 'receptior et communior Ovidii sententia'.

at the way he uses Acteon will enable us to see exactly where Scève has turned away from the narrative, allegorical and didactic aspects of the myth and attempted to use it in a much more condensed poem to present a number of different features of a love experience. Petrarch fell in love with Laura and he was changed into a bay tree: both the God of Love and Laura were hand in hand,

> Ei duo mi trasformaro in quel ch'i sono,
> Facendomi d'uom vivo un lauro verde
> Che per fredda stagion foglia non perde.  (lines 38–40)

The transformation into a bay tree is of course significant since the name of Laura, his mistress, is assumed to be in our minds when reading of his transformation into a *lauro*. This metamorphosis is accompanied by an allegorical assertion that constancy is always there: the bay tree never sheds its leaves even in the winter time. Hope disappeared and through despair he was changed into a swan and started to sing of his hopeless love,

> Ché, perch'io non sapea dove né quando
> Me'l ritrovasse, solo, lagrimando,
> Là've tolto mi fu, dí e notte andava
> Ricercando dal lato e dentro a l'acque;
> E già mai poi la mia lingua non tacque,
> Mentre poteo, del suo cader maligno;
> Ond'io presi col suon color d'un cigno.  (lines 54–60)

Laura forbids him to sing of his love; and because he disobeys he is turned into a stone unable to sing of anything

> Le vive voci m'erano interditte:
> Ond'io gridai con carta e con inchiostro:
> Non son mio, no; s'io moro, il danno è vostro.  (lines 98–100)

That is, so great were his confusion and dismay at being disdained by Laura that he became petrified. He pleads for mercy in his writings, while Laura shows the utmost contempt; and so, with great weeping and wailing he is changed into a fountain and begs Laura to love him; but instead he is changed into a flint

> i nervi e l'ossa
> Mi volse in dura selce; e cosí scossa
> Voce rimasi de l'antiche some,
> Chiamando morte e lei sola per nome.  (lines 137–40)

Finally he is transformed like Acteon,

> Ch'i' senti' trarmi de la propria imago,
> Et in un cervo solitario e vago
> Di selva in selva ratto mi trasformo;
> Ed ancor de' miei can fuggo lo stormo.     (lines 157–60)

He is punished by his cruel mistress for having approached her too intimately, and the physical transformation of Acteon symbolises the mental and psychological strangeness that the poet experiences. The reason for the punishment in Petrarch, as in Scève, can be attributed to a refined and non-sensual version of the suggestion made by Hyginus in his narration of the fable: *pastor Dianam lavantem speculatus est et eam violare voluit.* (*Fabulae,* Ch. 180.)

Petrarch throughout the *canzone* has been using allegorical means to stress his own incommunicability in love. Through the series of metamorphoses he has attempted to represent the intensity and stability of his love, which, however strange or new, remains unchanged in its basic features. Scève possibly remembered Petrarch's use of Acteon; possibly he knew of its use by Colonna in his *Hypnerotomachia* where the torments of a lover are described: 'plus esgaré que dedans un grand Labyrinthe: voire plus pressé qu'onque ne fust Acteon par ses chiens'.[1] Later in the story when Poliphile is watching Venus bathing, he is reminded of Acteon and Diana and describes the effect in this way,

j'en devins offusqué de mon entendement, je me senty ouvrir le cœur et y engraver la figure de ma bien aimée...n'y eut ni nerf ni artère qui de ce feu ne feust bruslé comme une paille seiche au milieu d'une grande fornaise...que quasi je ne me cognoissois plus et pensois estre mué en autre forme.

This description comes close to what Scève is saying in his dizain. So that in the woodcut we find a close connection with the emblems of Alciati and his followers while behind the woodcut there is a tradition of the personal use of the fable on which Scève is able to draw.

In the companion poem (no. 168) Scève is concerned with his emotions and state of mind:

---

[1] See the French translation of the work entitled *Hypnérotomachie ou Discours du songe de Poliphile*, Paris, 1561, p. 66 and pp. 127–8. The first edition came out in Venice in 1499.

Toutes les fois qu'en mon entendement
Ton nom diuin par la memoire passe,
L'esprit rauy d'vn si doulx sentement,
En aultre vie, & plus doulce trespasse:
Alors le Coeur, qui vn tel bien compasse,
Laisse le Corps prest a estre enchassé:
Et si bien à vers l'Ame pourchassé,
Que de soymesme, & du corps il s'estrange.
   Ainsi celuy est des siens dechassé,
A qui Fortune, ou heur, ou estat change.

If we read the first eight lines bearing in mind the figure and associations of the *impresa*, we find that the myth illuminates and enriches the argument. Acteon, when changed, experienced a strange feeling of loss of identity and estrangement from parts of himself. Scève is describing the effect of the memory of Délie on some of his faculties and analysing the disturbance that has taken place in the relationship between his body and heart. He begins with the words *Toutes les fois que*; the transformation wrought by Diana on Acteon was a unique occurrence, whereas Scève is concerned with a frequently recurring situation. The name of Délie and the particular quality it has in his memory. And so we must bear in mind the violent fate of Acteon in order to appreciate the full force of this oft-repeated event. In the first line too Scève reveals that it is not only his affective memory that is involved but the creative, intellectual faculty closely linked to *entendement*. The reaction of his intellectual faculty is ecstasy 'ravy d'un si doulx sentement', which causes it to leave its normal life linked to the body and pass over into a paradise of its own. Lines 5–8 then describe the estrangement between heart and body, since the mind seems to take with it the heart, seat of affections, and divert it to the *Ame*. This piece of psychological self-analysis is complicated and it would remain rather abstract and certainly schematic were it not that the *impresa* contains the second term of comparison, and therefore forms a rich counterpoint to the poet's own experience. The ecstasy, liberation from normal corporeal life and enjoyment of 'plus doulce vie' is accompanied by a feeling of dispossession emphasised by the totally different quality of Acteon's experience. With the explicit appearance of the motto in the last line complex analysis gives way to general statement. Scève points away from his particular experience to something on a wider plane, and from the purely psychological to the ethical. He has used the *impresa* as a suggestive comparison outside the poem, but one which, when we read the poem, we realise is an indirect or oblique statement intended to be 'read' with the poem. The vehicle of the metaphor is firmly implanted in the reader's mind by visual means and the poet can proceed to relate his own experience without having recourse to allusion or explicit metaphor. Furthermore Délie–Diana–Goddess and Mortal are all there, and the virtue of the poet's mistress is presented as totally different in kind from that of other women.

*Impresa* no. 26 'La Lycorne qui se uoit' is rather puzzling at first, for the picture seems to illustrate the well-known belief in the miraculous properties of the unicorn's horn. The animal was thought to use its horn to test and purify the water before the other animals drank of it. The belief appears for example in the *Physiologus Latinus* and in the sixteenth century even Gesner subscribed to it. Many emblems took this theme, illustrated it and gave it a title like *Venenum expello* or *Nihil inexplorato*. But the motto that Scève uses – 'De moy je m'espouante' – makes it clear that we are concerned here with a different situation, namely the unicorn gazing at its own reflection in a pool of water. The picture appears very much later in the *Symbolographia* of Jacobus Boschius (Augustae Vindelicorum et Dilingae, 1702. Class I, Tab. V. Symbol LXXXIX). It is surrounded by exactly the same motto, but there is nothing to indicate the source of the legend or the picture and it is possible that Boschius derived his picture and motto from Scève. The comment he gives is only apparent from the classification of this symbol under the heading *Conscientia* (the symbols in this section of the book are all given a religious connotation) and the description is simply 'Monoceros impetens effigiem suam in aquis expressam'. Apart from this isolated example, as far as I can see, there is no help from iconographical sources and very little evidence of any tradition concerning this aspect of the unicorn in literature. There is, however, one episode in a fifteenth-century Italian poem which may throw light on the situation depicted in the *impresa*.

The *Driadeo* of Luca Pulci tells the story of the shepherd Severe's love for the Dryad, Lora. He is on the point of winning her love, when Diana, enraged at his audacity, transforms him into a unicorn,

I ti transformo e facio uno elecorno
Con lunghi velli e nella fronte un corno.
  Severe il corpo suo visto cangiarsi
Volse gridere & venne un mormorio
Chello spaventa: onde non sa che farsi
Eglie veloce assai & corse al rio
Di fonte pietra nellacque aspecchiarsi
I stupefacto piu di se in oblio
Che non fu Chadmo...[1]

We notice immediately the similarity to Ovid's account of
Acteon's reactions to his changed state: both transformations
are wrought by Diana and both heroes are dumbfounded and
horrified at the realisation of their state. Furthermore Severe's
lament echoes the legend of Narcissus (*impresa* no. 7):

Quantera meglio il di chi mirai fiso
Quello splendor di quelle treccie bionde
Chio fussi suto dal viver reciso
Pietra mi specchio fiera alle tue onde
Quanta invidia ti porto o bel narciso
Che colla tua nympha ti risponde
Et vedi lombra tua nel fonte terso
Et non di fera quale ison converso.

His change into a beast means the loss of his human features
and when he looks at his image he is stunned. Then his
lamentation changes to curses against love;

I veggio ben dicea elfolle amante
Chi son propinquo almio stremo dolore
Ma po chi veggio quella luce sancte
Esser nel boscho: spero anco chamore
Non mi sara crudel: forse ignorante
Sono: & non penso che lalto splendore
Ma transformato in fiera acciochoio
Possa di lei adempiere eldisio
  Io so leforze damore & conosco
Che simile fiere sempre alle donzelle
Et alle vergine soglion drento alboscho
Dormir in grembo...

The connection between this *impresa* and the first one, in which
the unicorn is lying down with his head on the virgin's lap, is

---

[1] Luca Pulci (1431–1470) is the brother of the more famous Luigi Pulci to whom
this work is often wrongly attributed, as indeed it has been in the B.N. edition
(Rés. Yd. 734) which I have used. *Il Driadeo*, Florence, 1489, 4th part, p. hiiii
and ff.

made clear by this passage of Pulci. The context of love, the Goddess Diana, the suffering and eventual death of Severe (still as a unicorn) make the legend even more appropriate to *Délie* than one would have imagined – the motto stressing the personal isolation of the poet, his introspection and horror of himself. The allusive comparison to Narcissus in the Pulci passage evokes the basic theme of the mirror and the reflection of oneself in it. Moreover the two legends of the unicorn are present in Pulci's account, for after his transformation Severe decided to seek out his loved one. The maiden is struck with fear at the sight of him and becomes mad, and Severe is finally transformed into the river Sieve.

Now let us look at the companion dizain – no. 231:

> Incessamment mon grief martyre tire
> Mortelz espritz de mes deux flans malades:
> Et mes souspirs de l'Ame triste attire,
> Me resueillantz tousiours par les aulbades
> De leurs sanglotz trop desgoustément fades:
> Comme de tout ayantz necessité,
> Tant que reduict en la perplexité,
> A y finir l'espoir encore se vante.
>     Parquoy troublé de telle anxieté,
> Voyant mon cas, de moy ie m'espouuante.

The first eight lines describe the poet's state: his physical torment, his sighs, described in lines 3–5 with a touch of ironical humour in that his sobs are almost *aulbades* which awaken him to an awareness of the straits to which he has been reduced. The last two lines express his realisation of and reaction to his predicament. He is startled at the distance which he has travelled in his love and suffering, and we remember his anguished reaction to the new and strange state caused by unrequited love both in the Acteon *impresa* and throughout the cycle.

The last line, echoing the motto, introduces associations of both the mirror and the Narcissus theme and the possible fable lying behind the picture – the lover transformed by Diana into a unicorn. The figure of the unicorn has a double reference – to the first *impresa* and to the antithesis of mortal lover and immortal Goddess which is one of the leit-motifs of *Délie* – and is thus characteristic of Scève's density and compression. Furthermore, we can see in both the Acteon and the unicorn *imprese* one way in which Scève shakes himself free of petrarchist convention. He has managed by using the *imprese* to suggest certain things like strange metamorphoses (note how much Latin love-poetry of the Augustan period stressed metamorphosis) as a means of portraying certain aspects of the love experience. And these two *imprese* serve to highlight the psychological analysis in the companion dizains.

There are many instances where Scève deliberately turns away from the medieval accounts and goes back to the Classical poets. The famous *impresa* of Dido (no. 13) reveals that he is not following the version of the story found in Boccaccio, Petrarch or the sixteenth-century dictionaries of Classical mythology and collections of emblems and devices. Ronsard in the preface to his *Franciade* uses the other legend of Dido, stating that she would rather die by her own hand than break the vow of chastity she had made to her dead husband. This second version of the story stresses her fidelity to her husband Sychaeus, and Dido commits suicide in order to avoid the shame of a second marriage. Scève however, turning to Vergil, makes her a tragic queen who dies because of her irrational love.[1]

The woodcut of *Dido qui se brusle* (no. 13) shows Dido piercing her breast with a sword and surrounded by the flames of her funeral pyre. This is a faithful representation of Vergil's account in *Aeneid*, 4.642–65. Some other engravings and woodcuts show the Vergilian version that Scève used.[2] The motto *Doulce la mort qui de dueil me deliure* sets the tone and suggests the attitude to death which Dido shows when she has been forsaken by Aeneas. The last speech that Vergil gives her begins with the words

> dulces exuviae, dum fata deusque sinebat,
> accipite hanc animam meque his exsolvite curis (lines 651–2)

[1] Petrarch had deliberately rejected the Vergilian version of Dido in his *Triompho della Castità*, (Venetia, 1532).

> Quella che per lo suo diletto e fido
> Sposo non per Enea, volse ir al fine:
> Tacciail vulgo ignorante: io dico Dido
> Cui studio d'onestate a morte spinse,
> Non vano amor, com'è'l publico grido.          lines 155ff

In his *Senilium Rerum libri*, IV, 5, Petrarch gives fuller reasons for his interpretation and questions the accuracy of Vergil's account. Moreover Ruscelli shows an *impresa* in which a turtle-dove refuses to mate after her first mate has died, and in the commentary evokes associations with Dido, citing two sonnets of Petrarch in this connection. (*Le Imprese illustri*, op. cit. p. 170).

[2] For further details on iconographical evidence see D. G. Coleman, *The Emblesmes and Images in Maurice Scève's 'Délie'*, unpublished dissertation, Glasgow University, 1961.

and towards the end of it we read,

> dixit, et os impressa toro 'moriemur inultae,
> sed moriamur', ait 'sic, sic iuvat ire sub umbras'.
>
> (lines 659–60)

Queenliness, dignity and tragedy – all come out here. Her self-destruction, her suicide, her irrationality, her use of Aeneas' sword, her piling up of 'sweet relics' – all are aspects of Vergil's very moving account. This is exactly the context of intense, anguished love which cannot be reciprocated. A suggestion underlying this *impresa* is that the poet knows throughout that Délie cannot forsake her marriage to her husband. And in a paradoxical way Vergil's account of Dido's self-deception and Aeneas' refusal to let desire conquer duty is appropriate here. Dido's pretence that their love-affair was marriage,

> coniugium vocat, hoc praetexit nōmine culpam...    (line 172)

is echoed by Aeneas'

> nec coniugis umquam
> praetendi taedas aut haec in foedera veni.    (lines 338–9)

making it clear that even if she has interpreted their love as wedlock he has never said or done anything that suggested lawful marriage. Now in the dizain (no. 114) the impression of the dying Dido is in the reader's mind before reading the poem. The first six lines invoke time: the sweeping address to all units of time, from the longest down to the shortest,

> O ans, ô moys, sepmaines, iours, & heures,
> O interualle, ô minute, ô moment,
> Qui consumez les durtez, voire seures,
> Sans que lon puisse apperceuoir comment,
> Ne sentez vous, que ce mien doulx tourment
> Vous vse en moy, & vos forces deçoit?

and leading up to a single question – *Ne sentez vous?* Does not this suffering wear down time itself? If there is a certain pleasure in this martyrdom, then surely death itself will be sweet, since it will deliver the poet from time. This is an entirely emotional argument and the parallel with Dido provides an underlying point of comparison throughout. It enters more strikingly in the last four lines,

> Si donc le Cœur au plaisir, qu'il reçoit,
> Se vient luy mesme a martyre liurer:
> Croire fauldra, que la Mort doulce soit,
> Qui l'Ame peult d'angoisse deliurer.

Here the suicide and the discovery of the sweetness of death make a convincing case to reinforce the general conclusion of *Si donc...Croire fauldra...la Mort doulce soit.* Dido's motivation, like that of the poet himself, is presented as wholly convincing: because the psychological experience is intense and rules out as irrelevant all thoughts of anything besides love. At the same time the argument in the dizain – which is entirely emotional – is made more forceful by the paradoxical reversal of values: time should wear down pain but pain wears down time and the contrasting words in *plaisir/martyre* and *mort/douce* make the paradox poignant. The poem succeeds precisely because of the parallelism offered by the *impresa*.

This allusiveness, the echoing of a person's death as treated by Vergil, can be illustrated again in *impresa* no. 30. *Cleopatra & ses serpentz.* Scève envisages the two serpents that Vergil and Horace[1] mentioned as bringing about her death, rather than the perhaps more familiar prose accounts of Dio Cassius and Plutarch, in which a single serpent from Cleopatra's basket of figs fastened itself to her body. One of the scenes depicted on the shield forged by Vulcan for Aeneas is that of Cleopatra in Egypt, her flight and death. The relevant lines for us are,

> regina in mediis patrio vocat agmina sistro
> necdum etiam geminos a tergo respicit anguis.
>
> (lines 696–7)

This is a symbolic representation or warning of her death which she will welcome as Dido welcomed hers. The humiliation of being led through Rome in the arrogant triumphal march is something she cannot accept; as Horace says of her in an ode,

> Quae generosius
> Perire quaerens nec muliebriter
> Expavit ensem nec latentes
> Classe cita reparavit oras,
> Ausa et iacentem visere regiam
> Vultu sereno, fortis et asperas

---

[1] Vergil, *Aeneid*, 8.696–7; Horace, *Odes*, 1.37; Plutarch, *Antony*, Chs. 71 and 86; Dio Cassius, 11.14ff.

>       Tractare serpentes, ut atrum
>          Corpore combiberet venenum,
>    Deliberata morte ferocior...                    (1.37.21–9)

Again the solemnity and sense of drama are present; it is as if her death is the climax of the poem and through her defeat she achieves moral grandeur,

>       Saevis Liburnis scilicet invidens
>       Privata deduci superbo,
>       Non humilis mulier, triumpho.          (lines 30–2)

(Note *privata* – 'no longer a public figure' with also an allusion to *privare* – 'deprived of her power' and *humilis* – 'no mean woman'. Horace, through these epithets, reveals a sympathetic insight into Cleopatra's position.)

The first three lines of Scève's dizain (no. 267) 'je me sens...l'esperit trespercer/Du tout en tout, iusqu'au plus vif du sens...' already seem to convey the stinging, lethal sensations that are heightened by the visual impact of the picture and the legend behind it of the serpents biting into Cleopatra's breast and arms. We remember too the scene conjured up by Propertius (III.11.53–4)

>       bracchia spectavi sacris admorsa colubris
>          et trahere occultum membra soporis iter...

where we follow the route of the poison until her 'limbs absorb the hidden path of sleep'. The first three lines of the companion dizain stress *doulx, trespercer, au plus vif* and then give way to the beautiful

>       Tousiours, toute heure, et ainsi sans cesser
>       Fauldra finir ma vie...

The allusive echoes to Horace, Vergil and perhaps Propertius serve to add the dimension of superb triumph in death and the moral greatness that Scève can convey through the *impresa*.

Metaphors like Dido, Acteon or Cleopatra which are drawn from mythology enable the poet to achieve that density of expression which is characteristic of so much of *Délie*. For they introduce wide-ranging associations which it would otherwise have been impossible to evoke within a ten-line poem. There is a striking contrast with another sixteenth-century poet who used *imprese* (although no woodcut or engraving was published) as a starting point of his poems. Giordano Bruno's method in the

*Eroici Furori* consists of a description of an *impresa,* followed by the poem in which the objects of the device occur as poetic conceits and finally an exposition of the spiritual and philosophical meanings of the symbol. Take his use of the phoenix as a concrete example,

> Unico augel del Sol vaga Fenice,
> Ch'appareggi col mondo gl'anni tui,
> Quai colmi ne l'Arabia felice;
> Tu sei chi fuste, io son quel che non fui;
> Io per caldo d'amor muoio infelice,
> Ma ta ravvivu' il sol co raggi sui;
> Tu bruggi'n un', et io in ogni loco;
> Io da Cupido, hai tu da Phebo il foco.
>     Hai termini prefissi
> Di lunga vita, et io ho breve fine,
> Che pronto s'offre per mille ruine,
> Ne só quel che vivrò, ne quel che vissi.
>     Me cieco fato adduce
> Tu certo torni, á riveder tua luce.[1]

First he describes 'una Fenice volante alla quale è volto un fanciullo che bruggia in mezzo le fiamme, e vi è il motto. FATA OBSTANT.' In the poem that follows, Bruno uses the legend and qualities of the phoenix to establish points of comparison and contrast with himself. He explores the story in terms of his own passion and 'death' in love: the rays of the sun which burn the phoenix are contrasted with the fire of Cupid which burns the poet; the long life of the bird is in sharp contrast with his own short career. As it stands the poem is a typical love poem in the petrarchist tradition, similar to so many of Bembo's. But the philosophical commentary which follows explains the concept of death and rebirth used in the poem in terms of the 'intelletto inferiore' and the 'intelletto superiore', the 'amor sensuale' and the 'amor intellettivo'.

Bruno's poem is intellectual, learned and Neo-Platonic, but the one thing that differentiates him most clearly from Scève is that the allusions are to be explained in the course of reading the poem whereas Scève does not give the reader any elucidation. He requires the reader to move along a particular line of thought, guided by the clues that the picture and motto provide,

---

[1] *De gl'Heroici Furori,* Paris, 1585, unnumbered pages, ca. fviii. v°. For a full discussion see F. A. Yates, 'The emblematic conceit in Giordano Bruno's "De Gli Eroici Furori" and in the Elizabethan sonnet sequence', *Journal of the Warburg and Courtauld Institutes,* vol. 6, 1943, pp. 101–22.

towards the right tone and the right body of associations. It is
on this that the successs of his poems depended. The density of
Scève's technique is perhaps unique in the sixteenth century.
The relationship between the poetic form and the *imprese* and
images is brought into sharper light when we contrast Scève with
one of his contemporaries, Jehan de Boyssoné who also wrote a
series of dizains to his mistress Glaucie.[1]

> Je veis tailler des pierres l'aultre jour
> A ung tailleur qui, sans prandre grand poine,
> Sans se facher et sans trop long séjour
> Taillit rubis, diamant, cassidoine,
> Jusques a tant que feust la pierre idoine
> Pour enchasser en ung petit aneau.
> Lors luy priay me prester son marteau
> Et son burin pour mollir une femme:
> Mais je cogneu (cas estrange et noveau)
> Que la pierre est plus doulce que ma dame.　　　(p. 131)

Now let us see a typical companion dizain (no. 150) accompanying the *L'hyerre & la Muraille impresa*:

> Ou sa bonté par vertu attractiue,
> Ou sa vertu par attrayant bonté,
> Moytié bon gré, & viue force actiue,
> M'à tellement a son plaisir dompté,
> Que i'ay permis son vouloir ià monté
> Sur le plus hault de ma fermeté croistre:
> Et là s'estendre, & a tous apparoistre
> Pour ma deffence, & contre ma ruyne.
> 　Mais, comme puis a l'esprœuue congnoistre,
> Son amytié, peu a peu, me ruyne.

We are not concerned with the difference in theme (the first
being narrative, the second psychological), in idea-content, or
for the moment in the poets' attitude; we are looking for the
differences in structure. In both poems there are lines 9–10
which form a *pointe* to what has gone before. The pattern of
8/2 provides the two groups that a dizain frequently falls into.
As Henri Weber said,

la réussite du dizain présente déjà certaines exigences analogues à celles
du sonnet: elle veut un brusque mouvement de départ, qui nous jette
'in medias res', une articulation fondamentale qui répartit les vers en

---

[1] *Les Trois Centuries de Maistre Jehan de Boyssoné*, ed. H. Jacoubet, Toulouse,
1923.

deux groupes opposés suivant une formule variable, enfin une chute habilement ménagée sur un dernier vers bien frappé.[1]

However, with Boyssoné's dizain the argument is easily understood; he is concerned merely with the point 'Que la pierre est plus doulce que ma dame.' Scève is concerned with more than a leisurely approach to writing. The syntax is laboured and the movement of the argument rather heavy and tortuous. The poem is a combination of physical vocabulary (e.g. line 6 'Sur le plus hault de ma fermeté croistre') and the description of the abstract qualities involved in the ascendancy Délie gains over him. Since the *impresa* with its picture of ivy creeping over the old wall has been firmly imprinted on the reader's eye before the beginning of the poem, the vehicle of the metaphor – the parasitic plant grafting itself on the wall – provides a suggestive analogy for the whole process whereby Délie's will and personality have 'grown' on the poet. The argument in the dizain still follows a tortuous movement, and the paradoxical element (*contre ma ruyne/me ruyne*), as in so many dizains that we have already mentioned, is strongly there. But the analogy offered to Scève by the *impresa* is the vital element of difference from Boyssoné in dizain-structure here.

This difference between Boyssoné and Scève appears also when we consider dizains in which Scève's technique is not helped by *imprese*. One more comparison between the two poets will show how the 'oblique art' in Scève's use of the *impresa* is only one facet of his poetic creation. Boysonné is concerned in the next example with a theme which often appears in *Délie*, namely the separation of the two lovers for a certain period:

> Ces quatre jours que j'ay esté absent,
> Sans vous ouyr Madame, et sans vous veoir,
> Ils m'ont duré, me semble, autant que cent,
> Et cependant n'ay peu plaisir avoir,
> Combien que j'ay employé mon pouvoir
> Cercher plusieurs moyens de passe temps.
> Il faut doncq dire, et ainsy je l'entens,
> Que sans vous, belle, avoir je ne puys joye.
> Pour rendre doncq les miens espritz contens
> Fault pres de vous, Madame, que je soye.          (p. 154)

The argument of the poet is that he has known no pleasure during his absence from his mistress and therefore he concludes

---

[1] *La création poétique au XVIe siècle en France: de Maurice Scève à Agrippa d'Aubigné*, Paris, 1956, p. 222.

that, in order to be happy, he must be in her presence. The first six lines express the unhappiness that he has felt during their separation, and there is one comparison – between the four days of absence and a hundred ordinary days. Boyssoné is not interested in any metaphysical problem appertaining to the absence or separation of lovers, nor is he concerned to describe his feelings or suffering in detail. He is content to repeat his conclusions: lines 7–8 have already expressed it, but lines 9–10 put it in a different form without adding anything to the previous statement. The result is an extremely clear, pedestrian poem which reduces itself to the simple statement 'I am unhappy without you' and which does not enrich the reader's experience or understanding in any way.

Contrast this with dizain 367 in *Délie* where Scève begins with an evocation of the period of separation,

> Asses plus long, qu'vn Siecle Platonique,
> Me fut le moys, que sans toy suis esté:
> Mais quand ton front ie reuy pacifique,
> Seiour treshault de toute honnesteté,
> Ou l'empire est du conseil arresté
> Mes songes lors ie creus estre deuins.
>    Car en mon corps: mon Ame, tu reuins,
> Sentant ses mains, mains celestement blanches,
> Auec leurs bras mortellement diuins
> L'vn coronner mon col, l'aultre mes hanches.

The phrase *Siecle Platonique* refers to the Cosmic Year which was attributed to the Pythagoreans, and Plato in the *Timaeus* 39 gives it as 10,000 years: it was the period taken for the heavens to reproduce a specific arrangement. Cicero puts it clearly,

homines enim populariter annum tantum modo solis, id est unius astri, reditu metiuntur; re ipsa autem cum ad idem unde semel profecta sunt cuncta astra redierint eandemque totius caeli descriptionem longis intervallis rettulerint, tum ille vere vertens annus appellari potest

(De republica, VI.xxii)

This image is a richly allusive way of conveying the torturing length of time that this month of absence has been to the poet. If we look back at Boyssoné we see that the experience of absence *may* be the same for him, but he has not got it over to the reader in his 'four days like a hundred'. The difference in *texture* of the two poems is obvious – the one jejune, the other very dense. The *Siecle Platonique* further suggests the theme of separation of body and soul. This then leads directly to the description of the reunion of the two lovers which takes up the rest of the poem.[1] It is the power of the initial image that captures the imagination of the reader and illuminates the argument which follows.

What distinguishes Scève from Boyssoné is firstly the difference in attitude: Scève is concerned with the analysis of intensely personal experience – often in terms of current philosophical ideas – whereas Boyssoné records his love as a petrarchist lover does. And secondly there is the quality of the poetry. The function of the illustrated metaphors in *Délie* reveals a closer relationship between the image and the argument of the dizain than one would have expected, given the obvious decorative and sensuous appeal of the picture. Furthermore, the allusive technique, particularly with such richly emotive legends as those of Acteon or Dido, is a characteristic feature of Scève's best poetry. Characteristic too is the way in which the last line of a dizain containing the symbolic echoes of the figure or legend clinches the argument and allows the poem to end on a strong note by way of a *pointe* or gnomic statement.

Once the associations and suggestions are grasped we are in a position to look at the whole structure of the cycle with Délie herself providing both the focal centre and the leit-motifs to the theme of love.

[1] For a full analysis of this poem see O. de Mourgues, op. cit., pp. 21–2.

# 7

# THEMATIC STRUCTURE

One might be tempted to compare Marot and Scève here, in that both were writing in the 1530s and both were appealing to the court audience around François Ier. But Scève in his best dizains deals with a world which is very different from Marot's. Even in the conception of a French *canzoniere* dedicated to one mistress, Délie, Scève is different.[1] Marot's hesitation over the genres of poetry, his determination to recreate Graeco-Latin genres such as the elegy or the epithalamion, and his clear awareness of tradition in love poetry – all these points certainly make him akin to Scève in the renovation and reformation of poetry. Although not expressing the complexities of his personality, or the subtleties of his love, or the layers of change and uncertainty in his existence Marot succeeds in weaving within the framework of court poetry aspects of his witty and amusing turn of mind, and the ease of diction makes him a good court poet. His linguistic and prosodic cleverness may be demonstrated in one of his epigrams, *A la Bouche de Dyane*

> Bouche de coral precieux,
> Qui à baiser semblez semondre;
> Bouche qui d'ung cueur gracieux
> Savez tant bien dire & respondre;
> Respondez moy: doibt mon cueur fondre
> Devant vous comme au feu la cire?
> Voulez vous bien celluy occire

---

[1] One may note that Professor Mayer in his introduction to the *Epigrammes* (Athlone Press, 1970, *Les Epigrammes*, p. 16) has a strong conditional clause about Marot's *canzoniere*: 'On pourrait donc voir dans ce recueil d'une centaine d'épigrammes consacrées à une seule maîtresse une espèce de *canzoniere*, en l'occurence le premier *canzoniere* français, s'il n'etait que la plupart des poèmes dans ce Second Livre ne se rapportent ni à Anne, ni à l'amour du poète pour cette maîtresse.'

It is misleading to state as Professor Giraud and Professor Jung in their *Littérature française: La Renaissance, I, 1480–1548*, Paris, 1972, p. 220 did, that 'l'histoire de cet amour (of Marot and Anne) à notre avis domine toute l'œuvre marotique...Nous retrouvons...un poète profondément humain, nous sentons vibrer encore un homme tour à tour avide et apaisé, confiant et tourmenté, leste et profond, serein et tragique: bref, un grand poète de l'amour.'

Qui craint vous estre desplaisant?
Ha, bouche que tant je desire,
Dictes nenny en me baisant.

He exploits the stock-in-trade image of the lover melting like
wax in fire when looked at by his mistress' eye; he uses the
beauty of her lips 'de coral precieux' to lead up to a physical
event – kissing her. He recognises maliciously that a woman has
her pride to save and is (or imagines that she is) forced into
yielding. And the last two lines pinpoint the witty simultaneity
of refusal and kissing – both by the same mouth. Marot shows
both wit and playfulness in treating basic assumptions of the love
convention, allowing the physical, sensual side to rise to the
surface. He leads the reader to believe in the serious treatment
of the kiss but then dismisses it in the careless 'uncommitted'
attitude of the last line. The final flippant casualness throws an
amusing light on the whole mock-serious poem. Marot transforms the concrete, physical world into a framework of light,
witty verse. With him there is never any idea that love is being
taken seriously, and this is one of the things that separates him
from Scève. Scève, though he tries in many of his poems to
associate himself with the same reality – François Ier's court –
often fails to do so. He was inferior to Marot in his précieux
poems. But his non-précieux poems are a different matter. It is
not so much that in the non-précieux poems he lives 'in a
non-physical world of dreamings and imaginings'[1] but rather
that he transforms the physical world into an artefact. It is not
reality, nor dreams, nor striving that make up his poetry, but
the metamorphosis of these into another reality which is allusive
and intellectual, the whole being combined with a passion that is
taken seriously. Scève's poetry is an attempt to transform into
objective, rational terms the irrational desire to be loved. The
duality of love, which we have already mentioned (see p. 28) is
the basis of the cycle of poems to Délie and we must now look
at the structure as a whole.

The tradition of writing a series of love poems around one
mistress is well-known in Antiquity – Catullus and Lesbia, Propertius and Cynthia, Tibullus and Delia, Ovid and Corinna. The
reader knows that to enquire after the character of any one of

[1] D. B. Wilson, 'Remarks on Maurice Scève's "Délie"', *Durham University
Journal*, 1967, no. I, vol. LX, pp. 7–12.

these mistresses, or the attitude of the poet towards her, or to reconstruct biographical events from the details provided in the poems is not only inappropriate, it is to misread the convention of love poetry within which they were working. To deny the specificity of Lesbia and Cynthia is not to deny the reality of the sentiments expressed (any more than to assert their specificity necessarily guarantees that reality). Lesbia or Cynthia are foci for the poet's thought and experience in life generally. This convention became the model for the Italian *canzoniere* and their French followers including Scève. The Italian and Neo-Latin poets of the late fifteenth century and the first half of the sixteenth century also used this convention: for example, Marullus dedicates the majority of his Latin love elegies to Neaera, Andrelini to Livia, Jean Second to Julia and Salmon Macrin to Gelonis ('the woman who smiles'). It is a purely literary convention. Scève's use of the name Délie is an artistic device which enables him to give unity to the collection and to intertwine with his presentation of erotic themes a number of associations in legend and mythology. Given the extraordinary richness and complexity of ancient mythology, where most gods and goddesses have infinite ramifications of relationships through their adventures with others, any poet, Ancient or Modern, has in it an inexhaustible well to tap. Furthermore, there are not only family trees (e.g. Artemis, daughter of Zeus and Leto, sister of Apollo) – vertical ramifications, if one wishes to express it that way – but archetypal patterns and themes which give horizontal layers of associations. For example, running through many of the legends, there are themes of the avenging goddess, human and divine intercourse, nymphs fleeing from amorous pursuers, metamorphoses after frustration, crime, jealousy, chastity and fecundity, the relationship of Cupid to Venus, the hostility of Venus and Artemis. A veritable tangle of inter-connections results between one myth and any number of others. Lastly, the themes and leit-motifs correspond to basic human feelings, experiences and desires. The poet who uses this long chain of association is able immediately to refer personal feelings to a more universal plane and provide himself with a short cut to full versions of a story that are within the reader's memory and knowledge. In choosing the name Délie, Scève had at his disposal a vast number of legends, attributes and associations and a line of heroines to provide a tragic past to his story.

Délie was the virgin goddess born on Delos (Greek Artemis, Latin Diana); like her brother Phoebus Apollo, patron of hunting and healing, she was patroness of both chastity and child-birth, identified with Selene (Luna) the moon-goddess and the sinister Hecate, goddess of the underworld. She is one of the richest and most chameleon-like figures in Ancient mythology; hence peculiarly apt for the kind of love that Scève is celebrating. Délie is the virgin goddess, shunning the favour of men and serenely embodying the ideal of chastity. At the same time her unsubdued virginity has an element of wildness as in the violent treatment of Acteon: her rule over the world of nature and her relations with Pan and Endymion seem to place her on the borderline of chastity and sensuality. She is sufficiently ambivalent to suggest the chaste, pure, uncarnal love Scève sings of and yet, contradicting and interwoven with this is the perennial hope, the physical desire and, in rare moments, the physical satisfaction of the poet, his continual perseverance in 'taming' Délie by his *service d'amour*. The well-known episode of Diana and Pan may have been rationalised by later mythographical exegesis in terms of the dew dropping and fertilising nature, but the fact remains that the virginity is not untouchable. It is this ambivalence of the Diana figure in Antiquity which contributes to the power of Délie as a magic name. The wide-ranging associations linking Délie through specific myths or divine roles to Daphne, Hecate, Proserpina and Pandora serve to illuminate some of the basic antitheses of the cycle that Scève himself creates.

The preliminary huitain 'A sa Delie' posits the contrast between the 'ardentz estincelles' of Venus and the chaste love the poet bears his mistress.[1] Although the Neo-Platonic harmonics of the contrast between *amour charnel* and *amour divin* and the traditional distinction between the two Venuses, the one earthly, the other divine, are in the foreground here, there is also the mythological opposition between Diana–Artemis and Venus–Aphrodite, the former standing for chastity and the latter for lasciviousness. This opposition is implicit in the first four lines of dizain 9.

> Non de Paphos, delices de Cypris,
> Non d'Hemonie en son Ciel temperée:

---

[1] The opposition between *Cupido*, earthly love and *Amour*, spiritual love is fully discussed in R. V. Merrill, 'Eros and Anteros', *Speculum*, XIX, 1944, pp. 265–84.

Mais de la main trop plus digne fus pris,
Par qui me fut liberté esperée.

The poem is another variation on the *innamoramento* theme (cf. dizains 1, 2, 3, 6, and Ch. 2 *passim*), the last six lines taking the theme a little further since through the *Mariolaines* and *Œillet* he sees 'Beaulté logée en amere doulceur'. Scève attempts to describe his love first of all in opposition to the ideals of Roman poetry. He establishes this point by the rhetorical figure of the double negative *Non...Non*. Délie herself is rather baldly described; no associations with other mistresses are evoked in the phrase 'la main trop plus digne' (line 3); but this statement is only effective because the negatives have ensured that she differs totally from and surpasses Paphos and Haemonia. The geographical allusions recall to the reader the Venus associations: Latin lovers were all devotees of Venus, and Paphos, a town on the south-western extremity of Cyprus, was the scene of Venus' birth from the foam of the sea and hence one of the most important cult-centres. Goddess and town are often mentioned together, e.g. by Vergil (*Aen.* 1.415), Horace (*Odes*, 1.19.30) and by Ovid (*Am.*, 2.17.4). Boccaccio gave a fine description of the place, 'apud Paphos templum et ara fuit eamque aram solo thure et floribus redolentem faciebant eo quod Venus ex variis causis odoribus delectetur.'[1]

Sensuality, delightful perfumes and flowers were a background to the worship and practice of love. In the second line Haemonia, an ancient name for Thessaly often used by Roman writers, especially in Ovid's *Metamorphosis* (e.g. 1.568; 2.543 and 8.815), evokes an idyllic landscape, a soft sunny climate, good vegetation and tranquillity. But, of course, the main association which Thessaly had in love poetry, was with the practice of witchcraft. 'Drawing down the moon' was one of the most famous charms in antiquity and it was distinctly connected with Thessalian women, according to Aristophanes (*Clouds*, 749–50). In Tibullus and in Propertius this symbolic love charm is alluded to: Propertius, in his first poem, analysed in Ch. 2, says that *if* magicians can change Cynthia's heart, then he will believe *all*, including the moon-charm. By means of his two negative statements Scève has brought these associations to the reader's mind only to obliterate them by stating that neither Paphos nor

---

[1] *De Genealogia deorum*, Basel, 1532, Bk II, Ch. 2 *sub* Venus.

bewitching Haemonia had the power to enslave him. There is also Scève's delight in verbal wit in the first two lines: one recalls the epigram to Ducher (quoted in footnote 1 of Ch. 2 above) where the lines

> Delia si laetis blandum mihi ridet ocellis:
> Non mirum: mea nam *Delia delitiae* est.          (my italics)

contain the juxtaposition of *Delia/delitiae*. In this dizain we have *delices* (Délie?) *de Cypris* and *temperée/Tempe*(?) – the most famous landscape in Thessaly. In other words two puns. One recalls another dizain (no. 159) where Délie is called 'Et neantmoins delices de mon Ame' which plays again on the *delitiae* associations. And one may make the point that when he wrote in Latin he had a deliciously precious and fluid style but when he turned to French (e.g. the verse he sent to *Poésie Françoyse* in 1540, Saulnier, op. cit., t. 1, p. 124) the heavy obscurity of much of his poetry entered definitively. This does open up several points: is his verbal wit as strong in French as in Latin? Does this dizain hint at the various kinds of love that he wants to record? And does it tell us anything about the biography of Scève?

We shall take the last point first. Saulnier (op. cit., t. 1, pp. 219–23), examined the internal evidence provided by individual dizains for seeing two mistresses in *Délie* and concluded, 'Si telle est la densité d'expérience recélée aux vers de *Délie*, c'est qu'ils chantent des émois qui, sur le plan purement biographique, et pour ainsi dire dans le diagramme de ce destin, s'étaient trouvés inscrits éminemment deux fois. L'homme de quarante ans se retrouvait à vingt.' Now the years 1520–30 are a complete blank space in our knowledge of Scève's life. There are no records, and thus it is an entirely arbitrary interpretation to fix the first *innamoramento* at 1520. Secondly, the dating of the years during which *Délie* was composed is wildly variable. For instance Guégan (in the introduction, p. xxii, of his edition of the works of Scève op. cit.) and Parturier (in p. x of his introduction to *Délie*, Paris, 1916) have suggested that Scève was writing it as far back as 1526–7 whilst Saulnier, op. cit., t. 1, p. 155–6, and McFarlane (pp. 10–14) suggest that it was begun around the year 1536. In fact, the dates are equally arbitrary. This attempt at digging up some facts about the man Scève is largely unsupported. Conjecture or hypothesis is valueless when it is substantiated by an indiscriminate collection of 'facts', some gleaned from archives, some from the writings of contemporaries and some taken lock, stock and barrel from his purely fictional poetry. One cannot regard *Délie* as a kind of museum where everything is neatly labelled and beautifully enumerated. What one can see, however, is how carefully Scève has restructured his experience of love in order to impose a pattern on it.

Secondly, there is the type of love (singular or plural, chaste or sensual) that Scève is recording. Avignon must be seen as Scève's first experience of literature. Franco Simone[1] puts the point finely; 'during the splendour of the Renaissance proper Maurice Scève would come to Avignon. The Lyonnese poet would not discover Laura's tomb, but he would be frequently prompted by the still vivid reminders of Petrarch to a personal reading of the *Canzoniere*.' Certain features of the structure – the Petrarchan echoes in the first dizain and in the last – are well known. Three articles[2] have carried the question further and analysed closely how and where Petrarch and Scève are different. But there is the added point (which we saw in Ch. 2) of a totally different orientation. And this orientation depends largely on the kind of love that they are both recording. Let us take one dizain – 417 – to see a little more clearly how this reveals itself.

> Fleuue rongeant pour t'attiltrer le nom
> De la roideur en ton cours dangereuse,
> Mainte Riuiere augmentant ton renom,
> Te fait courir mainte riue amoureuse,
> Baingnant les piedz de celle terre heureuse,
> Ou ce Thuscan Apollo sa ieunesse
> Si bien forma, qu'a iamais sa vieillesse
> Verdoyra a toute eternité:
> Et ou Amour ma premiere liesse
> A desrobée a immortalité.

The sonnet of Petrarch that corresponds best with the dizain is, of course, the one where the river Rhône is addressed (*Rime*, 208),

---

[1] *The French Renaissance*, op. cit., pp. 63–4.
[2] Dorothy Coleman, 'Some notes on Scève and Petrarch', *FS*, XIV, 1960, pp. 293–303 and Doranne Fenoaltea, 'The poet in nature: sources of Scève's *Délie* in Petrarch's *Rime*', *FS*, XXVII, 1973, pp. 257–70. See also Dr. Fenoaltea's art. cit. p. 25 above.

Rapido fiume, che d'alpestra vena,
  Rodendo intorno, onde'l tuo nome prendi,
  Notte e dí meco disioso scendi
  Ov'Amor me, te sol Natura mena;
Vattene innanzi: il tuo corso non frena
  Né stanchezza né sonno: e pria che rendi
  Suo dritto al mar, fiso, u'si mostri, attendi
  L'erba piú verde e l'aria piú serena.
Ivi è quel nostro vivo e dolce sole
  Ch'adorna e 'nfiora la tua riva manca;
  Forse (oh che spero?) il mio tardar le dole.
Basciale'l piede o la man bella e bianca:
  Dille (el basciar sia'n vece di parole)
  – Lo spirto è pronto, ma la carne è stanca. –

Scève, by using the pun 'Fleuue rongeant' as the first words
of his dizain is immediately guiding his readers to this sonnet,
where the pun is explained (cf. footnote in the Carducci edition
of Petrarch referring one to 'cuncta rodens Rhodanus vorans
omnia' in *Senil*, xxv). The address to the river, the stopping of
the poet at Lyon, his idolising Laura, the main image of 'kissing'
(the river is asked to flow so swiftly towards Avignon and kiss
Laura) and the last line where 'the spirit is willing and the flesh
is weak' – these are all points that Scève wants his readers to
have in mind. He calls Petrarch 'ce Thuscan Apollo', thereby
bringing in the richness and density of mythology: Apollo as
the thwarted pursuer of Daphne/Apollo as god of poetry/Apollo
as brother to Diana/Apollo as god of the Sun – all of these
associations Scève will bring out in his poetry. The contrast lies
between the age of Petrarch, his attachment to a single mistress
and the *ieunesse* of Scève, seen through his recall of a first love –
'Et ou Amour ma premiere liesse'. Petrarch's flame will always
be strong and Scève's first love is the cause pushing him to write
poetry also. The rhyming-scheme in the dizain is crucial:
*nom/renom, dangereuse/amoureuse/heureuse, ieunesse/vieillesse/liesse,
eternité/immortalité*. The implications for Scève are enormous:
the immortality of Petrarch will be doubled by that of Scève;
the *vieillesse/ieunesse* theme is suggested; the use of the
Apollo/Daphne myth with all its carnal associations and the
identification of Laura/Avignon/Rhône is apt for Délie/
Avignon = Lyon/Rhône. Furthermore the verbal wit – the pun,
the echoing of Petrarch in the 'kissing' – 'Baingnant les
piedz' – is quite strong, and the following dizain 418 has an
architectural image ending with the line 'Pour l'eriger Colomne

de ma vie', echoing, perhaps, his first dizain – 'Constituée Idole de ma vie'. This is a denser, richer and more allusive kind of poem than the Petrarchan sonnet. To study it as the creation by Scève of one artistic love, let us look at dizain 388 and sonnet 6 of Petrarch's,

> Ce doulx venin, qui de tes yeulx distille,
> M'amollit plus en ma virilité,
> Que ne feit onc au Printemps inutile
> Ce ieune Archier guidé d'agilité.
> Donc ce Thuscan pour vaine vtilité
> Trouue le goust de son Laurier amer:
> Car de ieunesse il aprint a l'aymer:
> Et en Automne Amour, ce Dieu volage,
> Quand me voulois de la raison armer,
> A preualu contre sens, & contre aage.

> Sí travïato è l'folle mi'disio
>     A seguitar costei che'n fuga è volta
>     E de' lacci d'Amor leggiera e sciolta
>     Vola dinanzi al lento correr mio,
> Che, quanto richiamando piú l'envio
>     Per la secura strada, men m'ascolta;
>     Né mi vale spronarlo o dargli volta,
>     Ch'Amor per sua natura il fa restio.
> E, poi che'l fren per forza a sé raccoglie,
>     I'mi rimango in signoria di lui,
>     Che mal mio grado a morte mi trasporta;
> Sol per venir al lauro onde si coglie
>     Acerbo frutto che le piaghe altrui,
>     Gustando afflige piú che non conforta.

The whole sonnet is on the nature of the poet's desire and takes the form of a debate between his reason and his senses. The last three lines are an allegorical way of saying that he is dragged down by the effect of his passion: he is forced to eat the harsh bitter leaves of the bay tree. Scève guides us to the sonnet through lines 5–8: the play of words on the *Laurier*/Laura alerts us to the legend of Apollo and Daphne. The contrast *ieunesse/ vieillesse* and *Printemps/Automne* is reproduced strongly in the dizain. But what Scève is concerned with is a psychological analysis of love: in line 1 *doulx venin...yeulx distille*, in line 2 *M'amollit plus...*suggest that a stronger, more passionate love is holding the poet and he can contrast it with a sweet and fresh passion that he knew when younger. The contrast between him and Petrarch is immense: for Petrarch, although racked with passion for Laura, is still better off than Scève, the implicit argument runs, for Scève has a love where reason and senses are completely dislocated. The carnal side of love is recognised clearly here. It is a gross over-simplification of Saulnier's that there were two real mistresses in Scève's life (i.e. two women he possessed physically). There may have been fifty-two or there may have been none. The only relevant fact for us is the creation of a complex network of love-poems weaving multifarious threads around the human experience.

And finally there is the question of the extent of Scève's verbal wit, that is, when he is writing in the vernacular. Saulnier analyses (op. cit., t. I, pp. 131–3) *Scève et la facétie* and concludes, 'Où donc est le grave pontife sans sourire? Ne tenons-nous pas, non certes substitué au portrait traditionnel, mais le complément de singulière façon, une manière de Scève facétieux, amateur de plaisanteries joyeuses et un peu grosses?' This is incomplete; Saulnier takes love of language (inherited from the *Rhétoriqueurs*), and a feeling for the sound of words, and couples it to the rather childish joker of certain *imprese* (e.g. no. 25), or of puns like *Barbare a moy* = *Ile Barbe* at Lyon (no. 238). What is much more important is the way in which Scève can be subtle, allusive and witty in his Neo-Latin/French manner.

To revert to dizain 9, one can say that the allusions there are part of the technique of persuasion developed by a poet who was fully aware of what these proper names from the Graeco-Roman world could do. They contribute to Scève's object of convincing the reader of Délie's *nature digne* and of the over-whelming power of attraction that she exerts. Furthermore, they play an ambivalent part in calling up physical sensuality and then cancelling it. Paradoxically, although not a slave to sensuous emotion he is now enslaved by a higher, more worthy object of love. In the last six lines of the poem, carrying on the theme of the *innamoramento*, he combines high hopes and lofty thoughts with the symbolic *Œillet* and *Mariolaines* and these very common plants link with the initial allusions and emphasise the contrast between the exotic and the humble, the soft sweetness and the *amere doulceur*.

Numerous poems insist on the *quality* of their love which is infused with the virginity-associations of Diana: for example, dizains 6, 12, 28, 41, 97, 119, 185, 233, 285, 319, 322, 325 and 413. Diana as goddess of hunting comes into dizains 5, 67, 110, 131,

140, 250 and 327. Diana as the sister of Apollo comes into dizains 8, 44, 102, 120, 124, 149 and 322. These virginity-associations are fairly commonplace, and if they were all Scève drew from the name his use of a mythological framework for his love cycle would hardly be distinguished. But there are other associations, and in many ways he is at once Classical and petrarchist through his exploitation of both traditions.

Take for example, the favours granted by Diana to Endy-mion[1] which provides Scève with the starting point for a poem of longing and illusory possession of Délie, dizain 126.

> A l'embrunir des heures tenebreuses,
> Que Somnus lent pacifie la Terre,
> Enseuely soubz Cortines vmbreuses,
> Songe a moy vient, qui mon esprit desserre,
> Et tout aupres de celle là le serre,
> Qu'il reueroit pour son royal maintien.
>   Mais par son doulx, & priué entretien
> L'attraict tant sien, que puis sans craincte aulcune
> Il m'est aduis, certes, que ie la tien,
> Mais ainsi, comme Endimion la Lune.

Two aspects of the legend captured the imagination of Antiquity and the Middle Ages: the sleep of the beautiful youth Endymion and the love of an immortal goddess for a mortal. Erasmus quotes the saying 'to sleep the sleep of Endymion' and explains it thus, 'is erat puer adprime formosus ac Lunae adamatus. Cui quidem a patre Jove precibus impetravit ut quicquid optasset, id ferret. Optavit Endymion ut perpetuum dormiret somnum, id est immortalis perseverans et expers senii.'[2] The function and richness of the allusion in *Délie*, the theme and tone of the dizain are illuminated by a knowledge of a *sestina* of Petrarch's *Non ha tanti animali il mar fra l'onde* (*Rime*, 237). The general theme is the poet's suffering in love, and this is developed in six stanzas of six lines each, concluding with a three-line address to the

---

[1]  A favourite theme of Roman poets, and the sensual associations are explicitly mentioned by Propertius. In II.15 he explores the fact that it was the nakedness of Helen roused Paris and that of Endymion the Moon,

> nudus et Endymion Phoebi cepisse sororem
>   dicitur et nudae concubuisse deae.

There is no literary evidence for the statement but representation on vases and reliefs posits the nakedness. (See Roscher, *Lexicon Griech. und Rom. Mythol.*, I, 1246.)

[2]  *Adagia*, Basel, 1520, pp. 278–9.

poem. In structure it is thus a different kind of poem from the ten concentrated lines of Scève. Petrarch devotes the first half of the poem to demonstrating that he is the most unfortunate of men, that he never knows relief from suffering and that he can only hope for the peace brought by death. He longs for the evening, and

> Per lo dolce silenzio de la notte:
> Tal ch'io aspetto tutto'l dí la sera,
> Che'l sol si parta e dia luogo a la luna. (lines 28–30)

It is at this point that the poet longs to be with Endymion *addormentato in qua' che verdi boschi* and to know the peace of sleep. But he also longs for Laura to accompany the moon and visit him as Selene visits Endymion.

Scève offers a totally different viewpoint, but his opening line is an echo of the phrase in the *sestina* – *come imbrunir veggio la sera* (line 22). This time-setting is important: the sounds *heures, tenebreuses, vmbreuses* and the slow length of the first two lines emphasise the falling of night. The Petrarchan longing for night is not explicit, but through this description and through the phrase *qui mon esprit desserre* in line 4, the contrast between the anguish of day and the relief brought by night is felt. If we bear in mind that most rationalistic explanations of the myth (e.g. Boccaccio) make Endymion the personification of Sleep, and that Petrarch longed to be with Endymion *addormentato* we can see that the first two lines and the reference to Somnus create the sleep–dream sequence of the dizain and are linked to the final allusion to Endymion. Scève makes no explicit statement like *foss'io co'l vago de la luna* (line 31) and does not express the hope that Délie will visit him while he is asleep. But from line 5 onwards, in the light of the final allusion, it is as if the poet were re-enacting the Endymion episode with Délie as the Moon Goddess.[1] The *royal maintien*, the distance and coldness of the goddess–Délie as she appears in normal everyday life, give way to a *doulx, & priué entretien* (Cotgrave gives 'familiar' among other words for *priué* and this is precisely what is needed in the context) in the dream world of night. The poet has the illusion of possessing Délie but the encounter is condemned to remain

---

[1] Luna was the name given by Cariteo to his mistress in the sequence of poems called *Endimione*. But, as opposed to Scève, his mistress was the cold and distant woman extolled by the petrarchists.

an imaginary one and the sudden introduction of the Endymion parallel in the last line forces this point on the reader's understanding. Now this last line is ambiguous. It makes the reader hesitate between 'comme Endimion tient la Lune' and 'comme la Lune tient Endimion', thus suggesting the possible reciprocation of love in this encounter. Ironically, the familiar, intimate contact with the goddess is only achievable in a dream when the poet is *sans craincte aulcune*. Whereas in Petrarch the episode forms only a part of the longer poem, the Endymion myth in Scève, without being made explicit until the end, illuminates the whole.[1] This aspect of the Délie–Diana complex has far-reaching echoes in the love cycle. For the whole situation of a *doulx, & priué entretien* with Délie in a dream is linked to the occasions when reciprocation of love in some physical sense is implied (e.g. dizains 287, 364, 367, 400) and through this the possibility of 'taming' the wild virgin Délie is linked with the theme of sensual satisfaction (cf. dizain 429 on her *rusticité*, analysed in Ch. 2 above). For instance dizain 7.

> Celle beaulté, qui embellit le Monde
> Quand nasquit celle en qui mourant ie vis,
> A imprimé en ma lumière ronde
> Non seulement ses lineamentz vifz:
> Mais tellement tient mes espritz rauiz,
> En admirant sa mirable merveille,
> Que presque mort, sa Deité m'esueille
> En la clarté de mes desirs funebres,
> Ou plus m'allume, & plus, dont m'esmerueille,
> Elle m'abysme en profondes tenebres.

What strikes us first is the way the whole dizain seems an incantation on the sounds *m, em, im, um, em* leading up to what can be called a *rhétoriqueur's* line,

> En admirant sa mirable meruelle.

But this is not mere verbal gymnastics: it serves to evoke his state of mind, hesitating between the *desirs funebres* (a phrase from

[1] Another final image drawn from the parallel between Délie and the Moon Goddess is in dizain 194. In the first four lines we have Délie, the Goddess, and later the theme of death suffered by the poet in love. The sacrifices made to her are evoked by the reference to *mortz* and *tombes* and the last line 'Pour t'appaiser, mille, & mille Hecatombes' brings in associations with Hecate with whom Délie is also associated. The hundred sacrifices made to Hecate was a common explanation of her name found in Boccaccio, *De genealogia deorum*, and in the mythological dictionaries of the sixteenth century.

Scève's *Blason du Sourcil*) and their *clarté*: carnal suggestions with a spiritual meaning of higher love. Scève uses the leit-motif of light and darkness suggested by the moon-goddess to evoke the peculiarly complex and persistently ambivalent effect which Délie has on him. Lines 1–4 state the paradox of dying in himself while living in his mistress – *celle en qui mourant ie vis*. Then there is a strong re-assertion, with the intensive *mais tellement* and the move from *ma lumiere ronde* to *mes espritz rauiz*. This last phrase recalls the Neo-Platonic theory of the physiological effect that continual contemplation of the beloved has on the lover:

> où se porte l'attention continue de l'âme, là aussi affluent les esprits qui sont, soit les véhicules, soit les instruments de l'âme... L'âme de l'amant étant entraînée vers l'image de l'aimeé...les esprits sont également portés vers cet objet, et, volant continuellement vers ce but, s'épuisent.[1]

In line 6 Scève stresses both the miracle of Délie's being and his admiring contemplation of her by the use of a *figura etymologica* – words with the same root – *En admirant sa mirable merueille*. The paradox of line 2 is re-asserted in

> Que presque mort, sa Deité m'esueille
> En la clarté de mes desirs funebres...

which express in a more condensed, almost metaphysical, way his inner tension: on the one hand Délie awakens him to an awareness of a higher good; on the other hand, this very aspiration he knows is tinged with carnal appetite and doomed to failure. These tensions are emphasised further in the final paradox of

> Ou plus m'allume, & plus, dont m'esmerueille,
> Elle m'abysme en profondes tenebres.

The multiple and conflicting emotions set in motion by the moment of the *innamoramento* are recaptured by every aspect of this poem. There is the order of events: *embellit le Monde, ma lumiere ronde, mes espritz rauiz, sa Deité m'esueille, profondes tenebres*; and the juxtaposition of light and darkness, particularly in the phrase *la clarté de mes desirs funebres* where the two elements enter into a 'warring union'. Finally there is the growing intensity of the poem with the main pause following

---

[1] Marsile Ficin, ed. Raymond Marcel, *Commentaire sur le Banquet de Platon*, Paris, 1956, p. 214.

line 4 which is the real centre of the dizain, and then the vigorous new impulse that comes with *Mais tellement* of line 5. The distance covered can be measured by comparing the first line 'Celle beaullté qui embellit le Monde' with the last line 'Elle m'abysme en profondes tenebres.'

From this central episode open out the themes of the dual nature of his love and the dual nature of Délie herself. For in the first seven dizains he has studded his poetry with clues: the preliminary poem with its *renouelles*, the first dizain with its magnificent *innamoramento*, the second, through the allusion to Pandora (as we shall see later), the third with its allusion to hell, the fourth with his idolization of Délie, the fifth with his fleeing her eye, the first *impresa La femme & la Lycorne*, with its carnal suggestions, dizain 6 with the poet *continuellement* enslaved *en l'Auril de mon aage*, and the seventh with its metaphysical tension between carnal love and a more spiritual love. The time values are firmly placed in the ambivalent present and in the future: it is as if the poet were defining what it is, this love of his. One has springtime and absence of care as the setting in which the 'falling in love' took place; and he can not say what the meaning of the experience is, except by creating "approximations" to describe and analyse it.

The poet's hope of physical satisfaction is explicitly linked in dizain 394 to his choice of the name Délie. The allusion in line 6 *Comme la Lune aux Amantz fauorise* (cf. 41: 'le bien, qu'Amantz ont sur tout cher' is fairly strong, coming as it does in the middle of a poem on his sense impressions) evokes the theme dear to the Latin elegiac poets of the moon shining through the darkness of night and making easier the path of the lover to his mistress' home. Propertius for instance in III.16 stresses how kind the moon is to lovers,

> luna ministrat iter, demonstrant astra salebras,
>    ipse Amor accensas percutit ante faces...      (lines 15–16)

(cf. Philodemus' epigram *A.P.*, 5.123 for a different favour from the Moon). The moon is the tutelary deity of love at night and Propertius is able to exploit the theme richly and in an allusive way. As we saw earlier, Propertius is very close at times to Scève in the way he looks at love and expresses the experience. Scève like Propertius is concerned with intensely personal experiences, and both poets try to analyse their feelings in an intellectual way, thereby seeing the significance of those feelings against the background of their own literary tradition. Scève uses a number of leit-motifs that are found in Augustan poetry, like the moon charm (dizain 75), the astrological beliefs attached to the moon (see Tibullus, 1.2.43 and 1.8.21–2; Ovid, *Amor.* 1.8.6 and ii.26; cf. dizain 282) and the Cynthian images in dizain 356. In dizain 14 the whole 'binding' image is Roman. In this particular dizain Scève is concerned to expound the difficulty, the impossibility of union and the frustrating nature of the bond that actually exists betwen Délie and himself. The idea of a *magicus nodus* occurs in the love poetry of Tibullus and Propertius: binding recalls sorcery; knots that one cannot undo without knowing the necessary charm; the knot which is strong, indissoluble and wondrous and mysterious. Tibullus in 1.8.5–6

> ipsa Venus magico religatum bracchia nodo
> perdocuit multis non sine verberibus

– depicts the lover as a slave to Venus. Scève states his own position,

> Elle me tient par ces cheueulx lyé,
> Et ie la tien par ceulx là mesmes prise.
> Amour subtil au noud s'est allié
> Pour se deuaincre vne si ferme prise:
> Combien qu'ailleurs tendist son entreprise,
> Que de vouloir deux d'vn feu tourmenter.
>  Car (& vray est) pour experimenter
> Dedans la fosse à mys & Loup, & Chieure,
> Sans se pouoir l'vn l'aultre contenter,
> Sinon respondre a mutuelle fiebrue.

The latinism in *deuaincre* from *devincire* 'bind together, unite closely' is an allusive echo of Augustan poetry and the *Amour subtil* is perhaps an etymological pun, since *subtilis* had the meaning of *thread* in Latin (e.g. Lucretius, 4.88); thus it would mean both fine-spun and subtle. Lines 5–6 gives Love's purpose – to torment them both without any hope of untying the knot. At this point Scève introduces an illustrative image (i.e. an image which is a concrete example of something which would otherwise have to be stated in abstract terms) to emphasise that this proved the truth of his earlier statements. The unnatural mating of different animals was used as a topos in Antiquity, for example, Vergil, *Eclog.*, 8, lines 26–7 when the girl has left the goatherd to marry another man, the monstrousness of this new union is expressed by

> quid non speremus amantes?
> iungentur iam grypes equis.

The wolf and the goat were traditional enemies and the goat in particular was regarded as a lustful animal.[1] The mating of these two animals was such a preposterously impossible thing that Horace, for instance, uses it as an adynaton in one of his Odes.

> Sed prius Apulis
> iungentur capreae lupis,
> quam turpi Pholoe peccet adultero.                    (1.33.7–9)

The whole Ode is a demonstration that Venus, through a cruel joke, loves to match the couples in an odd way. Lastly, Love does not bring assurance or even hope with it. The force of the last three lines of the dizain lies in the way it depicts the monstrous action of Love and the mutual frustration and fever of the two lovers. The echoes from the love poetry of Horace, Tibullus, Propertius and Vergil bring out more powerfully the underlying passion that goes with the poet's love. But it is done so unobtrusively that it is only by recognising the clues in the structure of the poem and the Latinism of *deuaincre* that the reader draws the threads together.

The ambivalence of chastity and sensuality can be followed still further. By introducing Daphne and Dictynna, two figures closely associated and even fused with Diana,[2] Scève can display both sides of the coin – elusive flight from love and ardent pursuit. Daphne, according to Libanius, *Narrationes* 19 (cf. Ovid. *Met.*, 1.474–87) was a wild virgin like Artemis. But she was also the first love of Apollo (Ovid, *ib.* 452) whose unwanted attentions she managed to elude only by being transformed into a bay-tree.[3] In dizain 102 the final image

> Tu fuys Daphnes, ardeurs Apollinées

---

[1] See in Valeriano, *Hieroglyphica*, Basel, 1556, Bk 10. *De capra:* 'Libido et procacitas. Deque Satyris identidem capripedibus eadem omnium consensum feruntur, non posse quidem eos libidine satiari.' Later Valeriano says that 'sunt qui febrem ex Caprae simulachro significent propterea quod animal id eo semper incommodo laboret hinc anima illi semper ardentior ita ut attacta pastu exurere videatur.' He sums up the nature of a goat thus: 'natura instabilis lubrica atque mobilis.'

[2] Pausanias, *Descriptio Graeciae*, III.24.8: the laconian shrines of Artemis–Daphnaia and Dictynna–Artemis.

[3] Ovid, *Met.*, 1.545–67.

serves not only to illuminate the argument of the poem, which
concerns the elusiveness of Délie, always able to frustrate her
lover at the moment of success, but also to cast a suggestion of
erotic, carnal and physical desire over what otherwise would be
simply a description of a chaste conversation with Délie. The
poet reveals himself as always attempting, without success, to
transform the encounter into something un-chaste. His desire,
here again, is not spiritual or Neo-Platonic but human.

Another dizain – 310 – evokes the transformation when the
lover is left with the bay-tree as a bitter reward for his pains.
This time, the tense is future and the implication of the 'fruit'
or expectation is that of full physical satisfaction. We may
remember Ovid's sensual description of the frustration of Apollo
at the moment of Daphne's change:

> complexusque suis ramos ut membra lacertis
> oscula dat ligno: refugit tamen oscula lignum
> cui deus 'at, quoniam coniunx mea non potes esse,
> arbor eris certe' dixit 'mea...          (*Met.*, 1, lines 555–8)

Finally dizain 407 evokes the image briefly in the phrase *viuant
soubz verdoyante escorce* (line 9) which seems to echo Ovid's stress
on the human livingness of Daphne after her metamorphosis,

> hanc quoque Phoebus amat, positaque in stipite dextra
> sentit adhuc *trepidare novo sub cortice pectus.*
>                                  (*Met.*, 1, lines 553–4)

The other figure, of Dictynna, is exploited in a totally
different way to bring out a different aspect of the poet's pursuit
of his mistress. In dizain 353 it is again the sudden entry of the
allusion in the last two lines that startles the reader on first
reading the poem

> Sa vertu veult estre aymée, & seruie,
> Et sainctement, & comme elle merite,
> Se captiuant l'Ame toute asseruie,
> Qui de son corps en fin se desherite:
> Lequel deuient pour vn si hault merite
> Plus desseché, qu'en terre de Lemnos.
> Et luy estant ià reduict tout en os,
> N'est d'aultre bien, que d'espoir reuestu.
>   Ie ne suis point pour ressembler Minos,
> Pourquoy ainsi, Dictymne, me fuis tu?

A full account of the myth is given in *Ciris*, a poem once attributed to Vergil, and it is also recounted by Boccaccio and by sixteenth-century mythographers, so one can assume that it was fairly well known.[1] The legend in the *Ciris* poem is introduced into the account given by Scylla's nurse Carme of her mistress's insane passion for Minos. Carme remembers the loss of her own daughter Britomartis (called Dictynna after her death since she leaped into the sea from Dictaean rocks):

> te, Britomarti, diem potui producere vitae?
> atque utinam celeri nec tantum grata Dianae
> venatus esses virgo sectata virorum
> Gnosia nec Partho contenens spicula cornu
> Dictaeas ageres ad gramina nota capellas.
> numquam tam obnixe fugiens Minois amores
> praeceps aerii specula de montis adisses
> unde alii fugisse ferunt, et numen Aphaeae
> virginis assignant, alii, quo notior esses,
> Dictynam dixere tuo de nomine Lunam.          (lines 296–305)

Dictynna's virginity is stressed: she was a shepherdess and a follower of the chaste Diana. To escape the amorous attentions of Minos she fled to her death. The context of the story is important since the tale of Scylla's love and death and the story of Dictynna and her tragic end are both linked to Minos. The assertion that the poet is not like Minos makes an impact on the reader only if he thinks of Minos not as the wise ruler and judge of traditional legend but as the violent destructive lover who drove both Scylla and Dictynna to their deaths. The allusion illuminates the poem retrospectively. The first two lines declare Délie's virtue: *vertu* is closer to the Latin *virtus* or Italian *virtù* than to 'virtue'; for it signifies an energetic development of every faculty in man, not merely what is morally good. Erasmus uses *virtus* in this sense, and so do other humanists. In the dizain the associations of virginity and divinity are present, with the implication that Délie must not be sullied but rather worshipped with reverence. In line 3 there is a shift of emphasis from Délie herself to her effect on the poet: his soul, having left his body, now belongs to Délie and as a result of this total separation of soul and body his physical condition is pitiable. His body is 'plus desseché, qu'en terre de Lemnos': here there are a number of

---

[1] Boccaccio, op. cit. Bk IX, Ch. 25. An edition of *Ciris* appeared in 1517 in Venice. I have used the edition by de Gubernatis, Turin, 1930.

threads that Scève might be weaving together. Firstly, Lemnian earth was medicinal and called *terra sigillata* because it was impressed with a stamp, and that stamp, in ancient times, was the head of Artemis. Secondly, Lemnos was called *Aithaleia* in Greek, that is 'the fiery place' and was sacred to Hephaistos (Vulcan) and was therefore volcanic and dry. This dovetails neatly with Scève's *desseché* and his *reduict en os*. Thirdly, is there an echo here of Augustan love poetry? The bitterness and cruelty of Venus when angered are proverbial and illustrated by legends such as that of the women of Lemnos. The women murdered their husbands, and Scève might be alluding to his own murder by having his soul drawn from his body, leaving him as dry lifeless bones. Then, suddenly, comes the assertion, the protest against all this suffering, for it is *unmerited* since he is not a pursuer like Minos. He is giving Délie–Dictynna no cause to run away from him. This is very like the Narcissus dizain 60 which taken with the *impresa* makes its impact by negation: the poet is *not* like Narcissus,

> Qu'est il besoing de plus oultre m'occire,
> Veu qu'asses meurt, qui trop vainement ayme?

So far our examination of the allusive resonances of the name Délie has indicated a tension of opposites: the chaste unassailable goddess and the possibility of her submission, the reverent *serviteur d'amour* and the violent lover in pursuit. These themes become leit-motifs in the cycle as a whole, and we shall be looking at passion and rational self-control in a later chapter. Since it is specifically Classical mythology that provides Scève with a backcloth against which to set the non-spiritual, and the non-Neo-Platonic aspect of his love, we can perhaps say that there is nothing essentially of the thorough-going Neo-Platonic idea of progressing to higher spheres via love. This makes it impossible to accept the view that Délie is merely an anagram of *L'Idée*.[1] Furthermore, we have seen the non-Petrarchan aspects of Scève, the absence of any poems on the death of his mistress and the complete absence of Christ, the Christian God or the Virgin Mary. This makes the cycle a distinctly human one.

A further resonance is, of course, the inextricable mingling of love and death. This is a cliché of love poetry, but again Scève

[1] See the excellent *mise au point* of this question in Saulnier, op. cit., t. I, p. 249.

uses it startlingly. In the second dizain we have the retrospective working of the Pandora image not only on this poem's structure but over the cycle as a whole:

> Le Naturant par ses haultes Idées
> Rendit de soy la Nature admirable.
> Par les vertus de sa vertu guidées
> S'esuertua en œuure esmerueillable.
>    Car de tout bien, voyre es Dieux desirable,
> Parfeit vn corps en sa parfection,
> Mouuant aux Cieulx telle admiration,
> Qu'au premier œil mon ame l'adora,
> Comme de tous la delectation,
> Et de moy seul fatale Pandora.

The two important points in the Hesiodic account of Pandora (which Boccaccio follows closely) are first, that Pandora was created at the behest of Jupiter and endowed with gifts by all the gods and second, that she was the bringer of evil to earth.[1] The sixteenth-century mythographer Robert Estienne stresses so much the beauty, virtues and seductiveness of Pandora that she appears to be almost the prototype of the *femme fatale*, a 'deadly delight'. He describes her as a 'mulier fortissima et gratiosissima' and relates how each god gave her a specific virtue, 'cui singula dei sua dona dederunt, scilicet Pallas sapientiam, Venus decorem, Apollo musicam, Mercurius eloquentiam ...Hanc, ut ait Hesiodus, Jupiter in terram misit ut homines deciperet.'[2] The sixteenth-century reader would readily have understood Pandora to have been a consummate blend of blessing and curse, distributing good to some and evil to others. Furthermore, Pandora appeared in Orphic legends closely linked with Hecate. The interest shown in, and the use made of, Orphic theology and cosmology by Ficino and the Italian Neo-Platonists and Lefèvre d'Etaples suggest that this link would not be unknown to Scève himself and to some at least of his contemporary readers. In the *Argonautica* of 'Orpheus' this link is made perfectly clear as Orpheus invokes and then offers sacrifices to the goddesses of the Underworld:

Aussitôt, des enfers, elles s'éveillèrent à travers la flamme, terribles, effroyables, cruelles et on ne pouvait les regarder. L'une avait le corps

---

[1] Hesiod, *Works and Days*, 57–101, and *Theogony*, 570–612. Boccaccio, op. cit., Bk IV, Ch. 44. For a full discussion of the sources and development of the Pandora myth see D. and E. Panofsky, *Pandora's Box*, London, 1956.

[2] *Dictionarium...sub* Pandora.

en fer; c'est celle que les Infernaux appellent Pandore; avec elle venait un monstre funeste à voir, indestructible, aux formes changeantes, à trois têtes, l'enfant du Tartare, Hecate.[1]

Pandora is here a terrible, avenging, infernal goddess; the iron form is symbolic of the hardness and cruelty which she brings to earth and she is accompanied by the other infernal goddess, Hecate. The strength of Scève's allusion to Pandora lies primarily in the way it convinces the reader of the personal isolation of the poet. The first six lines of the poem deal with the actual creation of Délie, using scholastic terminology like *Naturant* in line 1 (*Natura naturans*) and *Nature* in line 2 (*Natura naturata*) and the faintly Neo-Platonic terminology of divine beauty and perfection infused into this mortal woman.[2] The perfection of Délie is stressed by means of nouns and adjectives in rhyming positions like *admirable/admiration/delectation*. The delight this unique woman brings everyone contrasts sharply with the surprise ending.

Secondly, the allusion, reflecting back on the dizain, endows the rather abstract description of creation with the concreteness of a myth. The creation of Délie is a parallel to that of Pandora. Lines 5–6

> Car de tout bien, voyre es Dieux desirable,
> Parfeit vn corps en sa parfection,

evoke the *omnia munera* with which Pandora was endowed and recall to the reader the specific talents and seductive attractions of Pandora. Thus the second poem of the cycle announces the theme of the avenging/delighting goddess, now baleful, now bountiful, which permeates the whole of *Délie*.

The iron form of Pandora lingers in our mind as successive dizains stress the incredible hardness of Délie: for instance dizains 88 and 239. Délie as the avenging goddess suggests the theme of the punishment or transformation of the intruding lover: so Diana punishing the audacity of the youth Acteon forms the subject of an *impresa* (no. 19) and it is likely that the *impresa La Lycorne qui se uoit* (no. 26) is another echo of the same theme.

---

[1] *Les Argonautiques d'Orphée*, ed. G. Dottin, Paris, 1930 lines 72–88. The Greek text had been published in 1500, 1517 and 1519; Latin translations appeared in 1519 and 1523.

[2] For a full analysis of this theme see L. Spitzer 'The Poetic Treatment of a Platonic Christian theme', *Comparative Literature*, 1954, VI, pp. 193 ff.

The harmonic range of the love-death theme is vast, extending through the Hecate–Proserpina–Diana–Luna complex of dizain 22 to the *mille Hecatombes* of 194, through moments when Délie is seen as a goddess of death and love, as in 403. Libitina is a strange goddess of Latin mythology, known primarily as the goddess of death but with one bizarre aspect: 'Les Latins ont mis en rapport *Libitina* avec *libet* d'où les formes *Lubitina*, et *Lubentina, Libentina*, et ils en ont fait une Vénus infernale'.[1] Ernout and Meillet quote one gloss which says, 'est dea paganorum, libidinis dea, quam quidam Venerem infernalem esse dixerunt: tamen et libitina dicitur lectus mortuorum uel locus in quo mortui conduntur', and then they add 'Mais ce n'est là sans doute qu'une étymologie populaire.' Now the dizain, it seems to me, does evoke love and death in this strange way,

> Tout le iour meurs voyant celle presente,
> Qui m'est de soy meurdryerement benigne.
> Toute nuict i'ars la desirant absente,
> Et si me sens a la reuoir indigne,
> Comme ainsi soit que pour ma Libytine
> Me fut esleue, & non pour ma plaisance.
>      Et mesmement que la molle nuisance
> De cest Archier superbement haultain
> Me rend tousiours par mon insuffisance
> D'elle doubteux, & de moy incertain.

There is a play in the line 'Me fut esleue, & non pour ma plaisance', the last four lines link the Cupid-archer associations with Venus; the whole context is of uncertainty: the poet does not know whether he is worshipping the corpses of the dead or the libidinous delights of Venus.

Other moments in the cycle call up Hecate, wielding her power over victims in Hades, and do so in an ambivalent way. Take dizain 376; this poem analyses the relationship between the poet and his mistress, taking as its starting-point two emotional facts. Firstly, love has reduced the lover to a shadow, and secondly Délie is to the poet as a body is to its shadow:

> Tu es le Corps, Dame, & ie suis ton vmbre,
> Qui en ce mien continuel silence
> Me fais mouuoir, non comme Hecate l'Vmbre,
> Par ennuieuse, & grande violence,
> Mais par pouoir de ta haulte excellence,

[1] *Dictionnaire étymologique de la langue latine*, by A. Ernout and A. Meillet, Paris, 3rd ed., 1951, *sub* Libitina.

En me mouant au doulx contournement
De tous tes faictz, & plus soubdainement,
Que lon ne veoit l'vmbre suyure le corps,
Fors que ie sens trop inhumainement
Noz sainctz vouloirs estre ensemble discords.

The allusion to Hecate in line 3 refers to the power of this goddess over the shades of the dead: she was thought to be called Hecate, 'vel que centum annos errare faceret insepultos, vel que centum victimis placaretur'.[1] But this power of Hecate is evoked only to be rejected in line 5, so as to emphasise the different quality of the poet's dependence on Délie. The real problem in the relationship and the real point of the extended negative comparison are revealed by the twist that comes in the last two lines. The metaphor of Body/Shadow is appropriate, but not for the discord that informs the lovers' relationship. The clash of *sainctz* and *discords* brings out fully the paradoxical nature of the total dependence of the poet on his mistress and gives a rather ironic twist to *saincteté*. The poem can thus be seen to be based on two negations: the poet is shadow to Délie's corporeal substance yet unlike shadow in that there is in this instance a basic clash between mover and moved; secondly Délie has the power to move him at will or to condemn him to wander in Hades, a power which has none of the violent infernal character of Hecate but springs directly from the divine power and virtue of Délie. The detailed exploration of the initial situation and the initial metaphor is a totally different technique from the startling entry of final images. It is more akin to Donne's technique of explaining and exploring a problematic relationship by means of a comparison.

The one dizain that states the ambivalent powers of Délie most clearly and most beautifully is no. 22:

Comme Hecaté tu me feras errer
Et vif, & mort cent ans parmy les Vmbres:
Comme Diane au Ciel me resserrer,
D'ou descendis en ces mortelz encombres:
Comme regnante aux infernalles vmbres
Amoindriras, ou accroistras mes peines.
  Mais comme Lune infuse dans mes veines
Celle tu fus, es, & seras DELIE,
Qu'Amour à ioinct a mes pensées vaines
Si fort, que Mort iamais ne l'en deslie.

---

[1] Calepinus, *Dictionarium...multo diligentius ab Ascensio repositum*, Paris, 1518 *sub* Hecate.

The initial image, Délie = Hecate – bringing in one of the associations around the name Délie – does more than start the argument of the poem, for in this dizain Scève draws on existing analogies of the Moon–Délie fusion to express something personal about the way Délie occupies his universe and whole being. The first two lines describe Délie as Hecate; the *Comme* expresses the meaning 'in her role or capacity as' Hecate, establishing not only a direct comparison but a fusion of the two beings so that Hecate is seen as Délie and Délie is seen as Hecate. Hecate as the 'dea triformis' is well established in classical mythology, in Vergil, Tibullus and Ovid. Hecate already contains both Diana and Proserpina (the two other manifestations used by Scève in lines 3–6). Boccaccio (op. cit., Bk 4) gives an exhaustive list of the names of the moon, which include Hecate, Diana, Proserpina, Trivia, Argentea, Phoebe, Ceres, Artea, Mena etc. Scève in these two lines evokes a psychological state – physical and mental bewilderment wandering between life and death in a kind of Limbo, as the victim of Délie–Hecate.

Lines 3–4 describe Délie–Diana. They may refer to the goddess as Queen of the Forests and Groves on earth, 'en ces mortelz encombres' or they may be an allusion to the love between the moon and Endymion. In the latter case the words 'D'ou descendis en ces mortelz encombes' would refer to the descent of the moon to embrace Endymion, and Scève would be, by analogy, contrasting the ecstasy that Délie–Diana sometimes brings with the extreme suffering inflicted by Délie–Hecate in the first two lines. Or finally they may be referring to the way in which Délie can help the poet to ascend to higher spheres through her love 'Comme Diane au Ciel me resserrer'.

Lines 5–6 make us see the Délie–Proserpina fusion: the goddess reigns in the underworld, in command of the pain and punishment of the inhabitants. The assertive *Mais* of line 7 puts these multiple associations in the background while Scève brings forward the Délie–Luna aspect. Luna was the 'planet' nearest the earth, the planet which, according to the astrological beliefs of the sixteenth century, controlled the liquid *defluus* which descended on humans and influenced their character and destiny. The personal intensity achieved by Scève in the last four lines is due partly to the phrase 'infuse dans mes veines', suggesting the intimate fusion, the immersing of Délie in himself, and partly by his manipulation of time through the verbs. The emphasis throughout the dizain has been on the future – 'tu me feras errer', *Amoindriras, accroistras,* with *descendis* in the past. Here in line 8 we have the positive assertion of *fus, es & seras,* bringing together all four allusions by means of this time – topos. By the use of these cosmic and Classical allusions Scève widens tremendously the scope of the pleasure–pain antithesis so that it fills his whole universe and is seen in psychological and spatial terms.

Finally, there is the multivalence of the light/darkness theme: Délie as the goddess of the moon (dizain 59), not because the moon is fickle (contrast Rabelais, *Tiers Livre,* Ch. 32) but because

> ...ie te cele en ce surnom louable,
> Pource qu'en moy tu luys la nuict obscure.

Sometimes there is a contrast between external light and inner darkness, but this inner darkness is often caused rather than illuminated by Délie; sometimes there is an analysis of the alternating states of light and darkness that Délie induces within him. The way in which Scève has used the various allusions and parallels is traditional, and their success depends on the reader's ability to call to mind the associations around the particular figure or goddess. The structure of the cycle as a whole forms a vast backcloth on which Scève interweaves themes, much as the Roman Augustan poets did, and conjures up the mythological allusions as well as the echoes of previous poets whether Roman or petrarchist.

# 8

## PASSION AND LINGUISTIC CONTROL

The duality of love represented by the figure of Délie – the chaste and the carnal – is implicit in the poet's attitude towards her. In one sense we never see or feel Délie in Scève's poetry. What we have is an exclusive concentration on the effects of her presence upon his psychological life. These effects are expounded through the leit-motifs that are an important structural feature of the collection. In the exploitation of the far-reaching symbols from the Bible and from Ancient mythology Scève has built up a private language which we can appreciate by reading one dizain juxtaposed with another, advancing until we feel we are participating in the poet's vision of human love.

The images[1] that Scève uses stand at the point of intersection between the external and internal world; they appeal to our emotions and our imagination. They disrupt the précieux and – in the modern sense of the word – artificial pattern, moulded by petrarchist tradition, which is exemplified by so many of the dizains, where he has not in fact gone beyond the pattern into reality. Indeed when he does so, a new pattern is constructed out of the raw emotions which are part of the reality of love. This is the vivid realisation of a significant emotion and it gives an emotional shock to the reader who can feel the experience in its intensity.

Changes in mood, changes in tempo, changes within a poem or between poems from the anecdotic or narrative to the severely intellectual, suggest that the poet was not recording his

[1] I have used the word *image* in two main senses throughout this book: on the one hand a picture made of words containing no element of comparison or similitude and on the other hand all the figures in which a comparison of two terms is implied, for example, simile, metaphor in its strict sense, personification, allegory and symbol. I have classified the images in Délie according to the function of each image within the context of a particular dizain. Certain descriptive terms are used based on the relation or intersection of the image's two parts, the tenor and the vehicle, and they enable us to discuss the effect of function of the image in a work. For detailed discussion of these points, see W. Nowottny, *The Language Poets Use*, London, 1962.

love experience in any chronological way or telling a connected story. In the ambivalence of love that the poet experiences in his whole relationship with Délie there is an interconnection between passion and the control of that passion by linguistic formulation. Ian Robinson[1] has observed concerning love poetry,

Seeing passion in life, in its splendour, terror and ridiculousness, is taking love with the appropriate seriousness made possible by language and guaranteed by the great creative uses of the common language. Love poetry is in that way the possibility of glory and terror in love. The poet has done his work if he shows us the possibility of this wrath and grace in our world.

How far does Scève communicate to his reader passion and control of that passion through the use of language and in particular its allusiveness? It will be useful to take some examples from Donne before proceeding to the analysis of certain dizains of Scève.

When Donne in *The Extasie* describes the physical situation of his mistress and himself he uses a series of sharply evocative images such as,

> Our hands were firmly cimented
> With a fast balme, which thence did spring,
> Our eye-beames twisted and did thred
> Our eyes upon one double string.

He concentrates the reader's attention on the hands and eyes and makes us feel the intense physical fascination, captivation and concentration of the lovers upon each other by means of metaphors evoking visual physical pictures. But Donne goes beyond this physical picture to explore the significance of the physical and spiritual: through the accuracy and audacity of the metaphor – threading 'bobble-beads' on a double string – he is able to show us the lovers' interdependence, the close connection between body and soul in the state of ecstasy in love. As units in the argument of a poem the images are logically useful as well as sensuously accurate or pleasing. Some modern critics like Eliot assume that good images are intended to direct our attention to the quality of the experience rather than to the universal meaning. But there are, as Rosamund Tuve showed conclusively in *Elizabethan and Metaphysical Imagery* (University

---

[1] *The Survival of English*, C.U.P., 1973, p. 216.

of Chicago Press, 1947), certain crucial differences between the poetics of the sixteenth and seventeenth centuries and those of the nineteenth and twentieth. In the sixteenth century each image is thought of as having a specific purpose, this purpose being controlled by the nature of the poem and the demands of decorum and significance. In the sixteenth and seventeenth centuries we must ask of such a poem as *The Extasie* 'Does it go beyond the world of personal sensations into the world of values?' It is quite evident that for the Donne poem the answer is 'yes' and, as we shall see, the same is true of, for instance, Scève's dizain 161 on jealousy. Take another example from Donne: *Love's Growth*, in which he sets out to convey some of the concepts of the nature of love. The increase in his love for his mistress invalidates the idea that love is pure essence. There are many clear statements in the poem and images that assist the development and understanding of the ideas. We do not feel the experience of increase in love until Donne offers us the image of concentric circles of water in a pool to express the seeming paradox of increase without dissipation or change in direction,

> If, as in water stirr'd more circles be
> Produc'd by one, love such additions take,
> Those like so many spheres, but one heaven make,
> For, they are all concentric unto thee.

This is a satisfying image because although concentric circles in a pond (the vehicle of the comparison) and the increasing love (the tenor of the comparison) are far apart and not normally seen in relation to each other, the way that they are brought together is plausible, natural and appropriately assists the idea Donne wants to express:[1] multiplicity but unity. The point of the image is to make the argument clearer. Donne is using rational terms to support an emotive statement of conviction.

---

[1] Compare this to exaggerated metaphors where the two terms of comparison are not only far apart but violently wrenched together. They give a momentary shock of astonishment to the reader and then fly apart again like

> Immortal Maid, who though thou woulds't refuse
> The name of Mother, be unto my Muse
> A Father...

(See James Smith's discussion which includes this illustration, in *Shakespearian and Other Essays*, C.U.P., 1974, pp. 262–78.) Female virginity/maternity/fatherhood – a marvellous jumble which cannot convince us that the analogy has established a hitherto unseen relationship that is permanent and satisfying.

Another example will show it even more clearly: Donne's *The Broken Heart,*

> He is stark mad, who ever says,
>   That he hath been in love an hour,
> Yet not that love so soon decays,
>   But that it can ten in less space devour;
> Who will believe me, if I swear
>   That I have had the plague a year?
>   Who would not laugh at me, if I should say,
>   I saw a flash of powder burn a day?
>
> Ah, what a trifle is a heart,
>   If once into love's hands it come!
> All other griefs allow a part
>   To other griefs, and ask themselves but some;
> They come to us, but us Love draws,
> He swallows us, and never chaws:
>   By him, as by chain'd shot, whole ranks do die,
>   He is the tyrant Pike, our hearts the Fry.
>
> If 'twere not so, what did become
>   Of my heart, when I first saw thee?
> I brought a heart into the room,
>   But from the room, I carried none with me:
> If it had gone to thee, I know
> Mine would have taught thine heart to show
>   More pity unto me: but Love, alas,
>   At one first blow did shiver it as glass.
>
> Yet nothing can to nothing fall,
>   Nor any place be empty quite,
> Therefore I think my breast hath all
>   Those pieces still, though they be not unite;
> And now as broken glasses show
> A hundred lesser faces, so
>   My rags of heart can like, wish and adore,
>   But after one such love, can love no more.

Here Donne has not transformed the idea (why it is stark mad to say one has been in love an hour) into the sensation (being a flash of powder burning a whole day). Evidently the flash of powder is introduced as an analogy; it follows a clear general statement about love's power of rapid destruction. An idea we might not grasp is made clearer and more intelligible by being put in an analogical relation with another idea we probably will grasp,

> Who would not laugh at me, if I should say
> I saw a flash of powder burn a day?

The familiarity and simplicity of this concrete situation makes the idea more intelligible. Similarly the image of his heart as glass is not due to free association but to Donne's conviction that shattered pieces of glass are a cogent analogy for experience. The fragility of glass, its sudden shattering, conveys the overwhelming experience that the blow of love is. Images perform a role exactly like that traditionally and ordinarily performed by metaphor or simile. Images must assist the argument of the poem, must bring out the full significance of a situation, must heighten the emotional tension, must illustrate a concept or idea; they must assist the persuasive motive of the poem and they are astounding when they work, as they do in *The Broken Heart*. For we admire the way Donne interweaves clear general statements about love's power of destruction with images which clarify the meaning by their familiarity and concreteness. The analogies are satisfying, and help the reader to grasp the general ideas of the poem. But at this point we realise that there are general ideas in that poem of Donne's; that he is talking about Love (and his experience of it) as much as about the hidden recesses of his own feeling or the twists and turns of his own mind. At this point we can turn appropriately to Scève's poem on jealousy,

> Seul auec moy, elle auec sa partie:
> Moy en ma peine, elle en sa molle couche.
> Couuert d'ennuy ie me voultre en l'Ortie,
> Et elle nue entre ses bras se couche.
>   Hà (luy indigne) il la tient, il la touche:
> Elle le souffre: &, comme moins robuste,
> Viole amour par ce lyen iniuste,
> Que droict humain, & non diuin, à faict.
>   O saincte loy a tous, fors a moy, iuste,
> Tu me punys pour elle auoir meffaict.          (no. 161)

Scève succeeds in communicating sensuality on both sides here: Délie is in her husband's arms, naked in the luxury of a feather bed – it is almost as if the poet in his misery is torturing himself with a visualisation of the embrace; and he is simply 'en ma peine'. After this rather abstract phrase to express his torment he evokes the stinging, prickling sensation of nettles, coupling this with an almost masochistic 'ie me voultre' which suggests an enjoyment of pain. But this is only the prelude to the argument, which is that Délie's husband in touching and possessing her is in fact violating the true bond of love 'par ce lyen iniuste' which is marriage. The basis of his argument is that 'droict humain, & non diuin, à faict'. This is remarkably like Catullus (72.3–4) or Propertius (II.6.41–2; or III.20) who regard the love-relationship as creating mutual obligation for both parties; so if one or other of the parties commits a wrong against this love-bond it is as if he or she is breaking an oath. This is an exciting poem in its description of intense and physical jealousy, through the evocation of concrete objects like *ortie* and *molle couche*, of physical pictures and also for the argument – appropriate from the lover jealous of his lady's husband and the non-divine bond of marriage.

I am not examining the poems that are 'passionate' in order to measure Scève against, say, Propertius or Baudelaire. Obviously, there are many poems where a direct sensual contact is implied.[1] What I am doing is trying to prove that in Scève, as in other great love poets, there is intrinsically in what they create a feeling that 'love is not trivial'; love is taken seriously. In this jealousy-poem of Scève there is a feeling of destructive love which is far removed from the petrarchist love tradition.

When we speak of images with an emotive function in Scève we think of the image which seeks to present the poet's emotional situation by evoking associations and parallels from Classical literature or from the Bible, and which uses these associations to convince the reader of the truth of the experience as well as to convey that experience in all its richness. However, while the description of sense impressions or personal experiences may be the sole *raison d'être* of a twentieth-century poem, a sixteenth-century poet is almost always concerned to go beyond the mere description and to direct the reader towards a particular evaluation of the experience or the general truth of it.

Take the famous dizain 143 with the jump in its final two lines into the field of comparison:

> Le souuenir, ame de ma pensée,
> Me rauit tant en son illusif songe,
> Que n'en estant la memoyre offensée,
> Ie me nourris de si doulce mensonge.
>     Or quand l'ardeur, qui pour elle me ronge,
> Contre l'esprit sommeillant se hazarde,

[1] See for example dizains 41, 133, 136, 169, 287, 290, 309, 349, 364 and 400.

Soubdainement qu'il s'en peult donner garde,
Ou qu'il se sent de ses flammes greué,
En mon penser soubdain il te regarde,
Comme au desert son Serpent esleué.

The association evoked here is Biblical: the Israelites have sinned against God and are punished by a plague of serpents. Moses intercedes on their behalf,

Oravitque Moyses pro populo, et locutus est Dominus ad eum: Fac serpentem aeneum, et pone eum pro signo; qui percussus aspexerit eum, vivet. Fecit ergo Moyses serpentem aeneum, et posuit eum pro signo; quem cum percussi aspicerent, sanabantur.
*(Liber Numeri,* cap. 21.8–9)

The episode was taken as typological in the Middle Ages and the Renaissance in view of Christ's explicit mention of it in the Gospel,

Et sicut Moyses exaltavit *serpentem in deserto,* ita exaltari oportet Filium hominis; ut omnis, qui credit in ipsum, non pereat, sed habeat vitam aeternam. *(Evangelium Secundum Joannem,* cap. 3.14–15, the italics are mine)

in connection with his own forthcoming crucifixion. The Brazen Serpent often figured in illustrated versions of the Bible such as Holbein's *Icones,* reprinted in Lyon in 1538, or 'potted versions' of the Bible, such as the *Figures du Vieux Testament* of Charles Fontaine or the *Quadrins historiques de la Bible* of Claude Paradin. Usually the serpent was shown on a cross and this enhanced the typological aspect.

But what is interesting here is the way Scève uses this image without any specifically Christian sense. The redemption, the elevation of Christ on the cross, the sin and blasphemy of the Israelites are all forgotten. Délie (in a purely human, non-religious sense) has taken over completely the role of the serpent-on-a-pole. Scève, very characteristically and boldly, has taken from the Bible an associative image and used it in the way he uses images taken from Classical literature. The poem is an investigation of the workings of the poet's memory; an evaluation of the role played in his mental and psychological life by the memory of Délie and the relationship between the memory and his other faculties. Lines 1–4: memory is the basis of his mental activity, it has almost become fused with *pensée* – the seat of his intellectual faculties – and wraps him in a soothing world of illusion. (*Illusif* in line 2 has the active meaning of 'illusion-creating'.) He is content to live in this dream-world, although he knows that it is an illusion, and his memory allows itself to be drawn into a purely emotional state. Lines 5–6: this memory of Délie, however, awakens his physical desire for her, which breaks into the soft world of dreams with a harshness suggested by the phrase 'l'ardeur qui pour elle me ronge'. The forces of passion and desire, stimulated by his affective memory, attack the *esprit sommeillant*. Lines 7–8 state how the alarm is given to his mind – with *greué* meaning *blessé* or *brûlé*. A counter-attack is made by the *esprit* against this physical, even sexual *dérèglement des sens*, the only cure for it being the appearance of Délie in his mind. The sudden emergence of the Brazen Serpent image brings in a whole range of associations – the healing, curing (Délie = Diana = Artemis, goddess of healing here?) effect of the Serpent *in deserto* and the fact that both the original wound and the healing, in the Biblical myth and in the poet's experience, are associated with serpents. The paradox inherent in the Biblical story – to cure the bite of serpents a serpent is needed – expresses an essential paradox of love. Thinking of the person you love creates the disturbance, and yet cure and order can only work through thinking of her (or him). The strong visual impression of the serpent erect and idol-like suggests the position that Délie occupies in his mind; once he gazes on her, the disturbance caused by his affective memory is calmed, and the dizain ends on a fixed static and contemplative note. Both the jump to another field of expression and the static gaze with which the dizain ends are hints that the movement in the content and structure of the poem is not circular but vertical; the movement undergoes a flash of dislocation at the end which seizes and transfixes it so that in a very concrete image there is also a certain kind of abstraction. The two planes interact so that at the same time the very concrete suggestions around serpents and the very abstract *mon esprit/mon penser* intensify each other in a warring, almost metaphysical way. Many images have the same kind of movement: for instance, the first dizain with its last line – 'Constituée Idole de ma vie' where again the immobility and the idol-like position are significant. Or no. 30 where both the *Serpent blessé* and the physical curing/non-curing are present in the last two lines,

Car, se sentant quasi Serpent blessé,
Rien ne le peult, non Dorion, guerir.[1]

Or dizain 224 where Scève calls up in a final image other associations surrounding the episode of the Israelites in Egypt. He contrasts the joyful renewal of life in Spring with the torturing renewal of his own suffering. The last three lines expand and reinforce the description of his own torment and give the result,

Ou le meurdrier m'a meurdry, & noircy
Le Cœur si fort, que playe Egyptienne,
Et tout tourment me rend plus endurcy.

The word *playe* here may have the two senses – the physical *blessure* and the moral plague – the specific allusion being to the plagues of Egypt. The analogy is between the way increased suffering hardens his heart and the way Pharaoh (*Exodus*, 7, 8, 9 and 10) hardened his heart after each successive plague.

But we shall look in detail at another dizain which has similar Biblical associations and is also concerned with the sheer physical force of love: dizain 372.

Tu m'es le Cedre encontre le venin
De ce Serpent en moy continuel,
Comme ton œil cruellement benin
Me viuifie au feu perpetuel,
Alors qu'Amour par effect mutuel
T'ouure la bouche, & en tire a voix plaine
Celle doulceur celestement humaine,
Qui m'est souuent peu moins, que rigoureuse,
Dont spire (ô Dieux) trop plus suaue alaine,
Que n'est Zephire en l'Arabie heureuse.

The poem starts off with two rich lines: the cedar being to the poet the balm against a serpent. *Cedrus* was the cedar or juniper tree and one may recall Vergil, *Georg.*, 3.414.

Disce et odoratam stabulis accendere cedrum
galbaneoque agitare graviis nidore chelydros.

where he urges the driving out of snakes by burning fragrant cedar wood, *juniperus oxycedrus*. Furthermore, in *Aen.*, VII.10–14 Vergil pictures Circe spinning to the fragrance of burning cedar wood,

[1] For a full discussion around *Dorion* – some herb which cured wounded serpents – see I. D. McFarlane, *FS*, XIII, 1959, pp. 99–111.

proxima Circaeae raduntur litora terrae,
diues inaccessos ubi Solis filia lucos
adsiduo resonat cantu, tectisque superbis
*urit odoratam nocturna in lumina cedrum*
arguto tenuis percurrens pectine telas.

The pun worked by Scève in *venin* for poison suggests *Venus* perhaps and the word *continuel* closes the two lines on a static, intensely anguished situation. The serpent has obvious sexual connotations, as well as, for Christian Europe, associations of temptation. Whereas dizain 143 was an investigation of the workings of the poet's memory and the relationship between his memory and his other faculties, this dizain provides another sidelight on what is basically the same situation – the perpetual torment that the poet undergoes in his love for Délie. Line 5 in the earlier dizain 'l'ardeur qui pour elle me ronge' is the starting point in the later dizain, but this time condensed and suggestive: she has become the balm, while within the poet there is the poison of sexual desire symbolised by the serpent. Whereas in the earlier dizain the only cure for this *dérèglement des sens* was to think intensely but not in a sexual way on Délie 'en mon penser', this time she is a cedar to his sexual desires and lust. Saulnier (op. cit., vol. I, p. 282) adds another association to the cedar–serpent image – 'on croyait aussi, en effet que le cèdre était funeste à l'homme'. And he cites a phrase from Du Perron's *Oraison Funèbre* on Ronsard: 'il conserve ceux qui sont morts et fait mourir ceux qui sont vivants'. In other words, it is perhaps akin to the power of the serpent – both tempter and redeemer – and thus contains and announces the ambivalence of Délie's effect which is analysed in this dizain. Note the way *continuel, perpetuel, mutuel* figure in the rhyming scheme, the way abstract and concrete are fused together – *cruellement benin, celestement humaine* and the way the whole poem is opened up through the allusions of the last few lines. The poem is concerned with the good effects that Délie has on his sexual desire and he now sings of 'celle doulceur humaine' which emanates from her breath and presence. The mysterious smell that emanates from women has always stirred poets and is conveyed here by *Arabie heureuse – Arabia felix –* which has associations with perfumes and riches and the softness of the Zephyrs.[1]

---

[1] The three-fold division of Arabia expounded by the Ancient geographers was well known to the sixteenth-century reader. We find for example in

But all these are surpassed by the power of Délie herself, and the ecstasy the poet feels in her presence. The precise qualities of softness that the poet breathes are certainly conveyed by the image of the last two lines but there is in addition implicit in the argument of the poem an evaluation of Délie herself and the constant desire of the poet.

Let us now look at another poem – no. 77 – where the unity lies in the complete identification of the poet himself with Prometheus. For Scève the Titan does not represent heroic stature but the suffering that he feels inside himself, so that there is an immediacy and a directness of torture conveyed by the long period, the rhyme schemes, the emphasis on certain recurring words, the antithesis and the repetition of the pattern:

> Au Caucasus de mon souffrir lyé
> Dedans l'Enfer de ma peine eternelle,
> Ce grand desir de mon bien oblyé,
> Comme l'Aultour de ma mort immortelle,
> Ronge l'esprit par vne fureur telle,
> Que consommé d'vn si ardent poursuyure,
> Espoir le fait, non pour mon bien, reuiure:
> Mais pour au mal renaistre incessamment,
> Affin qu'en moy ce mien malheureux viure
> Prometheus tourmente innocemment.

The mention of Mount Caucasus evokes a harsh, inhospitable and terrifying region. The description and epithets attached to it in Ravisius Textor's *Epithetorum opus*[1] are:

mons est Scythiae altissimus et multis scopulis frequens. Herodius ait altissimum montium. Riget perpetuis nivibus. Abundat arboribus, herbis, veneficiis et vulturibus. Horrens. Inhospitalis. ingens. nivalis. frigidus. asper.

Moreover the mountain was the scene of Prometheus' punishment, where chained to a rock he suffered the perpetual torture of having his liver devoured each day by a bird of prey only to have it grow again by night.[2] These associations of remote

---

Gregorius Reischius' *Margarita philosophica* (ed. Basle, 1535, p. 601) this description, 'Arabia triplex: videlicet Arabia deserta, Arabia petrea et Arabia felix unde thus venit et ob id thurifera dicitur.' Estienne and Torrentinus include these descriptions in their dictionaries. *Arabia felix* would conjure up a land rich in perfume and the powerful associations of beauty, softness of the zephyrs and sweetness are the climax in the poet's intention of persuading the reader.

[1] Basel, 1555, *sub Caucasus.*

[2] Hesiod, *Theogony*, 521; *Works and Days*, 47; Hyginus, *Poet. Astr.*, II.15.

desolation and heroic torment strengthen the force of the 'mon souffrir' of the first line and the idea of suffering is carried further by the associations of Hell and the punishment and torments of men – 'Dedans l'Enfer de ma peine eternelle'.[1]

Lines 3–4 make the reference to Prometheus more concrete and specific. Scève makes the bird *Aultour*, from the Latin *accipiter* meaning a hawk. Now Scève could not have had *le vaultour* in that line (as it makes one syllable too many) but he could have used *l'aigle*. According to some versions of the legend Jupiter sent an eagle to torment him, as Horace, *Carm.*, III.18.35 has it, while other versions suggest that it was a vulture. Boccaccio gives this latter interpretation thus; 'Quamobrem irati dii eum per Mercurium Caucaso alligari fecerunt, et vulturi seu aquilae iecur eius vel cor dilaniandum perpetuo dederunt',[2] and yet mentions *aquilae* without really making a choice. Could Scève be making a pun here? *Aultour* a hawk, a bird which preys usually not on mankind but on animals, *author* of my suffering? This makes the vehicle of a metaphor whose tenor is 'Ce grand desir de mon bien oblyé'. Thus the image is now complete and the torment, ever-fresh, is the parallel of the ever-increasing, ever-renewed one of the poet in his love for Délie. The extreme physical torture of Prometheus is never lost sight of: line 5 uses the word 'ronge' (a verb that Scève is fond of when physical activities are concerned; cf. line 5 dizain 143), in line 6 'consommé', in line 7 'reuiure', in line 8 'pour au mal renaistre incessamment'; lines 9 and 10 describe the poet's torment using still the metaphor of Prometheus who is finally named explicitly. The last line, 'Prometheus tourmente innocemment', with its apparently mild adverb *innocemment*, is at once harsh and wild. For Scève's experience is made to be seen as much worse than Prometheus' and the torture is itself given a poignant quality when seen as a playful, innocent, almost trivial game by Prometheus himself. Note too the way *innocemment* couples with *incessamment* in the rhyming scheme, so suggesting that hell is always present in the love vision of Scève. It is possible that the vulture associations add a connotation of sensuality, of the sexual

---

[1] This is, of course, skirting the medieval representation of perpetual devourings in the Christian Hell, where the 'enfer ou dampnez sont boullus' (Villon) is so brilliantly evoked in the frescoes of the Last Judgement by Taddeo di Bartolo in the cathedral of San Gimignano.

[2] *De gen.*, op. cit., 4.44, cf. Estienne who follows him closely.

torment of frustrated love, to the poet's description since the vulture was a well-known symbol of concupiscence. Tervarent (*Attributs et Symboles...*). gives under *Vautour* the vulture as a symbol of sensuality and Valeriano (*Hieroglyphica*, Bk 18) gives vulture under the heading of *concupiscentia*. Indeed Scève may be remembering a famous piece in Lucretius (*De rerum natura*, Bk 3, lines 984–94) where the link is made between the torments of Tityas and earthly love,

> nec Tityon volucres ineunt Acherunte iacentem
> nec quod sub magno scrutentur pectore quicquam
> perpetuam aetatem possunt reperire profecto.
> quamlibet immani proiectu corporis exstet,
> qui non sola novem dispessis iugera membris
> obtineat, sed qui terrai totius orbem,
> non tamen aeternum poterit perferre dolorem
> nec praebere cibum proprio de corpore semper.
> *sed Tityos nobis hic est, in amorem iacentem*
> *quem volucres lacerant atque exest anxius angor*
> *aut alia quavis scindunt cuppedine curae.*        (my italics)

The vulture devouring the liver of Prometheus is therefore an apt symbol of the torments of love. It is possible, too, to link the Promethean image here to the second dizain, whose last line is 'Et de moy seul fatale Pandora', since Prometheus was the creator of Pandora and hence the two dizains may have come from the same textual context. There is in this dizain 77 something almost clinical in the study of a body subject to a pathological condition. The continual regeneration, the inevitable eating away of the liver again and the suffering that does not end with death are all brought out strongly by the vocabulary. The physical place – the harsh Mount Caucasus – is linked with the notion of death, and the abstract and concrete are tied together in a powerful poem.

Where Scève feels frustrated and incapable of release by Délie, he either resorts to bare, often banal, petrarchist psychology or else attempts to bring into a pattern the disparate elements in his body and soul. Take dizain 118 as an example:

> Le hault penser de mes frailes desirs
> Me chatouilloit a plus haulte entreprise,
> Me desrobant moymesme a mes plaisirs,
> Pour destourner la memoire surprise
> Du bien, auquel l'Ame demoura prise:
> Dont, comme neige au Soleil, ie me fondz

Et mes souspirs dès leurs centres profondz
Si haultement esleuent leurs voix viues,
Que plongeant l'Ame, et la memoire au fondz,
Tout ie m'abysme aux oblieuses riues.

The poem is again concerned with the relationship between his
*memoire* and the rest of his passions and his mental faculties. It
is in the last two lines that the poem comes alive; it evokes the
river Lethe in the underworld which was traditionally regarded
as the river of oblivion. Vergil (*Aen.*, 6.713–15) says,

> 'animae, quibus altera fato
> corpora debentur, Lethaei ad fluminis undam
> securos latices et longa oblivia potant...

In other words, Lethe was the river through which, purified
by purgatory, souls passed before they were finally ready for
reincarnation. Boccaccio (op. cit., Bk 3, Ch. 17) comments on
the river,

> et ex illo dicit animas mundas et caelo dignas potare ut obliviscantur
> praeteritorum malorum quorum memoria felicitati perpetuae praes-
> taret impedimentum.

Petrarch in his poem *Pasco la mente d'un sí nobil cibo* (*Rime*, 193)
attaches the emotion of joy to the waters of oblivion and Scève
in dizain no. 147 uses the allusion with this same significance,

> Le doulx sommeil de ses tacites eaux
> D'obliuion m'arousa tellement.

But in the dizain under discussion, the associations seem to
be quite different. The poem starts with the statement that his
*frailes desirs* spur him on to greater enterprise and thus distract
his memory from the *bien* to which his *Ame* was attached. The
significance of this *entreprise* seems to be clear: it is driving him
towards a physical and emotional goal rather than a spiritual
one; the spiritual one is represented by the *bien* to which the soul
is attached. Thus the process described is that of his memory
and soul being drawn from their proper and serene states by
*desirs*, namely physical appetite. In line 6 the result is made clear
by the simile 'Dont, comme neige au Soleil, ie me fondz', where
the 'melting' process obviously betokens a dissolving into a purely
emotional state. The reaction or end-result as described in lines

7–10 is that of 'sinking' into the 'oblieuses riues' – which is surely
the climax of the abandonment of the *bien* which he mentioned
in line 5. Thus, far from referring merely to an ecstasy of
oblivion, this last allusion, put in the context of the argument,
is a clear pointer to a value judgement.[1] It invites the reader to
go beyond the understanding of the experience to share in the
author's evaluation of it, and the moral rejection of this oblivion
is founded on the terms and statements leading up to it in the
poem.

There are images which are contained in a single name taken
from mythology, like Argus, for example. Dizain 290 uses the
name in the last line,

> Comme gelée au monter du Soleil,
> Mon ame sens, qui toute se distille
> Au rencontrer le rayant de son œil,
> Dont le pouoir me rend si fort debile,
> Que ie deuien tous les iours moins habile
> A resister aux amoureux traictz d'elle.
> En la voyant ainsi plaisamment belle,
> Et le plaisir croissant de bien en mieulx
> Par vne ioye incongneue, & nouelle,
> Que ne suis donc plus, qu'Argus, tout en yeulx?

Line 10 calls up in the reader's mind the associations of the
legend as told by Ovid (*Met.*, 1.583–723): the jealousy of Juno
when she sees the intoxication of Jupiter for Io; the transformation of Io into a white heifer and Juno's appointment of Argus,
endowed with his hundred eyes, to guard her; his failure to do
so because the bewitching music of Mercury makes him fall
asleep; he is killed by Mercury and Juno sets his eyes in a pattern
on the peacock's tail.[2] But when we look at the context of this

---

[1] Saulnier (op. cit., vol. I, p. 243) analyses dizains with the same movement and
battle of the poet's faculties. He also points out that words like *bien* and *mieux*
are often ambivalent in Scève: 'Ce bien supérieur, c'est celui qu'il n'a pas.'
And far from being consistently used to indicate a superior or spiritual aim,
they often mean simply the attainment of a desired physical goal.
   There is an example in Bembo, *Gli Asolani*, Venice, 1505, p. 26, of the
undesirable effects of the river Lethe, 'che come se essi havessono la memoria
tuffata, d'ogni altra cosa fatti dimentichati, salvo che del lor male'. The context
is particularly interesting and illuminates the allusion in Scève. Bembo is
describing the nature of love – the passion which disturbs the mind and
invades all parts of the person who is in love. From the first desire a thousand
are born and the delight 'gli lascia ebbri del suo veleno'. It is at this point that
he introduces the allusion to Lethe.

[2] Ravisius Textor, *Epithetorum opus*, Basel, 1555, sums up these associations under
the rubric *Argus: Custos virginis, vigil, stellatus, centoculus.*

allusion the argument into which it fits is concerned with the poet's experience in contemplating Délie. The first three lines concentrate on conveying his sensation on encountering her, in terms of frost melting in the sun – 'Comme gelée au monter du Soleil' (cf. the last two lines of dizain 223 – 'Ie me deffis a si belle rencontre,/Comme rousée au leuer du Soleil'). This suggests emotional warmth which penetrates into his innermost being so that his *Ame* 'toute se distille'. The result is his increasing weakness and failure to resist her; counter-balancing this is his mounting pleasure described in lines 7–9. The associations around the legend of Argus are irrelevant except for the faculty of sight; the allusion immediately recalls Propertius' use of Argus in his famous elegy on Cynthia asleep at night and the poet watching her (*El.*, 1.3).

> sed sic intentis haerebam fixus ocellis,
> Argus ut ignotis cornibus Inachidos.          (lines 19–20)

The same sensations that Argus had, gazing in wonder on the strange (note *ignotis* here) form of the maid–heifer, the poet feels as he watches Cynthia with fascination. And again, we feel that Scève had in mind the way that Propertius used an allusion to fix precisely a sensation. The indirect note of envy in the dizain is not stressed. We are allowed to feel the experience at its fullest.

Another Classical image with a similar function is more explicit and the poem is straightforward. In dizain 443 Scève is concerned with analysing his reactions and sensations in Délie's presence.

> Combien qu'a nous soit cause le Soleil
> Que toute chose est tresclerement veue:
> Ce neantmoins pour trop arrester l'œil
> En sa splendeur lon pert soubdain la veue.
>  Mon ame ainsi de son obiect pourueue
> De tous mes sens me rend abandonné,
> Comme si lors en moy tout estonné
> Semeles fust en presence rauie
> De son Amant de fouldre enuironné,
> Qui luy ostast par ses esclairs la vie.

The outline of the argument, the ideas and indeed the illustration itself are taken from Speroni's Dialogue on love.[1] In the first

---

[1] For a full discussion of Scève's use of Speroni see McFarlane's ed., p. 27 and Appendix A.

four lines Scève takes the familiar experience of a person completely dazzled by the splendour of the sun and then narrows it down to his personal experience in love. In order to make this point he has recourse to a mythological comparison. All other aspects of the legend and the background are unimportant – Semele's prayer at Juno's instigation that Jupiter would appear to her in all his glory and the miraculous gestation and birth of Dionysus – and we are concerned exclusively with the moment of Semele's encounter with Jupiter, the thunder-clap, the intense heat and light, and the death-blow dealt to her by this epiphany. The way in which Scève goes beyond the experience to guide the reader in an evaluation of the ex-perience is conveyed partly by the explicit statements in the first four lines. The sun is a splendid and essential thing, but

> Ce neantmoins pour trop arrester l'œil
> En sa splendeur lon pert soubdain la veue.

It is partly conveyed too by the fact that Semele lost her life. The moral judgement is thus directed not against the lascivious and flirtatious Jupiter or the jealous and vindictive Juno, as it would have been if the associations of the rest of the legend were introduced here. It is rather against the effect of love upon the lover in general.

Let us now look at the treatment of death in dizain 378.

> La blanche Aurore a peine finyssoit
> D'orner son chef d'or luisant, & de roses,
> Quand mon Esprit, qui du tout perissoit
> Au fons confus de tant diuerses choses,
> Reuint a moy soubz les Custodes closes
> Pour plus me rendre enuers Mort inuincible.
>   Mais toy, qui as (toy seule) le possible
> De donner heur a ma fatalité,
> Tu me seras la Myrrhe incorruptible
> Contre les vers de ma mortalité.

This is a peculiarly difficult poem in that line 6 has given rise to two different interpretations. Odette de Mourgues gave this version in her book (op. cit., p. 19): 'the shock provoked by the sudden passage from nocturnal numbness and dreamy uneasi-ness to a state of lucid consciousness brings to the lover's mind the problem of how to transcend death. Awakening thus takes the form of a metaphysical crisis.' This version seems to depend on taking *plus* of line 6 in a negative sense meaning *ne...plus*.

This would be an unusual use of *plus*, although McFarlane claims it to be the same sense in dizain 17 line 10 (op. cit., p. 466) 'Car ferme amour sans eulx est plus que nue.' Neither Brunot (*Histoire de la langue française*, t. 2, Paris, 1906) nor Gougenheim (*Grammaire de la langue française du XVIe siècle*, Lyon, 1951) give any examples of *plus* being used for *ne...plus*. The interpretation is possible but rather far-fetched. McFarlane (*ibid.*) puts forward a second interpretation (although he opts for the first one) as possible: 'the poet's *Esprit*, on returning to him, makes him relatively immune from Death, but that this is nothing compared with Délie's influence for she will afford him complete protection from the worm and the canker.' I support this interpretation for a number of reasons.

If we read the poem in the context of *Délie* as a whole its meaning is perhaps partly illuminated by setting it alongside no. 79.

> L'Aulbe estaingnoit Estoilles a foison,
> Tirant le iour des regions infimes,
> Quand Apollo montant sur l'Orison
> Des montz cornuz doroit les haultes cymes.
> Lors du profond des tenebreux Abysmes,
> Ou mon penser par ses fascheux ennuyz
> Me fait souuent perçer les longues nuictz,
> Ie reuoquay a moy l'ame rauie:
> Qui, dessechant mes larmoyantz conduictz,
> Me feit cler veoir le Soleil de ma vie.

This poem, treating the same experience, does not show the same closely packed structure as no. 378. The first two lines of no. 378 set the scene of the coming of dawn in the same way as do the first four lines of 79. Lines 3–6 of 378 describe how his *Esprit* returns to him after the chaos and confusion of night, when it no longer belonged to his body. The lines

> Quand mon Esprit qui du tout perissoit
> Au fons confus de tant diverses choses,

state in less explicit form what lines 5–7 of dizain 79 had said. His state is not sleep but a trance, something between sleeping and waking, where none of the effects of either is fully present to provide him with something (it may be an awareness of himself, of his *moi* or of physical sensations which merely imply a *moi*) to grasp. The theme of the torturing length of night and the suffering it brings the poet occurs again and again in *Délie* –

e.g. no. 100 and 232 – and the relief that dawn brings is not only common in Scève but belongs also to the traditional petrarchist repertoire. Dawn seems to make the poet whole again after the disintegration of his personality in the confusion of night. Dizain 79 describes the feeling in its last three lines and there is no death here but simply an awareness of the 'Soleil de ma vie'. The poet has chosen the 'I' – the person he is acting in the poem – to give this resumption of life an active quality. 'Ie reuoquay a moy' is immediately followed by the simple petrarchistic formula – the Sun of my life. In dizain 378 it is seen as 'mon Esprit...Reuint a moy' followed by

> Pour plus me rendre enuers Mort inuincible.

With the return of his Spirit he is given a measure of invincibility against death. Even though dawn does not give him the illusion of immortality the chaos in which his faculties lay at night is restored by daylight to ordered shape; instead of being totally vulnerable to death, now at least he has the reminder of what the *moi* really is. In the last four lines of this poem the dramatic change of key at line 7 leads on to the superlative assurance that through their love he is able to conquer the concept of death. These lines suggest what every great love poet wants to suggest, that the assurance normally brought by dawn in the return of his consciousness is nothing compared to the certainty that even after death there is some immortality in love.

Now the meaning of the *Mais* in line 7 has troubled commentators as much as the *plus* in line 6. The meaning *But* has forced them into an opposition between the first six lines and the last four. It is not the meaning *But* that I read here; it is not a question of simple negation or opposition; it is that of the Latin *magis* – i.e. that of transcending 'rather' or 'but much more is' which cancels out the relative intensity of the experience in line 6 and leads on to the absolute statements of lines 7–10.[1] The first interpretation does seem to destroy the progression of the argument from the chaos of night towards the lucidity that dawn brings and interpolates a metaphysical crisis on the one line 6. It seems to me that the poet does feel more invincible against death when he is in full possession of his faculties than when he is sunk 'au fons confus de tant diverses choses' although the phrase 'plus...inuincible' may be an excessively forthright way

---

[1] Cotgrave and Huguet give many examples of *mais = magis*.

of expressing this feeling: which is why the *mais* is needed. It is worth noting the contrast in the tenses of the two verbs *perissoit* – the preceding state – and *reuint* – the decisive event that changed the state.

Furthermore we have to think of the life–death antithesis as the main statement of the last four lines. It is easy when we have decided that *Mais* is the Latin *magis* to recall Ovid's treatment of Myrrha (*Met.*, x) especially her dying prayer (lines 483–7),

> 'o siqua patetis
> numina confessis, merui nec triste recuso
> supplicium, sed ne violem vivosque superstes
> mortuaque exstinctos, ambobus pellite regnis
> mutataeque mihi vitamque necemque negate!'

Her prayer is granted by the Gods, and so she knows neither life nor death but is transformed into a tree. Whilst Scève can thus metamorphose Délie into Myrrha (forgetting totally the other associations of the legend, e.g. the incestuous aspect of love, and discarding the first half of the *vitamque necemque negate* to keep the power myrrh has of negating death) to be the *Myrrhe incorruptible* who alone can put a shape to his *fatalité*, the poet himself is treated as dead. The last two lines of the dizain are richly suggestive. The tense is future, and the comparison of Délie to myrrh is extended in the last line, where the myrrh is explicitly pitted against the *vers* and we are left with the concrete image, the actual decomposition of the lover's flesh as it is consumed by the worms. This concrete evocation is itself linked to the abstract *mortalité*: Délie enables him to transcend the idea of death – because her love makes it unimportant, and the fact of death – because their love will be immortal. And so death is metamorphosed into a completely different level and is seen to be on the level of inanimate nature – which is why the Myrrh allusion is so crucial.[1]

Throughout this chapter we have been coming to grips with allusiveness in poetry. It has meant that we were tackling allusions – where Scève was deliberately calling up associations

---

[1] The properties, partly scientific and partly legendary of myrrh would be well known to sixteenth-century readers of *Délie*. Calepinus for example has a full entry in his *Dictionary* under the rubric *Myrrha*: 'arbuscula est in Arabia praecipue nascens: cuius gutta quae sponte stilla viridis est amara. Eius virtus est: ut corpora imputribilia reddet. Fuit et Myrrha Cynarae Cypriorum regis filia: quae in arborem sui nominis fertur conversa.'

in order to negate them – by looking at the contextual linguistic formulae. This was one thing, we saw, that he was guiding the readers to perceive. Furthermore the combination of allusiveness, the command over language – of concrete and abstract connotations – made us see how Scève was fighting to say what he actually felt and thought. He was not concerned with any doctrine of love; he was not talking *about* love or immortality or death; he created these passions *within* the poems themselves. Thus the Argus, the Myrrha, the Promethean, the Lethean, the Semelian, the Brazen Serpent dizains are all 'original' precisely because Scève is saying something new, or making these allusions function in a way that seems new. Scève was making a metaphorical language work. And in so doing he makes us feel and see the world of love anew. He has moved into the field of actual experience. His omission of personal pronouns, his use of loan-words, his sparing recourse to the article, his breaking-up of a normal word-order – all give the impression of tautness and of concentration. There is at times in his use of images a warring or clashing juxtaposition which makes one think that he is fighting with language in an extremely individualistic way. There is also, among the weaker dizains, a hint that his readers can never fully understand the peculiar quality of his experience. This perhaps will be more evident in our next chapters.

# 9

## 'SIMPLE' THEMES

Although one still finds in Scève the simple attitude of a petrarchist lover, the last three chapters have explored some of the qualities in his poetry that set him far above the conventional stock-in-trade. A 'serious' approach to love poetry and a severe command of linguistic formulation are evident in his best dizains. Another aspect of his poetry – one that is regarded as vital by certain critics – comes through in a few poems; that is his interest in and indeed preoccupation with certain basic themes which have earned him the label of a 'metaphysical' poet. Themes such as the unity and duality of two lovers, the disunity of body and soul, the mortality yet immortality of love, the presence of the mistress in her absence and the subjective power of the memory were for Scève what the themes of *Le Cimetière Marin* were for Valéry: 'les plus simples et les plus constants de ma vie affective et intellectuelle'.[1] The adjective *simples* cannot be interpreted as 'simple to the reader'; for it has an intellectual connotation for both Valéry and Scève. Valéry can give in a few lines –

> Dures grenades entr'ouvertes
> Cédant à l'excès de vos grains,
> Je crois voir des fronts souverains
> Eclatés de leurs découvertes!

– a palpable mental configuration through an image which is so sensual that it seems to translate intellectual conceptions voluptuously. Valéry gives us a definition of intellectual poetry – 'composer dans une même œuvre les qualités de séduction immédiate qui sont essentielles à la poésie, avec une substance précieuse de pensée sur quoi l'esprit puisse revenir et s'arrêter quelque peu sans regret'.[2] The concentration and the density of Scève's best dizains set him, as we have seen in earlier chapters, alongside Propertius, Horace or Mallarmé; for the reader has to work simultaneously with the poet in comprehend-

---

[1] *Œuvres* (Pléiade ed.), t, I. p. 1503.    [2] Op. cit., t. I, p. 652.

ing poetry which is both voluptuous and intellectual. Scève is concerned with the analysis and significance of intensely personal experience in terms of current philosophical ideas. In the best dizains, both the syntax and the imagery communicate something about the poet's state of mind and something about his intellectualisation of that state of mind. In these, Scève shows real originality; neither the love experience depicted by the Latin Augustan poets nor that of Petrarch comes anywhere near the complexity of the love relationship as Scève conceives and presents it.

If, as Eliot once remarked, originality is simply development, then in Scève's case this means the development of all the allusiveness, all the raw philosophical materials and a firm grasp of language to form exquisite short love poems which show both emotional and intellectual strength. Brevity properly manipulated, a disruption, even harshness in the arrangement of words that contributes to their forcefulness, a lack of logical connectives, which at the risk of being obscure implies rather than explains and is a powerful element in the structure of the dizains, echo-effects of clashing vowels and consonants – all these features combine with the intellectual structure and Scève's way of expressing complexity through his blend of passion and thought.

Take for instance dizain 58, one of his best poems. It crystallises a moment in the flux of human existence:

> Quand i'apperceu au serain de ses yeulx
> L'air esclarcy de si longue tempeste,
> Ià tout empeinct au prouffit de mon mieulx,
> Comme vn vainqueur d'honnorable conqueste,
> Ie commençay a eslever la teste:
> Et lors le Lac de mes nouelles ioyes
> Restangna tout, voire dehors ses voyes
> Asses plus loing, qu'oncques ne feit iadis.
> Dont mes pensers guidez par leurs Montioyes,
> Se paonnoient tous en leur hault Paradis.

The content seems at first like an ordinary, rather banal petrarchist piece of praise for a moment of serenity amidst the darkness of love. But the treatment is entirely different. The initial metaphor is the break in the clouds of his suffering, conveyed through a vertical movement: looking up into her eyes. Her eyes are not described by an attributive adjective but by a

noun phrase 'au serain de ses yeulx'. (There are examples of
this comparison everywhere in Petrarch, as also the use of the
adjective *sereno* as a noun: for example, *Rime*, 160, line 5 'Dal
bel seren de le tranquille ciglia' or *Rime*, 264, lines 77–8 'E'l lume
de' begli occhi, che mi strugge/Soavemente al suo caldo sereno.'
It is precisely by separating the adjective *serain* into the noun
*au serain de ses yeulx* that Scève creates almost a concrete
abstraction.) The second line suggests the mood and attitude of
Délie through a landscape which is reflected in her eyes; here
are the germs of the method of suggestive analogy which
Baudelaire uses with great effect in poems like *Ciel Brouillé* and
*L'Invitation au Voyage* where the eyes of his mistress contain
the whole *paysage*. But whereas one of the dominant moods
expressed by Baudelaire through this analogy is that of an
autumnal season of 'mists and mellow fruitfulness' Scève's whole
mood is summed up in the serenity of Délie's eyes. Furthermore
the first word *Quand* prepares us for the brevity of the moment
caught by the dizain.

The first five lines are an upsurging upward movement ending
on *Ie commençay a esleuer la teste* and the calm of the first two lines
expands into the pride of victory and the vigorous impulse given
to the lover's striving towards a goal. The first is expressed in
the simile *Comme vn vainqueur d'honnorable conqueste* and the
second by means of the word *empeinct* which Huguet explains
as *poussé fortement*: Huguet cites two lines from Scève's *La
Saulsaye*,

> Jà sur le bort de la rivière empeintes
> De mort prochaine ayant les joues peintes

and Cotgrave gives the meanings as 'violently assailed, set on,
hard pressed, furiously hit or strucken'. The poet is violently
pressed towards his *mieulx* – which is allowed to remain ambiguous, as between the chaste love and the carnal appetite that
he always has for Délie.

The second half of the poem (6–10) describes the poet's
brimming joy and ecstasy, and suggests a spreading movement
which culminates in the second rise of the poem – 'Se paonnoient tous en leur hault Paradis.' The metaphor is still drawn
from nature but this time the second term of comparison is
water. Scève expresses his joy in terms of the overflowing of a
lake far beyond its normal size – 'le Lac de mes nouelles

ioyes/Restangna tout.' McFarlane has explained *restangna*: 'the sense requires the expression of exuberance' (*voire dehors ses voyes*). We have, almost certainly, another Latinism: *restagnare* means 'to overflow'.[1] He has thus rightly rejected the meaning 'stagnating, becoming stagnant, reverting to marshland' which Parturier and Saulnier both adopted for *Restangna*. But the context of the Tasso quotation he gives – in order to show how it was an Italian Latinism – is not very convincing, dealing as it does with Death and the nauseous sound of corpses on the water. There are two examples from Latin literature which have the right meaning but the context is also unlikely: Ovid, *Met.*, 11.364 and Lucan, 4.89. In the Lucan passage the meaning is appropriate, *alto restagnant flumina uallo* = the rivers formed pools within the high rampart; we can see the rivers becoming still and transforming themselves into calm waters, but the context is that of civil war. The Ovid passage,

> iuncta palus huic est densis obsessa salictis,
> quam restagnantis fecit maris unda paludem...

concerns a wolf emerging from this marsh, mad with rage and hunger, so it is not a good context either. I wonder whether *Restangna* is not like *deuaincre* of dizain 14 (discussed in Ch. 8) where through the use of one word Scève can go back allusively to the Graeco-Roman tradition? For by choosing *restagnare* he could make the reader remember certain poems by Augustan poets and particularly a very famous poem on Sirmio by Catullus. Poem 31 is a praise of the poet's home on Sirmio: the context is exactly what is needed for Scève's dizain: over-brimming joy and a strong emotion of happiness; high cliffs descending to the transparently blue water; the exquisite colour of the land and sky round about. Let us read a little of the poem,

> Paene insularum, Sirmio, insularumque
> ocelle, quascumque in liquentibus stagnis
> marique uasto fert uterque Neptunus,
> quam te libenter quamque laetus inuiso,
> uix mi ipse credens Thuniam atque Bithunos
> liquisse campos et uidere te in tuto.

Catullus makes a sharp distinction between *mare* and *stagnis*:

---

[1] P. 388 of his edition and see his article, 'Notes on Maurice Scève's *Délie*', *FS*, 1959, pp. 99–112.

the one being the sea, the other a lake. In the phrase *in liquentibus stagnis* he conjures up for his readers the transparency of this brimming water, which has stopped flowing. Ellis in his *Commentary on Catullus* says: '*liquentibus* defines *stagnis*, which in itself might be applied to any piece of water not river or sea, as sheets of flowing and therefore more or less clear, water. The two ideas seem to pass into each other, "liquid" and "clear"; Catullus has *liquidas undas* LXIV.2 "flowing waves"; Vergil, *liquentia flumina, campi liquentes,* "clear flowing rivers", "plains of clear flowing water": it seems to me certain that neither *liquens* nor *liquidus* ever mean simply "clear", but always convey the idea of fluidity in some form.'[1] This idea of fluidity fits exactly the mood of expansion and liberation of Scève's joy: calm water seen at the moment when it has stopped overflowing and just ripples, far outside its normal ways, in pools of blue water. Scève seems to combine both the movement of overflow in *Asses plus loing, qu'oncques ne feit iadis* with the feeling of calm and a visual suggestion from perhaps the half-remembered poem of Catullus.

In the last two lines the poet turns from the analysis of his sensations and emotions to the reaction in his mind, using another metaphor: *guidez par leurs Montioyes. Montioye,* although capable of diverse meanings in the sixteenth century, here clearly means a signpost or 'heape of stones layd neere a highway for the better discerning thereof' (Cotgrave). The context most frequently connected with this word is that of pilgrims being guided by 'heapes of stones' on their way to a shrine, and that upward movement is confirmed by the *Paradis* of the last line. The connotations of pilgrim and the word *Paradis* might lead one to interpret this poem within a Christian framework. But it is more likely that Scève is using the images in the same way as he used the Brazen Serpent in dizain 143 (see pp. 146–8 above) in a purely human secularised way, while retaining something of the emotive appeal of the religious association. The battle-cry of the French, *Montjoie Saint-Denis,* is perhaps a secondary suggestion, for the hill of Saint-Denis was regarded as a *lieu de joie* because the Saint received the reward for his martyrdom there. The verb *se paonnoient,* coming after such strong movement in the images previous to it, takes on concrete

[1] *A Commentary on Catullus* by Robinson Ellis, Oxford, 1889, p. 110.

force and 'wags' (as Cotgrave says in his entry for the word) 'struts it like a peacock'. In other words it suggests not only the free and proud movement of the poet's thoughts but also the 'opening out' or expansion in the realm of thought which like the sudden spreading of the peacock's brilliant tail is a parallel to the expansion in the realm of feeling expressed by the metaphor of the lake of joy, linked perhaps by the notion of brightness and blueness. One may again recall Baudelaire who in *Sed non Satiata* uses the modern form of the verb *se pavaner* in a similarly figurative sense, but one in which the movement conjured up is more languorous than vigorous, conveying the peacock's walk rather than its display. Everything in the Scève poem is unified and its mood and vertical movement together with the very judicious allusiveness make it stand out from his other poems of joy, especially as the analysis of his faculties has ended on thoughts which are themselves given the powerful imagery of the climax.

The commonplace philosophical idea of the lover being dead in himself and living in his mistress is the basis of many of Scève's intellectualised and rather abstract poems, for instance dizain 144. Here the opening lines fail to evoke for the reader the reality of the experience that Scève is concerned with:

> En toy ie vis, ou que tu sois absente:
> En moy ie meurs, ou que soye present.
> Tant loing sois tu, tousiours tu es presente:
> Pour pres que soye, encores suis ie absent.

But sometimes the argument is interwoven with the physical description – the analysis of the separation of body and soul, the lover's alienation from himself caused by the contemplation and complete conversion of self into Délie. The poet's loss of personal identity and re-living in Délie is the basis of dizain 100, where the poem starts not with an abstract notion but with a concrete experience which individualises the intellectual ideas,

> L'oysiueté des delicates plumes,
> Lict coustumier, non point de mon repos,
> Mais du trauail, ou mon feu tu allumes,
> Souuentesfois, oultre heure, & sans propos
> Entre ses drapz me detient indispos,
> Tant elle m'à pour son foible ennemy.
>    Là mon esprit son corps laisse endormy
> Tout transformé en image de Mort,

Pour te monstrer, que lors homme a demy,
Vers toy suis vif, & vers moy ie suis mort.

There is not the same density in this poem as in his more
concentrated dizains because there is more explanation here,
and yet, the disunity of body and soul is captured by the last line
(possibly a translation from Serafino's line *Che in me morto son
io, e in te son vivo*) which by the repetition of *vers* and *vif* and *mort*
contrasting with *toy* and *moy* contributes to the forcefulness of the
whole poem. But the way it starts with an evocative image –
calling to mind a marvellously delicate, soft, feather bed, con-
juring up sensual enjoyment before obliterating it, is a feature of
all good poetry: the expectation of something is aroused and then
cancelled. Indeed Scève proceeds to negate the suggestions of
peace and luxury already in lines 2–3. Setting the scene of his
nocturnal suffering in such physically pleasant conditions serves
to heighten the awareness of the torment which is even tied
down further to concrete reality in line 5. *L'oziose piume* occurs
in a Petrarchan sonnet (*Rime*, 7, 1 'La gola e'l sonno e l'oziose
piume') and is another example of a phrase that having caught
Scève's imagination is taken up and transformed into the line
*L'oysiueté des delicates plumes*.[1] The shift from the adjective *oziose*
to the noun of *oysiueté* means that the feeling of laziness
is separated from the feathers and given much more value.
Furthermore, the sonnet was concerned with a totally different
theme, since Petrarch was stressing the moral view of luxury,
greed and laziness which dispel active virtue, and this is placed
in the context of an exhortation to a friend. There may be
echoes of the theme of nocturnal insomnia in the Augustan
poets in this line, particularly Tibullus, 1.2.77–8.

Nam neque tunc plumae nec stragula picta soporem
nec sonitus placidae ducere posset aquae.

(Cf. Propertius, 3.7.50; Martial, 12.17.7 and Juvenal, 10.362 –
although these last two poets were referring merely to the luxury
of feather pillows.) Thus, the image of the first line may be an

[1] L. Hebreu, in *Philosophie d'Amour traduicte d'Italien en Françoys, par le Seigneur
du Parc Champenois*, Lyon, 1551 has at the end of the work an Appendix in
the form of a *Dictionnaire pour exposition des plus difficiles mots*. This interesting
commentary on the word *delicat* is to be found there: 'Délicatesses: douillet-
teries et accoquineries à quelques voluptés superflues, et non dignes d'un
homme robuste et ferme.'

amalgam of Petrarch's phrase and the theme of insomnia which is closer to the Latin poets.[1]

There is however a second reference to Petrarch, to the sonnet 'O cameretta, che già fusti un porto' (*Rime*, 234): the room which used to be a refuge of peace and solitude after the day's torments is now a perpetual torment, since he is afraid to be alone with his thoughts. This is much closer to the theme of the dizain in *Délie*. It is as if Scève remembers an isolated phrase from one poem, totally detached from its context, while having in mind the whole development of another sonnet whose spirit is close to his own treatment of the theme.

The strong concrete impressions of the initial line are echoed further in the poem by visual images of the poet *entre ses drapz* and then *transformé en image de Mort* – which suggests an elongated, lifeless and pallid corpse. This emphasis on the physical state of the poet, in the luxuriously soft bed, serves to prove emotionally to Délie that he is dead to himself. So the commonplace philosophical idea in this dizain is given new life through an intensely physical description.

In the poem just analysed, where Scève is investigating or at least expressing his experience of love, the style, images and psychological problems are not in such concentrated terms as we have seen them in for instance dizain 143 (the serpent image, see above, pp. 146–8) and dizain 129 (the hare image).

---

[1] See too Jean Lemaire de Belges, *Les Epistres de l'Amant vert*, ed. J. Frappier, Paris, 1948, in the second *Contes de Cupido et d'Atropos* where we find Cupido asleep

> Sur un mol lict de plumettes desliees...

with *volupté* being a niece of Venus on point of death. The end of the poem is also relevant,

> Dire qu'amour est mort dure et cruelle
> Quand pour un peu de douceur sensuelle
> On est ainsi de mortel mal atteint.

Or Gilles Corrozet, *Les blasons domestiques*, p16v°, Paris, 1539, the blason on the bed where the first few lines describe the softness and peace of a bed:

> Lict delicat, doulx & mollet
> Lict de duvet si tresdouillet
> Lict de plume tant bonne & fine...

Or Sannazaro, *Eleg.*, 1.1.61–

> quidve torus prodest pluma spectandus et ostro,
>   si non est gremio cara puella meo?
> si trahere infelix inter suspiria noctem
>   cogor et aeternos esse negare deos?

In both the latter poems the sudden jump to metaphor at the end leaves unexplained the whole field of associations on which the poem's meaning depends. The reader is forced to find for himself the right body of allusions to bring to the poem. Now this could work towards obscurity in the hands of lesser poets, but once the associations are grasped, the actual point of the comparison is simple. It does not rely on the reader's intellectual ingenuity in being able to tease out the likenesses between the hare and Délie. This is the dizain (129):

> Le iour passé de ta doulce presence
> Fust vn serain en hyuer tenebreux,
> Qui faict prouuer la nuict de ton absence
> A l'œil de l'ame estre vn temps plus vmbreux,
> Que n'est au Corps ce mien viure encombreux,
> Qui maintenant me fait de soy refus.
>   Car dès le poinct, que partie tu fus,
> Comme le Lieure accroppy en son giste,
> Ie tendz l'oreille, oyant vn bruyt confus,
> Tout esperdu aux tenebres d'Egypte.

The simplicity of the hare image, its exact position at the end of the poem and the fact that it is left unexplained contrast sharply, for example, with Donne's technique. For the reader *has* to know the nature of the hare as it was then understood before it can be seen as a good analogy for the poet himself. Erasmus quotes the phrase 'lepore timidior' in *De duplici copia*; Valeriano discusses at length the nervous nature of the hare, and Pierre L'Anglois says,

Par le Lievre, qui dort les yeux ouverts, les Ægyptiens signifioient le soing vigilent de celuy qui eust semblé estre bien endormy...Ils le mettoient aussi pour signe de l'ouy...Il est dedié à Venus...Il remarque aussi la peur...Par le Lievre qui se retire au giste, ont depeint l'homme solitaire, & qui se retire des compagnies, aussi n'y sont-ils iamais deux ensemble.[1]

The first layer of associations conveys the timidity and tension which the poet feels both in body and soul after the departure of Délie. The second layer introduces the sensation of hearing, and perhaps the association with Venus noted by Pierre l'Anglois. At the third layer is the solitariness of the hare. All three layers would only be present in the reader's mind when these associations, conventional for Scève's time had been understood.

[1] *Discours des Hieroglyphes aegyptiens, Emblemes, Devises, et Armoiries*, Paris, 1584, p. 47.

The reader's attention is drawn to the frightened hare, whose bodily position and nervous state convey the tension of the poet, then moves on to the idea of hearing in the phrase *oyant vn bruyt confus*. Here the notion of 'Il est dedié à Venus' combines with the hare's literal fear to convey the mental confusion and helplessness of the lover. Finally comes the allusion to the darkness of Egypt suffering from one of the plagues sent by God and reinforced by the Egyptian reference in Pierre d'Anglois' hieroglyphics thus clinching the Venus association. The simple analogy, based on the three sets of likenesses between the poet and the hare, opens out into vast associations of darkness, solitariness and the plague-ridden. It is further linked both by argument and by imagery to the rest of the dizain. For the first three lines have introduced the image of winter and darkness, the objective equivalents of Délie's absence, and the first six lines are concerned with analysing his physical and mental reactions to her departure and the relationship between his body and soul. Unlike Donne Scève does not rely on the exhibition of logical subtlety. When Donne introduces a startling analogy he is at pains to point out in detail its meaning and validity in the argument. In *A Nocturnal upon St. Lucy's Day* Donne uses the notion of love producing by alchemy a quintessence out of nothingness. He expounds its meaning carefully, introduced twice by the explanatory word *for*:

> Study me then, you who shall lovers be
> At the next world, that is, at the next Spring:
> For I am every dead thing,
> In whom love wrought new alchemy.
>    For his art did express
> A quintessence even from nothingness,
> From dull privations, and lean emptiness:
> He ruin'd me, and I am re-begot
> Of absence, darkness, death; things which are not.

The differences in structure between a poem of Donne's and a Scève dizain confirm the point. Donne chooses a longer, looser poetic form which permits a more leisurely introduction and establishment of an image and allows the idea to develop in two or three stanzas with subtle twists and turns and extended parallels. Scève on the other hand uses a condensed image to bring to the reader's mind parallels and associations which, although never explicitly elaborated, illuminate the whole argument of a poem. Since the associations would be familiar to sixteenth-century readers, Scève can rely on them to convey his record of emotional experience, his analysis of inner disturbances and his intellectualisation of reality. They refer an intensely personal experience to a more general background: for instance in dizain 2, whose basic starting point is the *innamoramento* of the poet, the experience of personal isolation, the general curse of women, the hyperbolical praise of the perfection of Délie, the celestial creation of the first woman, the ambivalent power of women in general and the power which Délie is going to exert throughout the whole cycle – all emerge convincingly from the allusion to Pandora: are unpacked from that box. In spite of the fact that the poetry is concerned with analysing the experience of love and the metaphysical and psychological problems appertaining to it, the images that are startlingly introduced at the end of the dizains do not rely on logical subtlety, on the sudden revelation of hitherto unseen relationships, but rather on traditional associations evoked by figures from classical mythology or the Bible or the legends of natural history.

But the fusion of abstract with concrete, the interweaving of philosophical ideas with concrete allusions, the movement into the final image, all have to be controlled, or the whole abstract and sometimes difficult argument does not crystallise as for instance it does in the hare poem. Dizain 46 demonstrates this point at its simplest and in many ways its crudest:

> Si le desir, image de la chose,
> Que plus on ayme, est du cœur le miroir,
> Qui tousiours fait par memoire apparoir
> Celle, ou l'esprit de ma vie repose,
> A quelle fin mon vain vouloir propose
> De m'esloingner de ce, qui plus me suyt?
>   Plus fuit le Cerf, & plus on le poursuyt,
> Pour mieulx le rendre, aux rhetz de seruitude:
> Plus ie m'absente, & plus le mal s'ensuyt
> De ce doulx bien, Dieu de l'amaritude.

The argument in the first six lines concerns the nature of the poet's desire for Délie and her constant presence in his being. It is developed tautly in psychological terms: if desire can be defined as the 'image de la chose que plus on ayme', and is 'le miroir du coeur', then it is in this mirror that Délie constantly appears and through the working of the poet's memory comes to dwell. The conclusion drawn from these propositions is expressed in the rhetorical question of lines 5–6. The argument is in a sense complete since we can see that the answers to this question are contained in the previous six lines. But Scève changes gear at this point and introduces the image of the stag fleeing from its pursuers. The last four lines serve to make the argument explicit and intelligible by giving us a concrete analogy from the world of nature. There is something super-fluous about the image here; not only is its surface worn thin through its being such a commonplace conceit but it also fails to provide any step in the argument. It merely puts the argument in more familiar terms. The image is not tied to the dialectic of the dizain as a whole.

Similarly when the argument is somewhat abstract a fine image in the last line does not always impel the reader to re-read the dizain in order to see that argument more clearly. An example of this is dizain 174:

> Encores vit ce peu de l'esperance,
> Que me laissa si grand longueur de temps,
> Se nourrissant de ma vaine souffrance
> Toute confuse du bien, que ie pretens.
>     Et a me veoir les Astres mal contentz
> Inspirent force au languissant plaisir
> Pour non acoup de vueil me dessaisir,
> Qui, persistant a ses fins pretendues,
> A mon trauail augmente le desir,
> Strigile vain a mes sueurs perdues.

The vowel and consonant dissonance in the last line holds us for the moment by the shock of the unexpectedly powerful line. But in the poem as a whole Scève has analysed the relationship between hope, suffering and persistent will: in lines 1–4 his hope nourishing itself in his torment; in 5–7 his 'stars', the astrological influences on his love and life, encourage him to persevere, so that his will persists in striving for its avowed end *du bien, que ie pretens*; in 8–10 this activity of the will, and this labour result in an increase in his desire; the last line introduces the image: the *vueil* is the tenor and the *strigile* is the vehicle of the metaphor. *Strigile* is the iron, horn or bone etc. instrument used to scrape the skin to remove dirt and perspiration and so refresh the body after labour. It thus evokes both a harsh scraping sensation and the relief from dirt and tiredness that it brings. But, paradoxi-cally, his *vueil* and his *desir* give way to his *sueurs perdues* – the poet's labours and persistence are in vain since they are neither rewarded nor relieved. Here the condensed image is rather obscure and ill-connected with the rest of the poem and so one is left with rather a tortuous investigation of an experience which does very little to bring the argument alive except through the sound of that last line. The harsh, unmusical effect of the whole dizain, apart from the last line, suggests the *durus* element of roughness in the arrangement of the words, the unrhythmical flow of the lines and the obscure syntax. It does indeed call up the line, in the preliminary huitain, 'Mainte erreur, mesme en si durs Epygrammes'. Thus in the two dizains discussed a moment ago – no. 46 and 174 – we see that a good last line is not enough to save the poems.

When Scève uses a leit-motif and out of it constructs a dizain which analyses his experience of love he manages to interweave the intellectual and the physical exceptionally well. Take dizain 200 as an example. It is a poem of separation constructed over the leit-motif of light and darkness, of the Moon Goddess and the poet. There are transitions from night to day, from suffering and torment to relief, running through the whole cycle, but here Scève has taken a cosmic phenomenon – the eclipse of the moon – and worked it into his own portrayal of separation.

> Phebé luysant' par ce Globe terrestre
> Entreposé a sa clarté priuée
> De son opaque, argentin, & cler estre
> Soubdainement, pour vn temps, est priuée.
> Et toy, de qui m'est tousiours deriuée
> Lumiere, & vie, estant de moy loingtaine
> Par l'espaisseur de la terre haultaine,
> Qui nous separe en ces haultz Montz funebres,
> Ie sens mes yeulx se dissouldre en fontaine,
> Et ma pensée offusquer en tenebres.

The first four lines are rather difficult; the syntax being 'Phebé luysant est priuée de son opaque estre par ce Globe entreposé à sa clarté.' The *priuée* in line 2 is the adjective 'familiar, intimate' and the *priuée* in line 4 is the past participle of *priver* to be taken with *de* in line 3. This recalls the Mallarmé sonnet analysed in Ch. 1, where the repeated *tu* jolted the reader into analysing intellectually and rationally which was the pronoun and which the past participle. Scève too jolts us into an active state of linguistic delight and perhaps makes us see here, more than in other examples, the sheer pleasure there is in handling

and ordering words. The syntax is not 'obscure' at all – to an
alert reader. The third line contains the apparent contradiction
between *opaque* and *cler*; the first refers to the fact that the moon
is in normal circumstances a reflecting body, receiving and
transmitting the light of the sun, whilst the second adjective
refers to the actual brightness of the satellite in that it receives
light from the sun.

The last six lines describe the separation of the two lovers in
terms of the eclipse of the moon; he, the lover, is deprived of
the source of his light just as the moon is deprived of the sun.
The *Montz funebres* have interposed themselves between him and
his mistress in the same way as the earth comes between the
moon and the sun when there is an eclipse. Scève also expresses
the results of this separation in terms of light and darkness.
*Offusquer* suggests both *obscurcir* and the mental darkness
experienced by the lover when separated from his mistress. (The
same motif and associations surrounding darkness are present
in the 37th *impresa*, *La Lune en tenebres*, and its companion dizain,
which deals with the obscuring of the poet's inner light and his
highest faculties, his *pensée* as opposed to his *cœur*.)

Overtones of the Neo-Platonic doctrine of the darkness of
carnal desire which obscures the light of the intellect may also
be present. Léon Hébreu for instance uses the image of the
eclipse when he discusses the relationship between *amour
honneste* and carnal appetite. He describes the eclipse of the moon
as 'interposition de la terre entre elle (the moon) et le soleil…Ce
qui advient semblablement à l'ame quand la corporalité et
terrestreité s'interpose entre elle et l'intellect'.[1] The poet's inner
light is destroyed and his highest faculties his *pensée* are plunged
into the mental darkness of death.

Similarly, Scève welds a commonplace scheme into something
larger, as he does in dizain 164, which starts

> Comme corps mort vagant en haulte Mer,
> Esbat des Ventz, & passetemps des Vndes,
> I'errois flottant parmy ce Gouffre amer…

The basis of this poem is the conventional analogy between
the ship tossed on a stormy ocean and the lover tossed on the
tumultuous sea of love. The analogy is conventionally introduced by the word *comme*, but Scève has broken through the

---

[1] Op. cit., p. 55.

convention by choosing as the vehicle of the comparison not a
ship but *corps mort*. Through this many associations with death
itself are evoked; the underlying idea is that the lover is dead in
himself anyway, a meaningless empty shell since his love is not
reciprocated. There is a much closer link between the two terms
of the comparison, the lover and a floating corpse, than between
the usual terms, a ship and the lover. The *dizain* develops into
a revocation of the lover's self from death by the sound of Délie's
name, and the reawakening of hope in him. This awakening is
given a strange concrete visual description in the last two lines:

> Et a ce son me cornantz les oreilles,
> Tout estourdy point ne me congnoissoys.

The verb 'corner' here suggests the tingling, prickling sensation
that one has on hearing one's own name or that of someone dear
to one and perhaps the visual suggestion of the poet straining,
cupping his ears to catch the sound.[1] In this reawakening Scève
also suggests the feeling of lostness in the quick transition from
the dead state, the feeling that his own identity is strange to
him. In this poem the initial deviation from a conventional image
has developed into a very personal statement.

Finally what is probably Scève's greatest poem, dizain 367,
on the subject of reunion after an absence. We have already
looked at this poem in Ch. 6 and the few brief remarks that
follow should be read in conjunction with the fine analysis by
Odette de Mourgues.

> Asses plus long, qu'vn Siecle Platonique,
> Me fut le moys, que sans toy suis esté:
> Mais quand ton front ie reuy pacifique,
> Seiour treshault de toute honnesteté,
> Ou l'empire est du conseil arresté
> Mes songes lors ie creus estre deuins.
> Car en mon corps: mon Ame, tu reuins,
> Sentant ses mains, mains celestement blanches,
> Auec leurs bras mortellement diuins
> L'vn coronner mon col, l'aultre mes hanches.

Délie only becomes a reality for the lover with the actual proof
of her physical presence; instead of losing themselves in the
overwhelming intensity of their emotion they reach a momentary and precarious perfection in the Rodin-like quality of the

[1] Cotgrave suggests for *corner*: to blow a horn or a cornet; and for 'les oreilles
me cornent': my ears glow or tingle.

embrace which does not suggest a succession of others but rather the marble and yet fragile quality of this unique one. Everything in this dizain leads up to the last four lines: the structure from 'Mais quand...' to 'Mes songes lors ie creus estre deuins', where there is no explanation, then at the beginning of line 7 the very firm logical word *car*; the leit-motif of Neo-Platonic philosophy – that without reciprocation of love the lover is nothing – used in an emotional way by the concrete evocation of the embrace; the fact that the reader is totally inside the experience from line 1 to line 10; the purely concrete character of the last line, which without any allusion or metaphor contains a very strong impression of the hands being *mortellement diuins* – all these features make us bless the artistic orientation and the emotional stability that Scève has shown in this greatest of love poems.

Quite obviously there are other dizains mentioned in earlier chapters which could be linked to this 'intellectual, voluptuous, simple poetry'. For example, the inevitable paradox of the serpent dizain or the basic phenomenon of 'expansion in love' in 'De toute Mer...' (which we shall look at in the next chapter). These basic themes of the love experience are evident whenever Scève writes well and so, in one sense, all his best dizains would come under the heading of 'simple poetry'.

# I 0

## NATURE AND SOLITUDE

The law of transience applies to both nature and man and a full recognition of it implies the willing submission of the self to the pattern of nature. Cicero (*De Senectute*, 2.5) expressed it in this way,

Sed tamen necesse fuit esse aliquid extremum et, tamquam in arboris bacis terraeque fructibus maturitate tempestiva, quasi vietum et caducum, quod ferendum est molliter sapienti.

He continues to express the metaphor in 19.71.

et quasi poma ex arboribus, cruda si sunt, vix evelluntur, si matura et cocta, decidunt, sic vitam adulescentibus vis aufert, senibus maturitas.

The death of youth is violent and unnatural; the death of old age is in complete accord with the laws of nature. It is a Roman commonplace to express man's cycle in the world in terms of spring, summer, autumn and winter: a man's prime is spring, his middle age is summer and his senility is compared to winter. Moreover Scève, unlike Petrarch, did not have a Christian outlook in his love poetry; neither did he have the Neo-Platonic concept of his love for Délie as leading him to Love as the ideal good. His love was not the supreme good which left Délie at the threshold. The nature of love seemed to be constant only in its vicissitudes, abiding only in its illogic. But Scève constructed out of his love a submission and a higher responsibility to the worth of love. His personal exploration of the conflicts and contradictions that he experienced in love sculptured for him a stability and a permanence in this human world, albeit a solitary one.

This permanence involves the value of his relationship with Délie and also the clear awareness that this world is transient. The cycle ends on solitude and the immortality of lover and mistress. A starting point for our analysis is the spectacle of Scève alone in nature. The lover's search for solitude in the heart of nature, his invocation to nature to witness, lament and

sympathise with his misfortune are topoi passed down to
European literature from Antiquity. The gift of artistic creation
is by nature isolated, and in Scève solitude is thought of as a
permanent state of the artist in the world, not in a religious sense
as Sponde or D'Aubigné certainly felt it, but in the sense that
Montaigne felt it. Let us test what is as yet only a hypothesis by
looking at dizain 423.

> Respect du lieu, soulacieux esbat,
> A toute vie austerement humaine,
> Nourrit en moy l'intrinseque debat,
> Qui de douleur a ioye me pourmeine:
> Y frequentantz, comme en propre domeine,
> Le Cœur sans reigle, & le Corps par compas.
>    Car soit deuant, ou apres le repas,
> Tousiours le long de ses riues prochaines
> Lieux escartez, lentement pas a pas
> Vois mesurant, & les champs, & mes peines.

The harmony between the poet, his mood, attitude and feeling
and the nature that surrounds him is striking. He escapes from
human company and seeks wild and deserted nature, but does
not thereby lose his problems; rather does the *lieu* nourish his
*intrinseque debat*. These two words are the key words of the dizain,
expressing the poet's state of mind and foreshadowing the last
line which contains the two aspects of the theme – *les champs, &
mes peines*. *Intrinseque* is translated by Cotgrave as 'intrinsecall,
familiar, secret, inward' – all of which echo the poet's attempts
to keep his inward secret from others but to reveal it to nature.
Lines 5–6 call up the harmony between the place the poet
chooses to walk and the state of his own heart and body. This
harmony is explained in the last four lines again, introduced by
the firm logical word *car* and the description of the solitary walks
he takes, *soit deuant, ou apres le repas*. The dizain is not without
blemish; the syntax of lines 1–3 is harsh, with *Respect du lieu* as
the subject of *nourrit en moy*, and *soulacieux esbat/A toute vie
austerement humaine* in apposition to it. But it is important for
the suggestion that in the end the solitary life without Délie is
the only one that the poet finds satisfactory.

Another dizain (262) emphasises even more the wildness of
nature where Scève seeks solace:

> Ie vois cherchant les lieux plus solitaires
> De desespoir, & d'horreur habitez,

> Pour de mes maulx les rendre secretaires,
> Maulx de tout bien, certes, desheritez,
> Qui de me nuire, & aultruy vsitez,
> Font encor paour, mesme a la solitude,
> Sentant ma vie en telle inquietude,
> Que plus fuyant & de nuict, & de iour
> Ses beaulx yeulx sainctz, plus loing de seruitude
> A mon penser sont icy doulx seiour.

There is an echo immediately of two lines of Petrarch (*Rime*, 35, 1–2)[1]

> Solo e pensoso i più deserti campi
> Vo mesurando a passi tardi e lenti...

and also the 'Cercato ho sempre solitaria vita (Le rive il sanno e le campagne e i boschi)' of another sonnet (*Rime*, 259). The reasons for preferring solitude are explicitly stated by Scève:

> Pour de mes maulx les rendre secretaires
> Maulx de tout bien, certes, desheritez.

In the same way Petrarch had said that nature alone knew

> di che tempre
> Sia la mia vita, ch'è celata altrui.             (*Rime*, 35)

But in Scève both the aspect of nature and the quality of his suffering are sharper and more anguished. *Les lieux* are *De desespoir, et d'horreur habitez*; and his *maulx/Font encor paour, mesme a la solitude*. By emphasizing this aspect, Scève makes the force of the last line even stronger,

> A mon penser sont icy doulx seiour

and the contrast between his anguish and the *beaulx yeulx sainctz* which are the cause of his pain.

Not only is this search for solitude rather harsher than in Petrarch's sonnets; it also seems as if it were a longing for the solitary life itself – which may be seen as a reason for the retreat that Scève actually took in the 1520s and also after writing *Délie*.[2]

---

[1] D. Fenoaltea, *The Poet in Nature*, art. op. cit., pp. 265–9; see also Luzius Keller, '"Solo e pensoso", "Seul et pensif", "Solitaire et pensif", Mélancolie pétrarquienne et mélancolie pétrarquiste', *SF*, 49, nuova serie, gennaio–aprile, 1973 for the treatment of this theme by sixteenth-century poets.

[2] See McFarlane's edition, p. 6 and Saulnier, op. cit., t. 1, Ch. 2 and Giudici, op. cit., Ch. 2. It may be that Saulnier is right in following up Nicolas Bourbon's suggestion that Scève was *Addictus Deo*; but this cannot be established on the internal evidence of *Délie*, as Giudici has suggested.

Several dizains hint at this inherent liking of solitude. For example in dizain 223 where the situation is a conventional meeting of Délie but the poet 'dissolves' in the presence of such an epiphany, there are the two lines

> Parquoy pensif, selon mon nayf vice,
> M'esbatois seul, quand celle me vint contre...

which suggest that he is doing something which is natural to him.

Scève knows solitary life even as a lover. Dizain 370 reveals the masochistic character of the lover's despair:

> Estant tousiours, sans m'oster, appuyé
> Sur le plaisir de ma propre tristesse,
> Ie me ruyne au penser ennuyé
> Du pensement proscript de ma lyesse.

This recalls the beginning of dizain 91

> Osté du col de la doulce plaisance,
> Fus mis es bras d'amere cruauté...

which evokes a lovers' embrace of gentle sensuality, the lover hanging physically around *plaisance*, even though the emphasis is on the abstract qualities. In dizain 370 the important words are *sans m'oster* and the concrete metaphor *appuyé/Sur le plaisir de ma propre tristesse*. Lines 5–10

> Ainsi donné en proye a la destresse,
> De mon hault bien toute beatitude
> Est cheute au fons de ton ingratitude:
> Dont mes espritz recouurantz sentement,
> Fuyent au ioug de la grand seruitude
> De desespoir, Dieu d'eternel tourment.

evoke the fact that solitary thought deepens despair until it is at its most violent and most stark. The whole tone of the poem is a downward movement – *appuyé, ruyne, cheute au fons* – and ends in a desperate flight in the last two lines.

The poems that we have just mentioned are closer to Petrarch than to the petrarchists – like Serafino – whom Scève began by imitating. Phrases in these poems might strike a chord in the reader's memory and evoke rich associations of their previous contexts in Petrarch. And yet, when we move on to other poems where the nature-imagery fuses the microcosm with the macrocosm, we become aware that Scève is not looking at the world in the same way as Petrarch. Take dizain 148:

> Voy que l'Hyuer tremblant en son seiour,
> Aux champs tous nudz sont leurs arbres failliz.
> Puis le Printemps ramenant le beau iour,
> Leur sont bourgeons, fueilles, fleurs, fruictz sailliz:
>   Arbres, buissons, & hayes, & tailliz
> Se crespent lors en leur gaye verdure.
>   Tant que sur moy le tien ingrat froit dure,
> Mon espoir est denué de son herbe:
> Puis retournant le doulx Ver sans froidure
> Mon An se frise en son Auril superbe.

The superb final line unifies the whole sequence of nature imagery. Lines 1–6 have already evoked a concrete picture of the succession of the seasons: Winter 'tremblant', 'champs tous nudz'; Spring with its renewal of beauty and colour and fecundity, culminating with a vision of trees, shrubs and hedges in which the verb *se cresper* finely depicts the tufted curls of foliage budding on the trees.[1] Line 7 introduces the tenor of the metaphor – 'Tant que sur moy', and the details of Winter and Spring become parallels for the poet's own situation. Within this extended comparison there are smaller ones of detail; for example in line 8 'Mon espoir denué de son herbe'. Part of the success of the metaphor is its congruity. The oncoming Spring 'le doulx Ver sans froidure' makes the last line (which corresponds to line 6 in the first half of the metaphor) a perfectly natural climax. *Se friser* has the same meaning and powers of visual evocation as the previous verb *se cresper* and may be compared to the suggestive phrase 'my green age'.[2] The poem relies for its effect on its sensuous evocations and the unity of its imagery.[3]

We pass now to one of Scève's most successful themes – the stability and transcendence over the future that his love brings

---

[1] Huguet on *se cresper* quotes this *dizain* as an example of the figurative use of the verb: 'se couvrir de feuillage comme d'une chevelure frisée'.

[2] Cf. Dylan Thomas:

> The force that through the green fuse drives the flower
> Drives my green age.

[3] Weber, *Création poétique*, op. cit., p. 204, shows that the originality of this poem lies 'pour une part dans les détails sobres, simples et pourtant saisissants qui évoquent l'hiver et le printemps et plus encore dans la fusion établie dans le dernier quatrain entre les saisons et les sentiments dans leur choc de l'abstrait et du concret obtenu grâce à d'étonnants raccourcis.'

him. Unlike the Pléiade, who promised to make their loved ones immortal through their own verse, Scève assigns to love itself the power of conferring immortality and makes it stand quite separate from writing about Délie. In particular he is concerned with the fame of Délie herself and only secondarily with the immortality of their love. Dizains on this theme are characterised by the combination of an image with the use of the future tense in the last few lines. When Scève is predicting the transcendence of Délie over death and the spread of her name and fame, the most powerful images he uses are those dependent on a geographical allusion. For example, in dizain 11 where this theme is dominant – further proof that he was not telling a love story chronologically – he proclaims Délie's conquest of time and space.[1] This affirmation is expressed in terms of an analogy: as flowers die and their perfume lives on, similarly Délie will know physical death but her moral virtues will not perish. There is nothing extraordinary about the argument, it is simply a strong emotional assertion by the poet of his faith in Délie's immortality, but presented as a proven fact rather than as a mere emotional statement,

> Les seches fleurs en leur odeur viuront:
> Prœuue pour ceulx, qui le bien poursuyuront
> De non mourir, mais de reuiure encore.

Already the verbs are in the future – *viuront, poursuyuront* and are given an important stress by being placed in the rhyming position. After this general statement Scève moves on to Délie, still using logical terminology for emotional affirmation – *Tes vertus donc*

> qui ton corps ne suyuront,
> Dès l'Indien s'estendront iusqu'au More.

The echoing effects of the future in the rhyme and the impression of length and breadth in the last line gained by the position of the verb *s'estendront*, still echoing the other future verbs, lead on to the fading and lengthening of *iusqu'au More*. (Cf. the same use of geographical allusions in dizains 283 and 284.)

At times Scève is involved in a prophecy of immortality for

---

[1] For the explanation of the complicated allusions of the first four lines see McFarlane's commentary.

himself as well as Délie: in dizain 90, for instance, where the argument concerns Délie's effect on the poet. The moral effect is first stated in the phrase 'Tu m'excitas du sommeil de paresse', which suggests that Délie awakened in him the awareness of a higher good and helped him ascend the ladder of virtue. This spiritual elevation alternates with the emotional despair she engenders in him

> Et par celuy qu'ores ie ramentoy,
> Tu m'endormis en mortelle destresse.

The alternation is brought to life through the repetition of the idea of *sommeil* in both parts. But if Délie is willing to help him, her virtue

> Agrandissant mes espritz faictz petitz,
> De toy, & moy fera la renommée
> Oultrepasser & Ganges, & Bethys.

It is only through the influence and aid of Délie's own qualities that Scève himself can hope for immortality. The extent of their fame is now conveyed by the two rivers, the Ganges and the Baetis (Guadalquivir) which mark the bounds of the world – India and Spain. (Scève is using a literary topos here, which in no way implies that he was unaware of recent geographical discoveries which had extended these limits.)

This transcendence of Délie beyond time and space finds its most complete expression in dizain 259, which deserves a brief glance. The first six lines are concerned mainly with space, and the last four with time, space and immortality.

> De toute Mer tout long, & large espace,
> De terre aussi tout tournoyant circuit
> Des Montz tout terme en forme haulte, & basse,
> Tout lieu distant, du iour et de la nuict,
> Tout interualle, ô qui par trop me nuyt,
> Seront rempliz de ta doulce rigueur.
>   Ainsi passant des Siecles la longueur,
> Surmonteras la haulteur des Estoilles
> Par ton sainct nom, qui vif en ma langueur
> Pourra par tout nager a plaines voiles.

The impression of space is conveyed in the first part both by the syntactic structure – one long sentence with the verb *Seront rempliz* occurring finally in line 6 – and by the judicious use of enumeration and conjunction. For instance, the first line immediately sets the tone by the repetition of *tout* and the placing of *et* which seems to lengthen the line by more than one syllable. Moreover the enumeration itself brings in places high and low, the sea, the earth, mountains, far off places by day and night, so that the whole universe seems present concretely in the dizain. Scève also uses vowel harmony to enhance the effect: for example, the placing of *tout tournoyant circuit* in the second line takes up and intensifies the *ou* echo of the first line, and the very difficulty of getting one's tongue around this phrase slows down the line. The sound recurs in important positions at the beginning of lines 4 and 5, so that the first six lines are, in terms of sound, a sequence of subtle variations on *ou, o* and *au*. The logic of this long enumeration is summed up in *Ainsi* and Scève can move on directly to the triumph of Délie's name over Time, and finally to celestial height, the *haulteur* of line 8 echoing the *longueur* of line 7 and the verb *Surmonteras* foreshadowing the *Pourra* of the last line. The final image which relies on an analogy between a ship 'sailing under full sail' and Délie's name bearing her aloft, sailing in air over time and space is beautifully done. The phrase *vif en ma langueur* is perhaps the one reminder of how Délie achieves this – through the love, the *doulce rigueur* (line 6), which has entailed his suffering. The image itself successfully conveys the sensation of *nager* because it is so closely linked to the sentiments and sensations of time and space already evoked in the first six lines. It is the climax to a poem which seems to defy the limits of the ten-syllable line and the ten lines of a dizain, and to evoke impressions of great length, breadth and spaciousness.

Other dizains which prophesy the future rely on an entirely different set of images from the geographical ones just noted. These are the poems where Scève represents Délie's immortality through images of 'greenness and perpetual flowering'. In dizain 175 this theme is set in the broad framework of human existence and the whole of nature.

> Voy le iour cler ruyner en tenebres,
> Ou son bienfaict sa clarté perpetue:
> Ioyeux effectz finissent en funebres,
> Soit que plaisir contre ennuy s'esuertue.
>   Toute hautesse est soubdain abatue,
> De noz deduitz tant foible est le donneur.
> Et se crestantz les arbres, leur honneur,
> Legere gloire, en fin en terre tumbe,

Ou ton hault bien aura seul ce bon heur
De verdoyer sur ta fameuse tombe.

The extraordinary, extra-natural quality of Délie's virtue emerges all the more strongly for being set against the normal course
of events. The central movement throughout the first eight lines
is that of falling: the lines show in various ways the decline of
glory in things human and natural. The first two lines evoke
the day falling into darkness,

Voy le iour cler ruyner en tenebres,

a line which conjures up physical darkness and carries the
suggestion of a slight moral judgement in the word *ruyner*, a
sense of degradation. The next two lines continue the movement but on an abstract plane. The fifth line is really the centre
of the poem since it contains the general statement, applicable
to both human and natural things – *Toute hautesse est soubdain
abatue*. The word *hautesse* leads through association back to the
sphere of nature, and lines 7–8 evoke concretely the tufted glory
of trees in spring and the inevitable falling of the leaves as
autumn succeeds summer. It is this evocation of Nature that
leads on to the image of Délie's virtue as green foliage
flourishing on her tomb and living on after her physical death.
She is the singular exception to the natural rule – 'ton hault bien
aura seul ce bon heur'. The great beauty of the poem lies partly
in this last image and partly in the skilful interweaving throughout the poem of concrete and abstract suggestions, of
physically specific and general statements. The vocabulary
expresses this ambivalence: words like *ruyner*, *hautesse*, *honneur*
and *legere gloire* have both moral and concrete harmonics. The
alternation of rhymes reflects the contrasting themes of perpe-
tuity and decline: for example in the first four lines *tenebres* and
*funebres* alternate with *perpetue* and *s'esvertue*, and *funebres* itself
retains some of the concrete suggestions of *tenebres* through the
echo of the rhyme. In the same way the concrete image of the
trees in the last six lines gives a particular colouring to the
general statement 'Toute hautesse est soubdain abatue'. And
the final image leaves the indelible image of the evergreen
immortality of Délie's virtue.

Dizain 407 uses the same kind of image.

En moy saisons, & aages finissantz
De iour en iour descouurent leurs fallace.

Tournant les Iours, & Moys, & ans glissantz,
Rides arantz defformeront ta face.
　Mais ta vertu, qui par temps ne s'esface,
Comme la Bise en allant acquiert force,
Incessamment de plus en plus s'esforce
A illustrer tes yeulx par mort terniz.
　Parquoy, viuant soubz verdoyante escorce,
S'esgallera aux Siecles infiniz.

This time the imagery permeates the argument and reaches a climax in the notion of her virtue living *soubz verdoyante escorce* where there is the additional evocation of the myth of Daphne and her metamorphosis into the evergreen bay tree. The nature imagery begins in the first line with the poet's lament,

En moy saisons, & aages finissantz.

This is strikingly similar to Shakespeare's

That time of year thou mayest in me behold
When yellow leaves, or none, or few, do hang
Upon those boughs which shake against the cold,

which relies for its beauty on the close fusion of microcosm and macrocosm summed up in the proverbial 'Autumn of my age'. The second two lines of the dizain pass to Délie. The prophecy that time will deface her beauty again recalls Shakespeare's

When forty winters shall besiege thy brow
And dig deep trenches in thy beauty's field.

In contrast to this warning however comes a confident affirmation that Délie's moral virtue will gather force, 'comme la Bise' – an analogy which suggests at once both strength and coldness. And it is her virtue, able to conquer time and space, that is extolled in the last couplet through the confident future tense of the verb at the beginning of the last line, the two images of 'greenness' and 'bise', the impression of infinity achieved by the last phrase of all, *aux Siecles infiniz*.

In the last dizain of all we find this same combination of an evergreen image and a future tense of the verb,

Flamme si saincte en son cler durera,
Tousiours luysante en publique apparence,
Tant que ce Monde en soy demeurera,
Et qu'on aura Amour en reuerence.
　Aussi ie voy bien peu de différence

Entre l'ardeur, qui noz cœurs poursuyura,
Et la vertu, qui viue nous suyura
Oultre le Ciel amplement long, & large.
Nostre Geneure ainsi doncques viura
Non offensé d'aulcun mortel Letharge.

This time Scève has chosen a particular evergreen shrub, the juniper, as a symbol of their love, which is immortal in the sense that it will never be forgotten or grow dim. The image awakens associations with the bay tree of Petrarch. The poem itself also exploits in condensed form the other images of immortality used by Scève: the ever-shining light or flame and the spatial transcendence of Délie's virtue – which echoes the dizain we have just discussed.

The last set of images which express immortality are worth mentioning for the personal attitude towards immortality that they reveal. Dizain 23 ends with the couplet,

Mais ton sainct feu, qui a tout bien m'allume,
Resplendira a la posterité.

The image here is not unusual in itself; it is used by all the petrarchist poets. But it is here employed in a dizain concerned with Délie's virtue. Furthermore Scève stresses that it is not through his poetry that she will gain immortality,

Doncques en vain trauailleroit ma plume
Pour t'entailler a perpetuité...

but through her own almost divine qualities.

In the dizains characterised by these nature-images the poet achieves a feeling of plenitude, distance and perhaps solitude. Visions of height, and depth, of being 'across' and 'above' the whole world suggests an inner force which comes from the solidity and worth of their love. Scève counsels an acceptance of human nature in all its capriciousness and all its inconstancy. Yet he achieves equanimity in his love – a kind of self-regulation. He advocates solitude, both in nature and in art – the cry to be left alone, far from the madding crowd, applies particularly to those poems where we are made to feel that public awareness can never be adequate to the peculiarly intense quality of one's own experience. This is one of the meanings that *durs epygrammes* carries in the preliminary huitain: poetry that is rough, virile, concise, hard-hitting and uncomplacent. The phrase also carries with it a certain allusiveness, to illustrate which we should look at dizain 408, where death and love dominate the foreground, but in the back-ground is the whole of Propertius' *Elegy*, III.2.

> Quant Mort aura, apres long endurer,
> De ma triste ame estendu le corps vuyde,
> Ie ne veulx point pour en Siecles durer,
> Vn Mausolée ou vne piramide:
>    Mais bien me soit, Dame, pour tumbe humide
> (Si digne en suis) ton sein delicieux.
>    Car si viuant sur Terre, & soubz les Cieulx,
> Tu m'as tousiours esté guerre implacable,
> Apres la mort en ce lieu precieux
> Tu me seras, du moins, paix amyable.

The convention on which Scève is drawing in this poem is that violent unrequited love eventually destroys its victim; the poet will die the cruel death that lovers expect *apres long endurer*. The fact that he can not and will not shake off the attraction Délie has for him is brought out by the adjectives *delicieux*, *precieux*, *amyable*. The lines

> Ie ne veulx point pour en Siecles durer,
> Vn Mausolée ou vne piramide...

contain an echo from Propertius' elegy,

> nam neque pyramidum sumptus ad sidera ducti
>    nec Iovis Elei caelum imitata domus
> nec Mausolei dives fortuna sepulcri
>    mortis ab extrema condicione vacant.          (lines 17–20)

The echo is too close for us to believe that Scève had not read the elegy. Furthermore he must have intended it to be heard by the reader with sufficient clarity to recall the original context. Propertius' lines are from a poem in which he sings of the power of his poetry over the minds of women and of the glory that his songs have won; indeed it is greater than if he had built for his love a Mausoleum. The Mausoleum or tomb of Mausolus, the satrap of Caria, erected by his widow Artemisia and decorated by four of the greatest sculptors of the age, was regarded as one of the wonders of the world. Even the pyramids, the temple of Zeus and the Mausoleum, for all their size, loftiness and splendour would come to nothing; but the poet who sings of his mistress will bring immortality to them both. The audience would catch the echo of these lines in Scève and with it the Propertian context of the mausoleum and pyramid, which are an image of grand mortality, a magnificent backcloth against which to set the assertion of immortality. Sixteenth-century poets did not, so to speak, grub around or expect their readers to grub around to find the quotation in some earlier poet, but rather assumed their readers' ability to recognise the quotation and so make the appropriate response. This is certainly what Scève is doing every time he employs the allusive process in his dizains. He has often been called 'a poet's poet' and in some senses this is true; but the whole Ancient tradition which Renaissance poetry grasps on to presupposes an élite audience.

There is a period towards the end of *Délie* in which the poet seems to have arrived at a kind of restful solution; and it is a period of solitude too. As Saulnier (op. cit., t. I, p. 160) says: 'C'est toute la fin de *Délie* (les dizains CDXII–CDXLIX forment le groupe le plus homogène de tout le livre) qui évoque, après l'abandon, la consolation grise d'une retraite solitaire, studieuse et calme.' Let us look at some of the poems in this period. Dizain 412 is a meditation on life, set in a framework of the antithesis between the active and contemplative life.

> Mont costoyant le Fleuue, & la Cité,
> Perdant ma veue en longue prospectiue,
> Combien m'as tu, mais combien incité
> A viure en toy vie contemplatiue?
> Ou toutesfoys mon cœur par œuure actiue
> Auec les yeulx leue au Ciel la pensée
> Hors de soucy d'ire, & dueil dispensée
> Pour admirer la paix, qui me tesmoingne
> Celle vertu lassus recompensée,
> Qui du Vulgaire, aumoins ce peu, m'esloingne.

Sitting on high on the top of Mont Fourvière in Lyon, he can see the rivers Saône and Rhône and their meeting in the city forming as it were a physical centre to his life. Looking out over the whole countryside from the mountain-top, the view is enormous and long, and earthly cares seem far away. He apostrophises the mountain and twice repeats *combien*: whereas with his heart he has chosen the active life, everything that he has done is now rewarded as he sits there away from the vulgar crowd. Scève is away from the mercantile care of the plebs, the merchants, the illiterate and the ambitious. He can now enjoy a lonely life with his introspective preoccupations. In dizain 413 he looks at his life from another angle: his desire and longing for Délie are expressed in the first lines, which stand as a sign of the ambivalence of his love,

> Honneste ardeur en vn tressainct desir,
> Desir honneste en vne saincte ardeur...

By applying the adjectives first to one term, then to the other, Scève is able to express the manifold effects of the experience. Following these two lines are several assertions in which he uses logical terminology; but they are merely emotional statements disguised beneath the cloak of logic. *Desir* and *ardeur* are juxtaposed to the *chaste esbat* of line 3

> En chaste esbat, & pudique plaisir
> M'ont plus donné & de fortune, & d'heur,
> Que l'esperance auec faincte grandeur
> Ne m'a rauy de liesse assouuie.

This is such a paradoxical conclusion that like Donne he is forced to give logical reasons for illogical statements,

> Car desirant par ceste ardente enuie
> De meriter d'estre au seul bien compris,
> Raison au faict me rend souffle a la vie,
> Vertu au sens, & vigueur aux espritz.

In the next dizain – 414 – the poet exhibits the aloof attitude in solitude. There is here a spiritual certainty and tranquillity also found in a number of other poems at the end of the sequence. There is moreover in this poem a suggestion that were the poet utterly unconcerned with love he would still like a

> Plaisant repos du seiour solitaire
> De cures vuyde, & de soucy deliure,
> Ou l'air paisible est feal secretaire
> Des haultz pensers, que sa doulceur me liure
> Pour mieulx iouir de ce bienheureux viure,
> Dont les Dieux seulz ont la fruition.

The way that Scève and Petrarch parted company over the *innamoramento* now seems obvious. The intellectual element in Scève avoided devices that were life and blood to Petrarch. Petrarch is allegorical where Scève is allusive. Petrarch's poetry is narrative where Scève is argumentative. Petrarch is lyrical where Scève is dense. Petrarch sang with *dolcezza* and *facilità* of his love where Scève's attitude towards his love was *dur*. Let us look finally at a dizain which brings in the theme of control and serenity – dizain 232:

> Tout le repos, ô nuict, que tu me doibs,
> Auec le temps mon penser le deuore:
> Et l'Horologe est compter sur mes doigtz
> Depuis le soir iusqu'a la blanche Aurore.
>    Et sans du iour m'apperceuoir encore,
> Ie me pers tout en si doulce pensée,
> Que du veiller l'Ame non offensée,
> Ne souffre au Corps sentir celle douleur
> De vain espoir tousiours recompensée
> Tant que ce Monde aura forme, & couleur.

The poem is the complement of *Le souvenir, ame de ma pensée* (dizain 143). The sleepless night is to the lover's mind a time of happiness. It banishes the pain that comes from the dissatisfaction of his senses of form and colour – things that belong to daytime, creatures of light. What is remarkable is the coherence of structure, the balance and control of the poet's technique. The first phrase – *Tout le repos* – sets the atmosphere through inversion; the first four lines are expressed calmly and perfectly with the visual image of the fingers and the clock. After this the poem changes into a narrative and then moves into the future tense with the confident statement that the body matters far less than the mind. The last line radiates peace and serenity,

> Tant que ce Monde aura forme, & couleur.

The order is mainly a closed one and is different from that of many other dizains which end with a startling image, forcing the reader to make a jump from one level to the other. For this one may quote Béguin's observation – 'Il y a, dans le lyrisme de Scève une perception étonnamment réelle de la personne humaine, de sa complexité, de ses contradictions, mais aussi de son indéfectible unité.'[1]

In this study I have endeavoured to shift the emphasis away from the 'startling modernity' of Scève, away from those aspects of his work which make him merely a sixteenth-century Donne or Valéry. Seeing him as a poet who was aware of the past – the Graeco-Roman and the Christian past – in fact serves not to diminish his stature but to enlarge it. I have also explored the ways in which *Délie* can be related directly to certain elements

---

[1] 'Sur la mystique de Maurice Scève', *Fontaine*, vol. vii, 1944, no. 36, pp. 74–97.

of sixteenth-century poetics. The *imprese* are a good example of how an understanding of the conventions, indeed of parts of literary history can enhance our sympathy and understanding. Once we leave behind the notion that the *imprese* are tiresome or even childish trappings of sixteenth and seventeenth-century taste, we can advance to a view of Scève as someone acutely aware of the value of pictorial love-conceits. Not only was he aware of the immediate and popular appeal to the eye. He knew also that this was reinforced by Neo-Platonic theories of intuitive knowledge of ideas or concepts derived from sense-impressions and communicated through the highest sense-organ of all. He was, moreover, aware of the differences between emblems and *imprese*; he knew that 'The emblem has only to feed the eyes, the device the mind. The former aims only at a moral; the latter is concerned with the ideas of things. The one is more delightful the more it is adorned with objects...The other sometimes has more loveliness to the eye when it is simple and bare, with no other ornament but a scroll.'[1] Scève also saw (what no one else seems to have seen) that the *imprese* provided a basis for illustrated metaphors and thus could be incorporated into a serious love *canzoniere* such as Délie.

Although there was little 'poetic' merit in the verses that were attached to *imprese* from the 1550s onwards, a serious love poet could use this précieux element and adapt it into a literary form. In seventeenth-century England poets like Donne and Herbert drew upon the emblem writers and transformed this raw material into a form of private and personal statement. Herbert in particular uses the emblematic method: for example when he starts from a comparison of two totally dissimilar things like the church floor and the human heart; there is no necessary connection between the two things fixed either by their common qualities or by tradition; but Herbert creates the meaning by creating the likenesses within the poem.

We can see how the *imprese amorose* allowed Scève to start from convenient visual analogies: either traditional images with well-known associations, in particular the mythological ones, or a startling comparison between two dissimilar things, as for instance *La Femme qui bat le beurre* (no. 47), where the tenor of the metaphor is in his *sens* and *raison*. He can then analyse his

---

[1] Observations of Capaccio quoted by Praz, *Studies*, vol. I, p. 70.

personal feelings and problems within the basic framework offered by the *impresa*. The *imprese* also provide Scève with the two most common ways of ending a dizain: by the use of a gnomic statement or proverbial saying or by the introduction of an image. This combination would appeal to a sixteenth-century poet in that it is one way of going beyond the analysis of a purely personal experience to point to the truth or general significance of it. In criticizing Scève for using proverbs and explicit statements of a general truth, critics have lost sight of the fact that a sixteenth-century poet was concerned as much with truth as with feelings and revelations of his personal character and experience. Set within their historical context, the *imprese amorose* appear much less obscure and irrelevant than modern taste would at first be led to believe. The density that Scève achieves by relying on associations and qualities of figures or animals being read through a group of poems is linked to the density of his poetry as a whole.

Scève's use of mythology is appropriated to the rest of his imagery: on each occasion he is concerned with specific sensations, emotions and attitudes. The sense of strangeness to oneself when one is in love is perfectly linked in dizain 168 to the Acteon myth and seen as a dissociation of the intellectual faculties from the physical body. Since Scève always points from his particular experience to something on a generalised ethical or moral level, this dissociation is seen as the basic feeling when human beings 'fall in love'. While Scève employs the three traditional elements – *corps, cœur, âme* – the *œil* is the first 'conductor of love' and it is only then that the higher faculties become involved. This is the basis of the view adopted by McFarlane and Staub that the whole cycle is as it were triggered off by the Eye.

The reader is struck throughout the work with Scève's intellectual vigour. This is a quality of the man himself and is not due to traditional influence. It is not always a virtue in the poet; for it can be responsible too for some of his failures, as when an abstraction is not kindled by his sensibility. Dizain 46 is a good example, where the psychological argumentation in the first six lines is not welded to the images of the last four lines. Or dizain 144, where the last six lines are not only difficult to understand but rely on excessively abstract terms. By contrast his successful poems are a complete blend of intellect and imaginative sensitivity, as for example *Le souvenir, ame de ma pensée* (143). Again, the logical formality is sometimes used only to pad out a rather conventional theme. For instance, in dizain 3 the feeble content – another variant on the *innamoramento* theme where the poison, the poet's credulous eyes and his loss of liberty are rather banal – is not redeemed by the strong articulation. There are plenty of logical connectives like *dont, pour, car,* and two *doncques* (somewhat reminiscent of Sidney's fondness for *but, for, so that, thus*) but the structure of the poem is merely a very elaborate shell with no pearl within. The intellectualisation of experience can fail too, as for example in dizain 166. The fine images in the last four lines (the whiteness of her hands)

> Ahontiroyt le nud de Bersabée:
> Et le flagrant de sa suaue alaine
> Apouriroyt l'odorante Sabée.

cannot make up for the difficulties of the dizain as a whole, which arise from the attempt to present an emotional statement couched in rational logical terms.

The faults in Scève are indeed numerous: an over-complication in structure (e.g. 448), a liking for obscure allusions (e.g. no. 11), a heaviness in the syntax (e.g. the last line in 448 – 'Pour beaucoup moins, qu'a Charles Landrecy', where one either has to read the modern *pour* for the *a* or invert Charles and Landrecy) which reads at times almost like poetry of the fifteenth century, a certain schematic abstraction which leaves the emotional feeling behind (e.g. no. 117) and a love for the materialisation of a metaphor like *L'humidité, Hydraule de mes yeulx* (no. 331). And finally, those précieux features, as I have called them in Ch. 5, which occur especially in many of the companion dizains to the *imprese*, and the treatment in some poems of hackneyed themes from petrarchist poets, and in others the mere elegant elaboration of stock conceits.

The poetic value of *Délie* does not lie in some illusory Neo-Platonic idea-content. Nor does it lie in the gradual progression that is discernible towards acceptance of the worth of suffering, and the role of Délie and of love in his life, although this progression, shot through with his struggles, physical frustrations and sufferings, is meaningful in itself as a record of human experience. The poetic value is to be seen

rather in the individual dizains, offering each in turn a moment
or aspect of experience, with the best of them exploring the full
significance of this experience *en profondeur*. The language, the
allusiveness, the imagery and the syntax lie at the heart of this
achievement. It is only in poems like no. 367 'Asses plus long,
qu'vn Siecle Platonique' that an intensely personal experience
is brought out strongly in physical and mental terms, and
through this the problems inherent in, and the frailty which is
a fundamental characteristic of, a human relationship are
conveyed to the reader. It is the judicious interweaving of
physical and spiritual terms, of literal and figurative language,
that makes us see the individual experience and the general
significance. Similarly it is through imagery that Scève is able to
bridge the gap between the simple, literal statement of a
personal situation, as in dizain 18:

> Mais moy: ie n'ay d'escrire aultre soucy,
> Fors que de toy, & si ne sçay que dire,
> Sinon crier mercy, mercy, mercy,

and an analysis which reaches out to the broader plane of human
experience.

Time and again Scève explored the paths that his own
experience of love had set, attempting in these various ways to
define himself in language that ranges from the severely abstract
to a degree of allusiveness that verges upon a private mythology.
If, in the last analysis, love is seen by him on a purely human
plane, this is surely what, for all his Venuses and Cupids,
Propertius would say. The feeling of double living corresponds
to the sense of expansion, of increased vitality, both physical
and psychological, that accompanies love. And if his sequence
demonstrates anything, it is that this fragile relationship between two human beings is worthwhile in itself. In our final
assessment as twentieth-century readers our own twentieth-
century prejudices and tastes must enter; but it has been the
object of this book to assist the postponement of that entry, so
that when it comes, it will be informed by relevant knowledge.
'Un beau vers renaît indéfiniment de ses cendres' (Valéry).

# BIBLIOGRAPHY

This bibliography is not exhaustive but contains some of the books and articles referred to in the course of the book.

### Sixteenth-century editions of 'Délie'

DELIE/OBIECT DE/PLUS HAVLTE/VERTV. A LYON/*Chez Sulpice Sabon, pour An/toine Constantin. Auec priuilege pour six Ans.* B. N. Rés. Y^e 1746.

DELIE./OBIECT DE/PLVS/HAVLTE/VERTV.A PARIS,/*Pour Vincent Norment & Ieanne Bruneau/rue neuue Nostre Dame, à l'image sainct/Iean l'Euange-liste, & au Palais en la gallerie par ou on/va a la Chancellerie/*1564. B. N. Rés. Y^e 1661.

### Modern editions of 'Délie'

*Délie, obiect de plus haulte vertu,* édition critique avec une introduction et des notes par Eugène Parturier, Paris, Hachette, (S.T.F.M.) 1916. Reprinted in 1931 and in 1962.

*Œuvres poétiques complètes de Maurice Scève, Délie, La Saulsaye, Le Microcosme, Arion et Poésies diverses,* réunies pour la première fois par Bertrand Guégan et publiées avec une Introduction, un Glossaire, des Notes et une Bibliographie, Paris (Garnier), 1927.

*The 'Délie' of Maurice Scève,* edited with an introduction and notes by I. D. McFarlane. C.U.P., 1966.

### Selections

*Sixty Poems of Scève,* Introduction, translation and comment by Wallace Fowlie. New York, The Swallow Press and William Morrow, 1949.

*Commentaire sur quarante-neuf dizains de la Délie* par Pierre Boutang. Paris, Gallimard, 1953.

### Works on Scève, particularly 'Délie'

Attal, J. P. 'État présent des études scéviennes', *Critique,* 1960, pp. 3–24.

*Maurice Scève. Un tableau synoptique de la vie et des œuvres de Maurice Scève et des événements artistiques, littéraires et historiques de son époque,* Paris, 1964.

Baur, A. *Maurice Scève et la Renaissance lyonnaise,* Paris, 1906.

Béguin, A. 'Sur la mystique de Maurice Scève', *Fontaine,* 1944, no. 36, pp. 74–97.

Brunetière, F. 'Un précurseur de la Pléiade: Maurice Scève', in *Études critiques sur l'histoire de la littérature française*, 6e série, Paris, 1899.

Coleman, D. 'Some notes on Scève and Petrarch', *FS*, XIV, 1960, pp. 293–303.

'Dizain 104 in Maurice Scève's *Délie*', *MLR*, LVIII, 1963, pp. 215–17.

'Scève's choice of the name *Délie*', *FS*, XVIII, 1964, pp. 1–16.

'Les Emblesmes dans la *Délie* de Maurice Scève', *SF*, no. 22, 1964, pp. 1–15.

'Images in Scève's *Délie*', *MLR*, LIX, 1964, pp. 375–86.

'Propertius, Petrarch and Scève', *Kentucky Romance Quarterly*, XVIII, 1971, pp. 77–89.

Fenoaltea, D. 'Three animal images in the *Délie*: new perspectives on Scève's use of Petrarch's *Rime*', *BHR*, XXXIV, 1972, pp. 413–26.

'The poet in nature: sources of Scève's *Délie* in Petrarch's *Rime*', *FS*, XXVII, 1973, pp. 257–70.

Frappier, J. 'Variations sur le thème du miroir, de Bernart de Ventadour à Maurice Scève', in *Cahiers de l'Association Internationale des Études Françaises*, 11, 1959, pp. 134–58.

Giudici, E. *Le opere minori di Maurice Scève*, Parma, 1958.

*Il Rinascimento a Lione e la 'Délie' di Maurice Scève*, Napoli, Liguori, 1962.

'Il problema dell'originalità della *Délie* di Maurice Scève', in *Zagadnienia Rodzajów Literackich*, 1962, t.v (1), pp. 121–46 and (2), pp. 67–107.

*Maurice Scève, poeta della 'Délie'*, Rome, 1965.

Greene, T. M. 'Styles of experience in Scève's *Délie*', in *Yale French Studies*, 47, *Image and symbol in the Renaissance*, 1972, pp. 57–75.

McFarlane, I. D. 'Notes on Maurice Scève's *Délie*', *FS*, XIII, 1959, pp. 99–111.

Mourgues, O. de. *Metaphysical, Baroque and Précieux poetry*, Oxford, 1953.

Mulhauser, R. 'The poetic function of the emblems in the *Délie*', *L'esprit créateur*, V, 1965, pp. 80–9.

Niedermann, W. *Versuch über Maurice Scèves Dichtung*, Zurich, 1950.

Pabst, W. 'Der Liebende im Akkusativ. Zu Maurice Scèves *Délie* XXII', in *Archiv. für das Studium der neueren Sprachen und Literaturen*, Band 199, Heft 5, 1962, pp. 189–298.

Parturier, E. 'Quelques corrections au texte de la *Délie* de Maurice Scève', *Revue d'histoire littéraire de la France*, XXIV, 1917–18, pp. 483– 6.

Perrat, C. 'Les relations de Maurice Scève et de Clément Marot; d'après le ms. 524 du Musée Condé', *Académie des Inscriptions et Belles-Lettres*, Année 1962 (publ. 1963), pp. 81–7.

Sainte-Beuve. *Tableau historique et critique de la poésie française et du théâtre français au XVIe siècle*, Paris, 1828.

Saulnier, V. L. *Maurice Scève*, Paris, 1948–9, 2 vols.

'Maurice Scève et Pontus de Tyard: deux notes sur le pétrarquisme de Pontus', *Revue de littérature comparée*, t. XXII, 1948, pp. 267–72.

'Maurice Scève et la clarté', *Bulletin de l'Association Guillaume Budé*, nouvelle série, no. 5, 1948, pp. 96–105.

'Maurice Scève et l'épitaphe de Laure', *Revue de littérature comparée*, 1950, p. 65ff.

'La cléricature de Maurice Scève', *BHR*, XII, 1950, pp. 14–19.

'Quelques termes de la langue de Maurice Scève', in *Festgabe Ernst Gamillscheg*, Tübingen, 1952, pp. 76–86.

'Sur trois dizains de Maurice Scève', *Annales de l'Université de Paris*, XXII, 1952, pp. 187–91.

'Objets et images dans la *Délie*', in *Médecine de France*, LXIII, 1955, pp. 32–39.

Staub, H. *Le curieux désir*, Geneva, 1967.

Stone, D. 'Scève's Emblems', *Romanic Review*, LX, 1969, pp. 96–104.

Weber, H. *Le langage poétique de Maurice Scève dans la 'Délie'*, Florence, 1948.

*La création poétique au XVIe siècle en France: De Maurice Scève à Agrippa D'Aubigné*, Paris, 1956.


### Greek and Roman literature

Atkins, J. W. H. *Literary Criticism in Antiquity, a Sketch of its development*, Cambridge, 1934 (repr. London, 1952), 2 vols.

Catullus. *Opera*, ed. R. A. B. Mynors (Oxford Classical Texts).

Grube, G. M. A. *The Greek and Roman Critics*, London, 1965.

Hesiod. *Works and Days* and *Theogony*. (Loeb Classical Library).

Horace. *Opera*, ed. H. W. Garrod (Oxford Classical Texts).

Brink, C. O. *Horace on Poetry*, Cambridge, 1963.

Wilkinson, L. P. *Horace and his Lyric Poetry*, 2nd ed. Cambridge, 1952.

Hyginus. *Fabularum liber*, Paris, 1578.

Ovid. *Opera*, ed. Merkel–Ewald–Lenz (Bibl. Teubneriana).

Plato. *Phaedrus*, ed. L. Robin, Œuvres complètes de Platon, t. iv, Paris, 1954 (Les Belles Lettres).

Pliny the Elder. *Natural History* with an English translation by H. Rackham and W. H. S. Jones (Loeb Classical Library).

Propertius. *Opera*, ed. M. Schuster (Bibl. Teubneriana).

Butler, H. E. and Barber, E. A., *The Elegies of Propertius*, London, 1905.

Quinn, K. *Latin Explorations*, London, 1963.

Quintilian. *The Institutio Oratoria of Quintilian*, ed. H. E. Butler (Loeb Classical Library).

Tibullus. *The Elegies of Albius Tibullus*, ed. Smith, K. F., New York, 1913 (reprinted Darmstadt 1964).

Vergil. *Opera*, ed. F. A. Hirtzel (Oxford Classical Texts).

*Ciris*, introduzione, testo e commento di M. Lenchantin de Gubernatis, Turin, 1930.

*Diversorum veterum poetarum in Priapum lusus. P. V. M. Catalecta* [sic]. *Copa. Rosae. Culex. Dirae. Moretum. Ciris. Aetna...et alia nonnulla quae falso Virgilii creduntur*, Venice, 1517.

Quinn, K. *Virgil's 'Aeneid'*, London, 1968.

Williams, G. *Tradition and Originality in Roman poetry*, Oxford, 1968.

*Emblems and 'imprese' sources*

Alciati, A. *Viri Clarissimi D. Andree Alciati Iurisconsultiss. Mediol. ad de Chonradum Peutingerum Augustanum, Iurisconsultum Emblematum liber*, Augsburg, 1531.

Amboise, F. d'. *Discours ou Traicté des Devises où est mise la raison et difference des Emblemes, Enigmes, Sentences et autres...pris et compilé des cahiers de feu messire François d'Amboise...par Adrien d'Amboise*, Paris, 1620.

Boschius, J. *Symbolographia sive de arte symbolica sermones septem*, Augsburg, 1702.

Bouhours, le Père Dominique. *Les Entretiens d'Ariste et d'Eugène*, Lyon, 1682.

Estienne, H. *L'Art de faire les devises*, Paris, 1645.

Farra, A. *Settenario dell'humana riduttione*, Venice, 1571.

Giovio, P. *Raggionamento di M. Paulo Giovio Vescovo di Nocera con M. Lodovico Domenichi sopra i motti e disegni d'arma e d'amore che communamente chiamano Imprese. Con un Discorso di Girolamo Ruscelli*, Milano, 1560.

Horus Apollo. *Hieroglyphica*, Paris, 1517.

*De la signification des notes hieroglyphiques des Egyptiens*, Paris, 1543.

La Perrière, Guillaume de. *Le Theatre des bons engins*, Paris, 1539.

Le Moyne, P. *Devises héroiques et morales*, Paris, 1649.

*De l'Art des devises*, Paris, 1666.

Menestrier, le Père Claude François. *L'Assemblée des sçavans et les presens des Muses. Pour les nopces de Charles Emmanuel II, Duc de Savoye...et de Marie Jeanne Baptiste de Savoye princesse de Nemours*, Lyon, 1665.

*La Philosophie des Images*, Paris, 1682.

*Devises des Princes...ou la Philosophie des Images*, tome second, Paris, 1683.

*L'art des Emblèmes*, Paris, 1684.

*La science des devises*, Paris, 1686.

Paradin, C. *Devises héroiques*, Lyon, 1551.

*Quadrins historiques de la Bible*, Lyon, 1555.

Percivallo, B. *Rime e Imprese*, Ferrara, 1588.

*Rime degli Accademici Occulti con le loro Imprese e Discorsi*, Brescia, 1568.

Ruscelli, G. *Le Imprese illustri*, Venice, 1572.

Tasso, E. *Della realtà e perfettione delle Imprese di Hercole Tasso*, Bergamo, 1614 (second edition).

Valeriano, P. *Hieroglyphica*, Basel, 1555.

Villava. *Empresas*, Baeça, 1613.


*Italian literature*

Bembo, P. *Gli Asolani*, Venice, 1505.

*Opere*, Milan, 1808.

Colonna, F. *Hypnerotomachia Poliphili*, Venice, 1499.

*Hypnérotomachie ou Discours du songe de Poliphile déduisant comme Amour le combat à l'occasion de Polia...nouvellement traduit de language italien en françois* (Edité par Jean Martin et traduit par le C^al de Lenoncour), Paris, 1561.

Ebreo, L. *Dialogi d'Amore*, Venetia, 1535.

*Leon Hebrieu De l'Amour*, A Lyon par Jean de Tournes, 1551.

*Philosophie d'Amour de M. Leon Hebreu. Traduict d'Italien en Françoys par le Seigneur du Parc Champenoys*, Lyon, G. Roville et T. Payen, 1551.

Ficin, Marsile (Marsilio Ficino). *Commentaire sur le Banquet de Platon*, Paris, 1956 (Les Classiques de l'Humanisme).

Petrarca, F. *Rime*, ed. Carducci and Ferrari, vol. xii of the Bibliotheca Carducciana, Florence, 1957.

*Il Petrarcha con l'espositione d'Alessandro Vellutello...*, Venetia, 1532.

Wilkins, E. H. *Studies in the Life and Works of Petrarch*, Cambridge (Mass.), 1955.

Bishop, M. *Petrarch and his World*, London, 1964.

Petrarchism. Sozzi, B. T. *Petrarca* (Storia della Critica), Palermo, 1963.

Baldacci, L. *Il petrarchismo italiano nel cinquecento*, Milan, 1957.

Baldacci, L. *Lirici del cinquecento*, Florence, 1957.

Spagnoletti, G. *Il petrarchismo*, Milan, 1959.

Forster, L. *The Icy Fire*, C.U.P., 1969.

Pulci, Luca. *Il Driadeo*, Florence, 1489.

Serafino. Barbara Bauer-Formiconi, *Die Strambotti des Serafino dall' Aquila: Studien und Texte zur italienischen Spiel- und Scherzdichtung des ausgehenden 15. Jahrhunderts*, Munich, 1967 (Freiburger Schriften zur romanischen Philologie, 10).

Speron Speroni. *I dialogi*, Vinegia, 1542.

### Other works before 1800

Boccaccio, Giovanni. *De Genealogia Deorum Gentilium*, Basel, 1532.

Calepinus, Ambrosius. *Dictionarium...multo diligentius ab Ascensio repositum*, Paris, 1518.

Cotgrave, Randle. *A French English Dictionary*, London, 1611.

Equicola, Mario. *Libro di natura d'amore*, Venice, 1554.

Erasmus, Desiderius. *Adagia*, Basel, 1520.

*De duplici copia verborum ac rerum commentarii duo*, Basel, 1519.

Estienne, Robert. *Dictionarium nominum virorum mulierum populorum idolorum urbium et quae passim in libris prophanis leguntur*, Paris, 1541.

Fontaine, Charles, *La Fontaine d'amour*, Paris, 1545.

Fulgentius. *Mythologiarum libri tres*, Basel, 1535.

*Fabularum liber*, Paris, 1578.

*La Magnificence de la superbe et triumphante entrée de la noble et antique Cité de Lyon faicte au treschrestien Roy de France Henry deuxiesme de ce nom et a la royne Catherine son Espouse, le xxiii de septembre M.D.XLVIII*, Lyon, 1549.

Perottus, Nicolaus. *Cornucopiae sive linguae Latinae commentarii denuo recogniti*, Basel, 1521.

Reischius, Gregorius. *Margarita philosophica*, Basel, 1535.

Textor, Ravisius. *Epithetorum opus*, Basel, 1555.

3

39321

off

off

low

3

39321

off

off

low

3

39321

BIBLIOGRAPHY

off

off

low

3

39321

*General books and articles after 1800*

off

off

low

3

39321

off

off

low

3

39321

off

off

low

3

39321

off

off

low

3

39321

off

off

low

3

39321

off

off

low

3

39321

off

off

low

3

39321

off

off

low

3

39321

off

off

low

3

39321

Baudelaire, Charles. *Les Fleurs du Mal*, ed. J. Crépet et G. Blin, Paris, 1942.

Boyssoné, Jehan de. *Les trois centuries*, ed. H. Jacoubet, Paris, 1923.

Castor, Graham. *Pléiade Poetics*, C.U.P., 1964.

Close, A. J. 'Art and Nature in Antiquity and the Renaissance', in *Journal of the History of Ideas*, xxx, no. 4, 1969, pp. 483ff.

Cocking, J. M. 'Imagination as Order and as Adventure', in *Order and Adventure in Post-Romantic French poetry. Essays presented to C. A. Hackett*, edited by E. M. Beaumont, J. M. Cocking and J. Cruickshank, Oxford, 1973, pp. 257–69.

Curtius, E. *European Literature and the Latin Middle Ages*, translated from the German by Willard R. Trask, London, 1953.

Donne, John. *The poems of John Donne*, ed. H. J. C. Grierson, 2 vols, Oxford, 1912.

Freeman, Rosemary. *English Emblem Books*, London, 1948.

Gardner, Helen. *The Business of Criticism*, Oxford, 1959.

Jackson, C. W. 'Molle atque facetum', in *Harvard Studies in Classical Philology*, vol. xxv, 1914, pp. 117–37.

Lee, R. W. '"Ut Pictura Poesis": The Humanist theory of Painting', *Art Bulletin*, xxii, 1940, no. 4, pp. 197–270.

Lemaire de Belges, Jean. *L'Epitre de l'Amant Vert*, ed. J. Frappier, Paris, 1948.

Mallarmé, Stéphane. *Œuvres complètes*, Pléiade edition, Paris, 1945.

Marot, Clément. *Œuvres complètes*, ed. C. A. Mayer, London, 1958–73.

Mayer, C. A. and Bentley-Cranch, D. 'Clément Marot, poète pétrarchiste, Jean Marot', *BHR*, t. xxvii, 1965, pp. 183–5.

Montaigne. *Essais*, ed. Plattard (Les Textes français), Paris, 1959.

Nowottny, W. *The Language Poets use*, London, 1962.

Panofsky, E. *Studies in Iconology; Humanistic themes in the art of the Renaissance*, New York and Oxford, 1939.

Peletier du Mans, Jacques. *Art Poetique* (1555), ed. J. Boulanger, Paris, 1930.

*Physiologus Latinus*. ed. F. J. Carmody. Éditions préliminaires. Versio B, Paris, 1939.

Praz, Mario. *Studies in Seventeenth-century imagery*, London, 1939, 2 vols.

Proust, Marcel. *À la recherche du temps perdu*, Pléiade edition, Paris, 1954, 3 vols.

Raymond, Marcel. *L'influence de Ronsard sur la poésie française (1550–1585)*, Geneva, 1927, reprinted 1965.

Réau, L. *L'iconographie de l'art chrétien.* 3 tomes in 6 vols, Paris, 1957–9.

Richards, I. A. *Principles of Literary Criticism*, London, 1950.

Saint-Gelais, *Œuvres complètes*, ed. P. Blanchemain, Paris, 1873, 3 vols.

Salza, Abd-el-Kader. *Luca Contile, uomo di lettere e di negozi del secolo XVI*, Florence, 1903.

Santangelo, G. (ed.) *Le Epistole 'De imitatione' di Gianfrancesco Pico della Mirandola e di Pietro Bembo*, Florence, 1954.

Sebillet, Thomas. *Art poétique françois*, ed. F. Gaiffe, Paris, 1932.

202

Shepard, O. *The lore of the Unicorn*, London, 1930.

Simone, Franco. *The French Renaissance. Medieval Tradition and Italian influence in shaping the Renaissance in France*, translated from the Italian by H. Gaston Hall, London, 1969.

Smith, Pauline. *Clément Marot, Poet of the French Renaissance*, London, 1970.

Tervarent, F. de. *Attributs et symboles dans l'art profane, 1450–1600, Dictionnaire d'un langage perdu*, Geneva, 1958.

Tuve, R. *Elizabethan and Metaphysical Imagery*, University of Chicago Press, 1947.

Valéry, Paul. *Œuvres*, Pléiade edition, Paris, 1957, 2 vols.

Weinberg, B. *A history of literary criticism in the Italian Renaissance*, University of Chicago Press, 1961.

White, M. 'Petrarchism in the French Rondeau before 1527', *FS*, vol. xxii, 1968, pp. 287–95.

# INDEX

Alamanni, Luigi, 52, 65
Alberti, L. B., 24
Alciati, A., 54, 101
  verses, 58, 81, 82
  woodcuts, 54–6, 101
Ammirato, Scipio, 63–4
Andrelini, 117
Angeriano, 51
anti-Christian attitudes, 25, 134–5, 147, 178
Aquinas, St Thomas, 1
Aretino, 55
Ariosto, 61
Aristophanes, 119
Aristotelian
  manner, 94, 98
  mimesis, 38–9, 43
Aristotle, 1
assimilation, *see* innutrition
association(s)
  animal, 27–8, 75, 194
  Biblical, 146–50
  Classical, 151–61
  guidance to a body of, 110–11, 140, 181, 194
  layers of, 117–18
  linguistic, 11
  mythological, 109
  use of, to convey personal experience, 170–2
  of death, 176
  on the part of reader, 3
  *see also* images, literary allusiveness, Nature–love symbols, simple themes
Augustan
  poetry, poets, 49, 53, 130, 134, 140, 163, 165, 168
  *see also* Catullus, Horace, Ovid, Propertius, Tibullus, Vergil
Avignon, 16, 64, 121, 122

Bargagli, Scipio, 64
Baudelaire, Charles, 42, 146 164, 167
Béguin, A., 192

Bembo, Pietro, 40, 59, 110
Biblical associations, 146–50, 161, 166, 169
Blake, William, 13, 31
*blasons*, 16, 56, 65–6
  *see also imprese*, woodcuts
Boccaccio
  on Actaeon myth, 99
  on Dictynna, 133
  on Dido, 106
  on Endymion, 126
  on Lethe, 154
  on moon-names, 139
  on Pandora, 135
  on Paphos, 119
  on Prometheus, 152
Bonhomme, Macé, 54
Boschius, Jacobus, 103
Bouchet, Jean, 51, 52
Bouhours, le père Dominique, 98
Boutang, P., 11, 14
Boyssoné, Jehan de, 111–14
Brunetière, F., 7, 73
Bruno, Giordano, 109–10
Busson, H., 37

Caburacci, 64
Camerarius, 57
Carrafa, Ferrante, 83
Catullus
  an epigrammist, 15
  and love relationship, 146
  and *miser* epithet, 22
  and 'mistress convention', 116
  and water-image, 165–6
  poetic style of, 40, 48–9
Charles Emmanuel II, 63
Christ, 80, 147
Christian
  attitude to love, 24, 29–30
  past, 192
  poetry, 80–1
Cicero, 27, 40, 47, 49, 113, 178
Coleman, D., 55–6, 61, 106
Colonna, 101

205